# PUBLISHER'S NOTE

Ancient Chinese classic poems are exquisite works of art. As far as 2,000 years ago, Chinese poets composed the beautiful work *Book of Poetry* and *Elegies of the South*. Later, they created more splendid Tang poetry and Song lyrics. Such classic works as *Thus Spoke the Master* and *Laws Divine and Human* were extremely significant in building and shaping the culture of the Chinese nation. These works are both a cultural bond linking the thoughts and affections of Chinese people and an important bridge for Chinese culture and the world.

Mr. Xu Yuanchong has been engaged in translation for 70 years. In December 2010, he won the Lifetime Achievement Award in Translation conferred by the Translators Association of China (TAC). He is honored as the only expert who translates Chinese poems into both English and French. After his excellent interpretation, many Chinese classic poems have been further refined into perfect English and French rhymes. This collection of Classical Chinese Poetry and Prose gathers his most representative English translations. It includes the classic works *Thus Spoke the Master*, *Laws Divine and Human* and dramas such as *Romance of the Western Bower*, *Dream in Peony Pavilion*, *Love in Long-life Hall* and *Peach Blooms Painted with Blood*. The largest part of the collection includes the translation of selected poems from different dynasties. The selection includes various types of poetry. The selected works start from the pre-Qin era to the Qing Dynasty, covering almost the entire history of classic poems in China. Reading these works is like tasting "living water from the source" of Chinese culture.

We hope this collection will help English readers "understand, enjoy and delight in" Chinese classic poems, share the intelligence of Confucius and Lao Tzu (the Older Master), share the gracefulness of Tang poems, Song lyrics and classic operas and songs and promote exchanges between Eastern and Western culture. We also sincerely invite precious suggestions from our readers.

Oct. 2011

# 出版前言

中国古代经典诗文是中国传统文化的奇葩。早在两千多年以前，中国诗人就写出了美丽的《诗经》和《楚辞》；以后，他们又创造了更加灿烂的唐诗和宋词。《论语》《老子》这样的经典著作，则在塑造、构成中华民族文化精神方面具有极其重要的意义。这些作品既是联接所有中国人思想、情感的文化纽带，也是中国文化走向世界的重要桥梁。

许渊冲先生从事翻译工作70年，2010年12月荣获"中国翻译文化终身成就奖"。他被称为将中国诗词译成英法韵文的唯一专家，经他的妙手，许多中国经典诗文被译成出色的英文和法文韵语。这套"许译中国经典诗文集"荟萃许先生最具代表性的英文译作，既包括《论语》《老子》这样的经典著作，又包括《西厢记》《牡丹亭》《长生殿》《桃花扇》等戏曲剧本，数量最多的则是历代诗歌选集。这些诗歌选集包括诗、词、散曲等多种体裁，所选作品上起先秦，下至清代，几乎涵盖了中国古典诗歌的整个历史。阅读和了解这些作品，即可尽览中国文化的"源头活水"。

我们希望这套许氏译本能使英语读者对中国经典诗文也"知之，好之，乐之"，能够分享孔子、老子的智慧，分享唐诗、宋词、中国古典戏曲的优美，并以此促进东西文化的交流。也敬请读者朋友提出宝贵意见。

2011年10月

PROJECT FOR TRANSLATION AND PUBLICATION
OF CHINESE CULTURAL WORKS
中国文化著作翻译出版工程项目

CLASSICAL CHINESE POETRY AND PROSE

# LOVE
# IN LONG-LIFE HALL

HONG SHENG

TRANSLATED BY XU YUANCHONG & FRANK M. XU

许译中国经典诗文集

长生殿 | 【清】洪升 著
许渊冲 许明 译

五洲传播出版社
China Intercontinental Press

中华书局
Zhonghua Book Company

# CONTENTS
# 目　　录

## ACT III
## 第三本

CLASSICAL CHINESE POETRY AND PROSE

# LOVE
# IN LONG-LIFE HALL

HONG SHENG

TRANSLATED BY XU YUANCHONG & FRANK M. XU

China Intercontinental Press    Zhonghua Book Company

# PREFACE

*On seventh day of seventh moon when none was near,*
*At midnight in Long-life Hall he whispered in her ear:*
*"On high we would be two birds flying wing to wing;*
*On earth two trees with branches twined from spring to*
*spring."*

Such is the love story of Emperor Xuan Zong of the Tang
Dynasty and his favorite Lady Yang, as told by Bai Juyi in his *Song
of Everlasting Regret*. Such is also the theme of the tragedy of *Love
in Long-life Hall* written by Hong Sheng of Qing dynasty. The
emperor's love for his Lady which ends in the army's revolt and in
her tragic death is considered as a turning point of Tang dynasty's
decline and fall. Since olden days the rise and fall of dynasties
hinge more or less on the fate of a beauty. It is true not only in the
East but also in the West; for instance, the fate of Roman Empire
might have been altered by the life or death of the Queen of Egypt.
As Pascal said, if the nose of Cleopatra, Egyptian Queen, had been
an inch longer, the history of Roman Empire might have been
rewritten, for if she were not so bewitching, the Roman General
might not have fallen in love with her and lost the empire.

Cleopatra was hundreds of years earlier than Lady Yang of
the Tang dynasty. Her contemporary was Lady Li, favorite of the
Martial Emperor of the Han dynasty, whose beauty is glorified in
the following poem:

*There is a beauty in the northern lands,*
*Unequalled, high above the world she stands.*

1

*At her first glance, soldiers would lose their town;*
*At her second, the monarch would lose his crown.*
*How could monarch and soldiers neglect their duty?*
*For crown and town are overshadowed by her beauty.*

But the Martial Emperor did not neglect his duty. Instead, he sacrificed the beauty for his empire, and after her death he wrote an elegy, in which he said how lonely and dreary he felt on seeing her robe without finding her person, and on walking along the marble steps without seeing her foot print. Even when he found a fallen leaf on the threshold of her bedroom deserted and empty, he would think it transformed by her soul unwilling to tear herself away from her former abode. Her bedroom, her silk robe, the marble steps belong to the external world, while the emperor's grief and loneliness to his internal world. Here we see the external world is described to reveal the internal world. In other words, scenic expressions are used as lyric expressions. Such is the method used in poetry.

In the *Book of Poetry* compiled in the 5th Century B. C., poetry may be divided into three kinds: songs, odes (including feastful and epical odes) and hymns. As for the art of versification, three methods are used, that is, narration, comparison and association. This tradition has been inherited and developed, in scenical as well as lyrical expressions. For instance, we may read Li Bai's description of the beauty of Lady Yang:

*Her face is seen in flowers and her dress in cloud,*
*A beauty by the rails caressed by vernal breeze.*
*If not a fairy queen from Jade Mountain proud,*
*She's Goddess of the Moon in crystal hall one sees.*

In the first two lines we see the poet compares the lady to a flower, and in the second she is associated with a fairy queen and the Moon Goddess. That is to say, comparison and association are used. In Bai Juyi's *Song of Everlasting Regret*, we find verses describing Lady Yang:

*Turning her head, she smiled so sweet and full of grace*
*That she outshone in six palaces the fairest face.*

In the first line narration is used, while in the second the lady is compared with or contrasted against the fairest face to emphasize her beauty.

In Hong Sheng's *Love in Long-life Hall*, we see the three methods inherited and developed. For instance, we may read the dialogue between the two maids about Lady Yang in the Scene of *Spring Siesta*:

*She keeps straight her waist slender*
*Like willow trees;*
*Her skin's so tender*
*We fear it might be ruffled by the breeze.*
*Behold her headdress quiver*
*And her skirts softly spread!*
*Her feet are light enough to tread*
*On ripples of the river.*

We may say the first line is narration, the second comparison, the fourth association, but the rest is three methods used together, and we can hardly say whether it is narration, comparison or association. The same is true in the Scene of *the Bath*. Let us read their dialogue about the Emperor's love for his lady:

*Hand in hand by day, cheek to cheek by night,*

*They have enjoyed love's all delight.*
*She follows him like a shadow true;*
*They can't be parted as water can't be cut in two.*

Here we see the double comparison of shadow and water.

*No tongue can tell with how much love they're fed,*
*No word can describe their lovebirds' bed,*
*Where they'd enjoy their fill,*
*And their love blazes still.*
*See her private vernal bower!*
*Spring hides there where our lord would bring fresh shower*
*For thirsting flower.*

Here we see comparison and association developed into metaphor. How does the English poet describe Antony's love for Cleopatra? Let us read their dialogue in Act One:

*Cleo. If it be love indeed, tell me how much.*
*Ant. There is beggary in the love that can be reckoned.*
*Cleo. I'll set a bourn how far to be beloved.*
*Ant. Then must thou needs find up new heaven, new earth.*

Shakespeare uses concrete words to describe abstract thing, and visible heaven and earth as bourn for the invisible feeling. We may say that he is more direct than the Chinese playwright. How does Shakespeare describe the inner world of his character? Let us hear what Cleopatra says to her maid sent to find Antony.

*See where he is, who's with him, what he does.*
*I did not send you. If you find him sad, say I am dancing;*
*If in mirth, report that I am sudden sick. Quick and return!*

Lady Yang and her maid say what they believe, but the Egyptian queen tells her maid to say what they do not believe in order to deceive Antony. Here we see Shakespeare's characters more complicate than the Chinese. We may compare the dialogues between the Emperor and Lady Yang with that between Antony and Cleopatra before their death:

> Lady: *Dry sorrow gnaws my heart.*
> *How can I from you part?*
> *Like a pair of lovebirds in stormy turbulence,*
> *How can we suffer such violence?*
> *My soul has fled*
> *While tears are shed.*
> Emp.: *High as Imperial Majesty,*
> *From grief I am not free.*
> *How can I forget*
> *The first night we met?*
> *Without you by my side,*
> *To live is worse than to have died.*

We see the Chinese Characters just say what lovers think and feel in elaborate language. But what do Antony and Cleopatra say before their death?

> Ant. *Not Ceasar's valour hath overthrown Antony,*
> *But Antony's hath triumphed on itself.*
> Cleo. *I am fire and air, my other elements I give to baser*
> *life.*
> Maid: *Dissolve, thick cloud, and rain, that I may say*
> *The Gods themselves do weep!*

Here we see only blood of Lady Yang and sympathetic tears of the Tang emperor in the *Long-life Hall*, while in Shakespeare we see the blood of a heroic Roman general and tears of an unconquered queen of Egypt: That is one of the differences between Chinese and Western civilization, and one of the reasons why the East may learn from the West just as the West may learn from the East. Such is the importance of G2, ChinAmerica or AmeriChina.

*Frank M. Xu* at OKC, USA.

February 2009

# ACT I

## Scene 1 Prologue

**Tune: The River All Red**

Since olden days how few
Lovers have remained ever true!
If they love each other heart and soul,
They'd be united from pole to pole.
A thousand miles could not keep them apart,
Nor even death could sever heart from heart.
If o'er your hapless fate you wail and weep,
In love you are not deep.
What could move earth and sky,
Melt stone and gold,
Shine like the sun on high
In history of old
But affectionate deeds done
By loyal and filial son?
The ancient sage did not undervalue love song,
The modern playwright should make music of
The story of beautiful Lady Yang
To glorify true love.

**Tune: Spring in Pleasure Garden**

The Emperor Bright and Lady Jade Ring
Were at the height of their love in Hot Spring,

Where she was bathed in imperial light.
Then in the Hall of Love as Long as Life
They pledged to be forever man and wife.

She performed dances divine
And he composed music fine
Till rebels beat war drums to blast their hope.

On the Soul-Searing Slope
Imperial armies would not farther go
Unless the fair Jade Ring received her fatal blow.

The western journey broke the Bright Emperor's heart;
The living and the dead were kept far, far apart.

Fortunately her soul repented her sin
And she became an immortal heroine.

When he sought for her body in the burial mound,
Nothing but her fragrant pouch was found.

The Weaving Star had not witnessed their vow in vain;
A Taoist flew to bring back from above
The golden hairpin and its case, token of their love.

In Lunar Palace Hall the lovers met again.

The poet would sing the song
Of their rainbow dance for long.

### Summary of the Scene

The emperor was fond of music, dance and feast;
His favorite fair Lady lost her life and all.

In the lunar palace she met the Taoist priest;
The Weaving Star witnessed their vow in Long-life Hall.

## Scene 2 The Pledge

(The Bright Emperor enters with two eunuchs.)

**Emperor** sings to the tune of *The First Branch in the East Breeze* :

Wearing imperial crown

And dragon-broidered gown,

I've ruled this land with measure.

I shower favors with spring breeze;

My palace's full of blooming trees.

Peace prevails far and near;

Prosperous is the year.

Why don't I spend my days in pleasure?

To end my life in palace hall with love o'er flowed,

I would not envy gods above the cloud.

To our forbidden palace come best days:

In royal gardens trees shed vernal rays,

Heaven is pleased that happy times last long;

People enjoy peace and nothing goes wrong,

Nine Songs spread wide our government's renown;

Six dances are performed in courtier's gown.

I brought fresh shower for the Divine Flower

Ten nights ago in our Love-making Bower.

**I am the Bright Emperor of the Tang Dynasty. Third son to His Late Majesty, I succeeded to the throne thirty years ago. Since then I have appointed such able ministers as Yao and**

Song at my court and such wise counselors as Zhang and Han in the State Council. I am glad that they have well governed my empire as far as the frontier and my people have had good harvests from year to year. It is indeed the reign of peace as in the time of my grandfather, and the penal law has long been out of use as in the Golden Age of old. Lately I have spent my leisure enjoying music and beauty. I have noticed that a maid of honor named Jade Ring Yang is gentle and beautiful. Choosing this auspicious day I am making her my sovereign lady. I have ordered to give her a bath in the Hot Spring of the Flowery Pool, and told Ever Fresh and Mindful Maid to wait on her. My eunuch Gao should be bringing her here now.

(The eunuch Gao enters with two maids holding fan, who are leading Lady Yang.)

Lady Yang sings to the tune of *Spring in Jade Pavilion*:

I'm glad a wave of favor comes down from on high.

Dressed after bath, I'll follow my lord by and by.

Maids sing, continuing the same tune:

On marble steps neglected ladies stand in line,

And peep with envious eyes at her beauty divine.

(They walk forward, and the eunuch Gao kneels before the emperor.)

**Gao:** Your slave Gao reports that the newly appointed Sovereign Lady Yang is at the palace gate, awaiting your pleasure, Sire.

**Emperor:** Send her in.

**Gao** (Turning back): His Majesty orders Lady Yang to the Audience Hall.

**Lady Yang** (Advancing and kneeling before the emperor): Your slave Jade Ring wishes a long, long life to Your Majesty.

**Eunuch:** You may rise.

**Lady Yang:** Born of a humble family and with common quality, I was fortunate enough to be chosen a maid of honor. Now I am exceedingly honored to be selected as sovereign lady, but I am afraid I cannot prove worthy of this high honor.

**Emperor:** You are born of an illustrious family and unequalled in character as well as in beauty. I am happy to have you serving in the palace.

**Lady Yang** (Curtseying): Long live Your Majesty!

**Gao:** You may rise.

(Lady Yang gets up.)

**Emperor:** Let the feast begin!

(As Gao passes on the order, music is heard offstage. Lady Yang offers wine to the Bright Emperor, and the maids hand a goblet to her. The emperor takes his seat in the center of the stage, and she sits beside him.)

**Emperor sings to the tune of *Charm of Mindful Maid*:**

For miles and miles all over the land,

I've looked for a beauty's hand

To lead fair ladies in imperial hall.

Today the fairest of them all

Is sent me from on high;

She is truly matchless 'neath the sky.

I'll shower

My favor on her jasper bower,

And ennoble her in the Book of Jade;

She shall outshine my fairest palace maid.

**All sing in chorus:**

We wish that love

May reign below as long as above.

**Lady Yang sings to the same tune:**

Overwhelmed by your praise,

Long and deep I meditate.

Afraid my humble ways

Unworthy of such honor great.

Your sudden favors raise

Your slave from earth to sky.

I'd imitate

The heroine who would defy

Danger, or the lady historian moderate

Who would not ride

With her lord but stand

A pen in hand,

Ever at his side.

**All sing in chorus:**

We wish that love

May reign below as long as above!

**Maids sing to the same tune:**

Now we admire

The first lady in best attire

In palace of today,

Like Lady Swallow bathed in sunny ray.

The royal favor from now on

Will be lavished on her alone.

Do not decline!

Dressed up in golden bower,

You sing in jasper tower

And hand him brimming cups of wine

From spring to winter, rain or shine.

**All sing in chorus:**

We wish that love

May reign below as long as above!

**Eunuchs sing to the same tune:**

Let us look up!

The dragon-broidered robe bright as sunshine.

Like clouds waft pheasant feathers fine.

The Heaven's Son delights in her new attire.

Drink cup on cup!

The vernal breeze sweetens the palace we admire.

The golden moon's radiance displayed

And rainbow clouds spread like brocade!

The Heaven's Son would bring fresh shower

In the evening for thirsting flower.

**All sing in chorus:**

We wish that love

May reign below as long as above!

**Gao:** May it please Your Majesty, the moon has risen.

(The table is cleared.)

**Emperor:** I'll watch the moon from the courtyard with Lady Yang.

(Music is heard offstage while the emperor leads Lady Yang forward, leaving the others in the background.)

**Emperor sings to the tune of *Ancient Tower*:**

I leave the hall gilded by lantern light

To gaze at her under the moon bright.

The courtyard flowers are not so fair

As her charming air.

She lowers her head and leans on my arms,

Her cloudlike hair casting shadow on her radiant dress

Sets off her charms

Really numberless, (Laughs gently.)

So happy I'm tonight

In vernal breeze and in moonlight,

I envy not the Southern King bringing fresh shower

To his dream lover in her nymphean bower.

**Lady Yang continues to sing to the same tune:**

From now on how happy am I

To serve my lord in feast with pleasure high!

On marble steps to him I cling,

Hearing his words breathe spring.

Fragrance floats from his retinue

My dress is moist with chilly dew.

I gaze till lovebirds rest

In palace eaves, in their nest.

**Emperor: Attendants, lanterns! Light the way to the western palace!**

(Gao shouts assent. Eunuchs and maids carry lanterns to light the way.)

**All sing to the same tune as above:**

What splendor

To be escorted by ladies slender

And lanterns casting shade on shade!

Look back! We see the screens inlaid

With pearls and the Milky Way

Shedding flickering ray.

Through corridors everywhere

A perfume's floating in the air.

How goes the night?

Above the bronze statue rides the moon bright,

You may enjoy your fill tonight.

Under canopies crimson and green

A pair of phoenixes amid the cloud are seen.

Songs of "Jade Tree" and "Jasper Flower"

And "Moonlit Spring River" are sung by all,

When the moon sinks behind the palace wall.

Let's lift the silken screen!

Let drunken lovers enter their orchid-sweet bower!

**Gao:** May it please Your Majesty, we have reached the western palace.

**Emperor:** Attendants, leave us!

**Gao:** Through purple curtains the vernal breeze blows.

**Eunuchs:** From pearl-decked tower heavenly music flows.

Emperor continues to sing:

Flowers whisper in candlelight

To the moon over the casement bright

About our love on such a happy night.

**All:** Do not ask ladies of the other bowers

How they will pass their lovely hours.

(The maids bring fresh pyjamas to the emperor and Lady Yang, then retire. The emperor and Lady Yang sit down.)

**Emperor:** The candles shed silvery light on your silken dress.

**Lady Yang:** I have received imperial favors numberless.

**Emperor:** Tonight all other beauties may frown with sorrow.

**Together:** But all will sing of "New Treasure" tomorrow.

**Emperor:** I pronounce my vow that, from tonight on, I will live together with my dear lady forever and ever. (Taking from his sleeve an ornamental pin for her hair and a jewel case.) I have brought you this gold pin and this jewel case to pledge our love. Let us love each other as long as we live.

Emperor sings to the tune of **Cotton Fluff**:

This hairpin made of gold

And this case set with emerald,

I put them close to my heart as a treasure

Beyond measure.

Tonight I give you this pin for your cloudy hair

To make it look more fair,

And this case wrapped in a scarf to weave

Fragrance in your silken sleeve.

Like lovebirds on the pin together we may fly;

Our hearts become one like the case's love-tie.

(Giving them to Lady Yang, who curtseys.)

Lady Yang sings to the same tune:

I thank Your Majesty

For the hairpin and case carved with flower.

I fear my humble quality

Unworthy of the favor you shower.

(Looking at the gifts.)

I peer at phoenix and dragon carved on the face

Of the golden case;

How I love the twin

Of gold hairpin!

May our love be as firm as gold in heart!

May the hairpin and case never be set apart!

### Epilogue of the Scene

**Emperor:** The vernal moon shines on the blooming tree.

**Lady Yang:** It's the first time you shower love on me.

**Emperor:** I'm long drunk with your beauty by my side.

**Together:** Happy from year to year, we're satisfied

(Exeunt.)

## Scene 3 The Bribe

(Enter An Lushan in arrow-proof coat and felt hat.)

An sings to the tune of *Song of Cavalry*:

I grieve for my fellows in vain:

I fall into a trap again.

Can I subdue my aspiration high?

Hidden by cliffs, can my ambition lie?

Be patient awhile and stand by!

My belly's big and mighty I appear;

I'm full of wit and brave without a peer.

How can a fiery dragon conquered be?

The world would tremble when I stir the sea.

I am An Lushan from Liucheng. My mother prayed to the Lushan Mountain to give her a son, came back and gave birth to me whom she called Lushan. At my birth our tent was overflowed with light and all beasts and birds fled away. Then my mother married a second husband An Tingyan, chief of a tribe, so my surname became An. I enlisted under Military Governor Zhang Shougui. Struck by my uncommon appearance, he adopted me. I was then appointed as a lieutenant and sent to fight the western tribesmen. Boasting of my courage, I advanced recklessly and was badly defeated and forced to take flight. Luckily Governor Zhang was too lenient to have me executed, but sent me to the capital for punishment. I arrived yesterday, uncertain of my fate. Fortunately I have a sworn brother named Zhang Qian, who is a steward in Prime Minister Yang's office. Having bribed the escort to release me awhile, I have sought out my sworn brother and through him sent presents to the Prime Minister. Now I am going to learn the outcome. (Walking round the stage) Alas! An Lushan, you are a brave fellow. Can this be your end? Damn it!

An sings to the tune of **Way of Brocade**:

Like an unruly dragon, I
Would have stirred up the sea to brave the sky.
But out of water, like captured turtle or fish,
Brave as I am, I'm trapped and can't do what I wish.
 Had I known that defeat meant I must lose my head,
I'd have my blood in battle shed.
Now suddenly on air my chained feet tread
Can I rely on bribes given at dead of night
To make good my escape from the sad plight?
O since Heaven favored me with the day,
Should I allow myself to be killed in midway?
I see this is the Prime Minister's court and I must wait for my sworn brother here.

(Enter Zhang Qian.)

**Zhang:** The emperor's kin's Prime Minister of the state;
As his steward I'm as good as a magistrate.
(Greeting An): So you have come. His Grace has accepted your gifts, and will give you an audience.

**An** (Bowing): I must thank you for your help.

**Zhang:** His Grace has not yet entered the court. Let us wait in the antechamber.
It is all in the Prime Minister's hand.

**An:** To save one beaten on the borderland (Exeunt.)

(The Prime Minister, Yang Guozhong, enters with his retinue.)

Yang sings to the tune of *Immortals at the Magpie Bridge*:

Related as a kin

To our great sovereign,

Both my cousin and I

Have received favor high.

As Prime Minister I alone govern the state.

Beware! I am in power and splendor great.

The imperial government is now in my hand;

My position's most respectable of the land.

After the audience when I leave the court with ease,

All courtiers bow before me as if bent by breeze.

I am Yang Guozhong, a cousin to Lady Yang. As Prime Minister, I share the glory of the sun and the moon, and give orders like wind and thunderbolt.

(Laughing sardonically)

Living in luxury, I believe a man should enjoy himself while he can. Accepting bribes, I have the power to shape the imperial decisions. Attendants, leave me!

(His retinue goes out.)

Zhang Qian reported a short time ago that a frontier lieutenant, An Lushan, who lost battles, has been brought to the capital for court martial. But he has sent me presents, begging his life be spared. I think victory or defeat is a matter of common occurrence, and to be defeated occasionally is excusable.

(Laughing) If I spare him, I shall be saving a useful officer for the state. I have already sent for him and shall make up my mind when I see him.

(Zhang enters.)

**Zhang:** Your Grace, An Lushan is waiting outside.

**Yang:** Bring him in.

**Zhang:** Yes, Your Grace.

(He goes out. then leads in An Lushan in a blue coat and cap.)

Come his way.

**An:** (Advancing on his knees): The wretched An Lushan salutes Your Grace.

**Yang:** Rise.

**An:** A criminal who should be sentenced to death dare not.

**Yang:** Zhang Qian has reported to me your purpose in coming here. Now give me your own account of your offence.

**An:** Your Grace, I was ordered to attack the western tribe…

**Yang:** Rise and speak.

**An** (Rising) sings to the tune of *Thrice Awake from Wine*:

Relying on our strength, we charged the foes,

And overran all. those on our way. But who knows

By surprise they surrounded our camp at night;

How could we pit our bare hands against their swords bright?

**Yang:** How did you escape?

**An:** I fought my way and broke through.

Alone I saved my life on a horse with a spear.

I hoped to be pardoned for past services done.

But now before a court martial I should appear.

(Kowtowing) I beg Your Grace for mercy on the beaten one.

**Yang** (rising from his seat):

To lose an army is against the law.

Though I have power, how can I the verdict withdraw?

The sentence, when once passed, unaltered shall remain.

I fear I cannot change the wind and rain.

**An** (Shedding tears on his knees): Only if Your Grace take mercy on me can I be saved.

**Yang** (Laughing):

E'en if the court will follow what I say,

It is not easy to tell you the way.

**An** (Kowtowing): My life is in the hands of Your Grace.

**Yang:** Well, tomorrow when I go to the court, I'll see what can be done.

I'll try to save your life and set

You free from the law's net.

**An** (Kowtowing): I owe Your Grace such gratitude that I can repay you only by serving as your dog or horse. Would Your Grace allow me to take my leave?

**Yang:** Zhang Qian, show him out!

**Zhang:** With hopeful flag in sight,

You'll see good news alight.

(Zhang leads An out.)

**Yang** (Reflectively): This An Lushan is a junior officer at the frontier, who has by no means distinguished himself. Now he shall be sentenced to death. If I try to save him, it might arouse the emperor's suspicion. (Laughing) Ah, I've got it. The other day Governor Zhang stated in his memorial to the throne that An's knowledge of barbarian languages and military skill qualified him for the post of a frontier general. I'll drop a hint to the minister of war to propose to the emperor that An be summoned to court to be tested by His Majesty. That will give me the opening I need. Yes, that's it.

### Epilogue of the Scene

I know well how to use my power;
My face may change from hour to hour.
Gold can save one from punishment;
The premier is the government.

(Exit.)

## Scene 4 Spring Siesta

(Enter Lady Yang attended by Ever Fresh and Mindful Maid.)

Lady Yang sings to the tune of **Slow Song of Zhu Yingtai**:

> Waking from dreams
>
> Of spring sunbeams,
>
> I feel too tired to dress with grace.
>
> Before the mirror I
>
> Linger long and feel shy
>
> To rouge my lips and powder my face.

**Maids:** Ere the sun leaves

> The lofty eaves,
>
> The curtain's rippled by the breeze.
>
> Why not enjoy awhile the incense sweet with ease?

(Ever Fresh and Mindful Maid kowtow.)

**Lady Yang:** Rise. (Singing to the tune of **Crabapple in Spring**):

> Outside the window orioles' warbling song
>
> Aroused me from my sleep lasting not long.

**Ever Fresh:** In morning cool the green quilt chills the eyes.

**Mindful Maid:** From burners wreaths of incense rise.

**Lady Yang:** Not recovered from last night's wine, I've heard the maid.

**Maids:** Say music in the other bower played.

**Lady Yang:** I'd ask how many crabapple blossoms bright

**Together:** Began to blow last night.

**Lady Yang:** I am Yang Yuhuan, born in Hongnong District. My father Yang Yuanyan held a government post and died early, so I was brought up in my uncle's home. I was born wearing a jade ring with two words "Ever True" on it, so I was called by the name of "Jade Ring" and of "Ever True". I'm gentle and beautiful. When I wipe my eyes with my silken sleeves, my tears drip like rosy ice; when I try my rainbow dress, sweat rolls on my fragrant jadelike skin. Favored by the emperor, I was raised from the rank of a palace maid to that of an imperial lady with all the prerogatives of a queen. My cousin Yang Guozhong is prime minister and my three elder sisters have been made duchesses, so my whole family has been greatly honored. Last night I was with the emperor in the west palace. As he brought fresh shower for my thirsting flower, I felt a pleasant lassitude in my limbs. I did not rise from my couch till noonday.

**Maids:** All is ready for Your Ladyship's toilet.

**Lady Yang** (Walking to the mirror and singing):

> The window's pearly curtain steeped in morning sun,
> The precious mirror waits to see my toilet done.

(Sitting before the mirror and singing to the tune of ***Zhu Yingtai***):

> Lightly I comb my hair and dress it in a bun;
> I peer in the mirror to see if it's well done.

**Ever Fresh:** Here is an emerald hairpin, my lady.

**Lady Yang:** I put it on my head.

**Mindful Maid:** Here is the rouge, my lady.

**Lady Yang:** I'll smooth it on my lips red.

**Ever Fresh:** Please pencil your eyebrows, my lady.

**Lady Yang:** I trace my eyebrows with care.

(Rising) I linger

And keep straight my waist slender

Like willow trees.

**Mindful Maid:** Ah! you have forgotten this flower, my lady.

(Pinning on the flower for her)

I add some cherry blossom with my finger.

**Maids** (Looking at Lady Yang):

Your skin's so tender

We fear it might be ruffled by a breeze,

**Will your Ladyship let us change your clothes?**

(Helping her into another dress)

What perfume rare

Wafts in the air!

She takes her gold-embroidered dresses down

And puts on her apricot-colored gown.

(Lady Yang takes a few steps while her maids watch her.)

Behold her headdress quiver

And her skirts softly spread.

(Lady Yang puts on her slippers.)

Her feet are light enough to tread on river,

But she won't go ahead.

(Lady Yang looks down at herself.)

Her grace is matchless in the gentle breeze.

(Lady Yang looks in the mirror.)

Before the mirror she is charming at her ease.

(Lady Yang yawns sleepily and the maids support her.)

Your Ladyship's still tired.

Why not take a siesta as desired ?

**Lady Yang:** Yes, I am still tired and will rest a little longer. Draw the bed curtain for me.

> Why should spring beauty fill with drowsiness the air?
> I feel sleepy again after combing my hair.

(Lady Yang sleeps and the maids put down the curtain.)

**Ever Fresh:** Can the emperor have gone to see Lady Mume Blossom, that he has not yet come?

**Mindful Maid:** But don't you know that Lady Mume Blossom has moved to the east wing of the Upper Sunny Bower?

**Ever Fresh:** Is it true?

**Mindful Maid:** Yes, it is true. The emperor is so devoted to Lady Yang that he spends all his leisure time in the west palace. He does not even bring his attendants. So you and I, we must wait on them well.

(Enter the emperor.)

Emperor continues to sing to the same tune:

> What a delight
> To see my mistress fair and bright!
> I am insatiate
> Of caressing her early and late.

(As the emperor approaches, the maids curtsey to him.)

**Maids:** Long live Your Majesty! Our lady has just gone to sleep.

**Emperor:** Do not wake her. (Raising the curtain)

> Parting the silken curtain, I can't tell
> The aroma from her fragrant smell. (Looking at her)
> I love her lying like rose jade
> On the embroidered quilt of brocade.

**Maids** (Aside): Such gallantry

Has made him king of lovers to the highest degree.

**Lady Yang, waking, sings in a low voice to the same tune:**

O who is it

That parts the curtain of my bed?

Drowsy, I rub my starry eyes.

(Sitting up, she rubs her eyes and smoothes her hair.)

**Emperor:** The powder fades

On her face fair,

The rouge on her lips not so red,

And disheveled her hair.

(The maids help her up. She opens her eyes, then closes them again as she sits down once more.)

I'm moved to see her held up by her maids,

So frail she seems

Nor able to rise

Nor to sit.

(The maids support her as she sits, and the emperor assists them.)

I'd better wait, while she still dreams.

**Lady Yang** (Seeing him): Long live Your Majesty!

**Emperor:** It would be pleasant to enjoy this sunny morning outside. Why do you sleep at noon?

**Lady Yang** (Speaking low): Last night I was favored by Your Majesty, You brought fresh shower for my thirsting flower so that I, laden with your favor, became too weak to rise and dress up, so I fell asleep again. That is why I failed to welcome Your Majesty just now.

**Emperor** (Laughing): So the fault is mine, isn't it?

(Lady Yang blushes without a word.)

My dear, you still look drowsy. Let us go to the front pavilion to enjoy awhile.

**Lady Yang:** As Your Majesty wishes.

(They walk forward, followed by the two maids.)

**Emperor:** The setting sun retains the Western Queen.

**Lady Yang:** On gentle breeze the beauties lean.

**Maids:** The palace pleasure won't be shown,

So to few outsiders it's known.

(As the emperor and Lady Yang sit down, the eunuch Gao enters.)

**Gao:** The water clock is heard at noon from tower high,

The sovereign's joy known to the eunuch near by.

Long live Your Majesty! On your order the prime minster has given An Lushan a test and he is now waiting outside to make his report.

**Emperor:** Let him come in.

**Gao:** His Majesty orders the Prime Minister to approach.

(Prime Minister Yang enters.)

**Yang:** Through my office pass all the reports from the land;

I've heard all palace gossip, being close at hand.

(Bowing to the emperor and Lady Yang)

Long live Your Majesty! Long live Your Ladyship!

**Gao:** You may rise.

**Yang:** On Your Majesty's order, I have tested An Lushan, and beg to report that I find him a stout fellow skilled in archery and horsemanship.

**Emperor:** Yesterday I read General Zhang's report that An Lushan knew six barbarian languages and the arts of war, and that he would make a good frontier general. But, as he had been defeated in war and was to be court-martialed, so I sent you to test him. Since you find him an able man, you may tell him that his disastrous mistakes are pardoned, and order him to appear in court tomorrow morning. I shall appoint him to a post in the capital, and see how he conducts himself.

**Yang:** It shall be done, Sire.

(Going out)

**Gao:** The peonies are in full bloom, Sire, at Aloes Pavilion. Would Your Majesty and Your Ladyship care to enjoy them?

**Emperor:** Very good. With such a beautiful lady and such beautiful flowers, you must send for Li Bai to the Pavilion to compose a beautiful poem for us.

**Gao:** I will send for him at once, Sire!

**Emperor** (To Lady Yang): My dear, let us go to enjoy the flowers.

### Epilogue of the Scene

**Emperor:** By balustrade the flowers bloom impearled with dew.

**Lady Yang:** Around bowers and pavilions we enjoy the view.

**Emperor:** A song newly-composed will highly be admired.

**Together:** We wait for laurel poet's coming as desired.

(Exeunt.)

## Scene 5  Spring Excursion

(Enter Eunuch Gao.)

Gao sings to the tune of *Congratulations to Imperial Court*:

In inner court I hold the highest place;

Early and late I wait on the Imperial Grace.

In gold and sables, jade belt and embroidered gown,

I follow His Majesty up and down.

I, Gao Lishi, General of the Imperial Guard, control the six palaces and enjoy greater power than any minister. I seize every opportunity to please the emperor and anticipate his wishes, and thanks to my discretion and eagerness to please, I have become a great favorite of His Majesty. Today is the third day of the third moon and the emperor, who is going to visit the River Bend with Lady Yang, has ordered me to instruct the Prime Minister and the three duchesses to accompany them. I am going now to carry out my instructions.

To tell the lady's kins I'm on my way;

His Majesty requires their presence today. (Exit.)

(Enter An Lushan in official dress, followed by attend-ants.)

An sings to the tune of *Congratulations to Imperial Court*:

Since I paid court to man in power,

Imperial favors on me shower.

A prisoner turns to favorite, I again may aspire high.

I, An Lushan, have been held in great favor since I regained office through imperial mercy. It is lucky to have a big belly, reaching nearly to my knees. One day when His Majesty noticed it, he asked me what was in it, and I answered, "Only my loyal heart!" The emperor was pleased, and since then he has become fond of me and more convinced of my loyalty, promising I shall soon be made a prince. This is unlooked-for fortune. Attendants, leave me!

(His attendants go out.)

Today is the third day of the third moon, and the emperor and Lady Yang are visiting the River Bend with the three duchesses in their train. Men and women of the capital are going to watch. Why not change into civilian dress and ride there to enjoy the spectacle?

(He changes his dress and mounts his horse.)

Now I have passed the city gate. Behold! The road smells sweet with fragrant dust and carriages and horses run like fleeting clouds. What a brave show!

The catkins on the road bewilder drunken eye,

And birds call out from flowers to the passers-by.

(Enter two young lords in magnificent dress.)

Lords sing to the tune of **Night Sailing Boat**:

How enchanting the vernal land!

Amid lovely blossoms the breeze

Blows as if it were fanned.

A screen of willow trees

Stand in array

On the pathway.

We can't tell if it showers

Red silks or violet flowers.

(They greet each other.)

**First Lord:** It is the third day of the third moon today. Shall we go to the River Bend to have a good time?

**Second Lord:** Yes, let's go. A string of carriages is passing there.

It must be the procession of the three duchesses. Let us hurry over to have a look!

**Together** (walking): Look, on the way

The splendid carriages with embroidered screen

Blazing with jewels red and green

Vie on display.

The winds compete

In fragrance with the scent of musk and orchid sweet.

The gems adorning brilliant gown

Outshine each other up and down. (Exeunt.)

(The Duchesses of Han, of Guo and of Qin enter, each in a carriage, accompanied by an attendant and a maid.)

Three Duchesses sing together to the tune of *Night Sailing Boat*:

Stop here and feast the eye

On silken gowns as bright as cloud!

Ladies in beauty vie

With chignon proud,

Black like cicada's wing

And eyebrows painted with grace.

It's pleased His Majesty for us to come in spring

By riverside to follow royal trace.

**Han:** I am the Duchess of Han.

**Guo:** I am the Duchess of Guo.

**Qin:** I am the Duchess of Qin.

**Duchesses:** By the imperial command we are summoned to the River Bend. Attendants, drive on!

**Attendants:** As you say, your ladyships. (The carriages move forward.) Duchesses continue to sing:

Wheels red

On flower-strewn rivershores tread

With dropping trinkets and slanting hairpins,

Among fallen petals imperial kins

Are honored to ride

By riverside.

Palace robes in a string

Sweep forward to enjoy spring. (Exeunt.)

(An Lushan rides up and gazes after the duchesses.)

**An:** Ah, what beauties!

(Singing to the tune of **Night Sailing Boat**):

When they cast back their glances,

How their unmatched loveliness entrances!

O let my horse pursue

Their carriages to have a closer view!

On my way to the River Bend, I have caught a glimpse of the three duchesses, each of them a celestial beauty. Ah, Son of Heaven, emperor of Tang! You have not only the beautiful Lady Yang, but her three sisters too. How fortunate you are!

All flowers belong to His Majesty.

How grand an emperor is! See!

Let me spur on to feast my eyes on them.

Scanning the cabs ahead with greed,

Now and again I whip my steed.

(He whips his horse and gallops forward, but the attendants bar his way.)

**Attendants:** Halt, there! The Prime Minister is here. How dare you try to charge past?

(Prime Minister Yang rides in.)

**Yang:** What is all this fuss?

(Yang and An look at each other; then An turns away in haste.)

**Attendants:** Just now we saw this man galloping wildly forward, so we stopped him.

**Yang** (Laughing): It is An Lushan. But why did he run away from me like that? (Thinking)

Where are the carriages of the three ladies?

**Attendants:** Just in front.

**Yang:** So? How dare An Lushan be so impolite?

(Continuing to sing to the same tune):

It's hateful not to pay

Respect before imperial kinsmen on the way.

How impolite to ride

By fragrant carriages' side!

How can I keep apart

The sudden anger in my heart!

Attendants, escort the carriages closely and drive away all passers-by!

(Attendants assent.)

**Yang:** Go forward! Clear the road with golden whip!

Let your steeds follow painted carriages on their trip!

**Attendants:** Let passers-by

Never come nigh,

Lest you incur the displeasure

Of the Prime Minister at leisure! (Exeunt.)

(Enter a country woman, a plain lass, a flower girl and a country squire.)

All sing to the tune of *Perfumed Dress of Brocade*:

In clothes new,

With made-up face,

Clumsy in view,

We pretend to grace.

Our robes are green with grass,

Our hair red with flowers, alas!

(They greet each other.)

**Woman:** Are you going to visit the River Bend?

**Others:** Yes, the emperor and Lady Yang will be there today.

(We are going to see royalty.)

**Lass:** It is said that the emperor loves Lady Yang as a precious jewel. I wonder how her looks compare with mine.

(The flower girl laughs, and the squire looks the lass over.)

Why do you look at me like that?

**Squire:** I find your face has its share of jewels too.

**Woman:** What jewels?

**Squire:** Her eyes are cat's eye stone;

Her wrinkled forehead has the agate's line;

Her teeth are made of amber-bone,

Her lips of coral fine.

(The country woman laughs, and the lass strikes the squire with her fan.)

**Lass:** You glib-tongue, don't you have your share of jewels?

**Squire:** Try to tell me what they are.

**Lass:** Your skull looks like a silver mine. How many diggers were buried therein?

**Woman:** Enough of that. I've heard that wherever the three duchesses pass, many things are dropped on the way. Let's go and see what we can find.

**Lass:** Then let us hurry up!

(They walk on, the lass teasing the squire.)

**All:** In the breeze light

Floats the cloud bright.

The ducal carriages bring

To woods and grass fragrance of spring.

**Squire:** Let's see if we can find anything left in the grass.

**Girl:** I will leave you now.

I'll cry and sell my flowers before

The rich men's painted door.

(She goes out, crying "Flowers to sell!" The others search in the grass and each picks something up.)

**Lass** (To the country woman): What have you got there?

**Woman:** A hairpin.

**Lass** (Examining it): It is made of gold, with a ruby on it. How lucky you are!

**Woman** (To the lass): And what have you?

**Lass:** An embroidered phoenix slipper.

**Woman:** Well, try to put it on.

**Lass** (Trying): Confound it! I cannot even get my toe in. I'll keep the pearl on it though.

(Taking off the pearl, she throws the slipper on the ground.)

**Squire:** Let me pick it up and put it in my sleeve.

**Lass:** You know to take advantage of me. Show me what you have got.

**Squire:** A gold box wrapped in a silk handkerchief.

**Woman** (Taking the box and opening it): Oh, it is something brown, in thin slices with rather a sweet smell-could it be some love potion?

**Squire** (Laughing): No, this is scented tea.

**Lass:** Let me try it. (She and the country woman taste some, but spit it out.)

Pah! It's bitter. How can people eat this?

**Squire** (Taking back the box): All right. Let us go on.

(They walk on.)

**All:** The butterflies are busy with the bees

Flying among the flowers and the willow trees.

Behold! The Dragon Tower high

Reflected in water! River Bend is nigh.

(The country woman and squire walk off.)

**Lass:** Wait for me! I'll pass water, but where can I find a water closet?

What can I do but make water in the open air?

(Exit.)

(Enter the three duchesses with their attendants and maids.)

Duchesses sing to the tune of *Song of Juice*:

Our perfume's mingled with the fragrance of the flowers;

The orioles' songs are interspersed with laughing words.

See willow catkins fall like snow over duckweed white,

Pairs of bluebirds

Pecking red petals falling in showers.

Gone are two-thirds of season bright.

What a sunny day!

Let our carriages drive on their way!

**Attendants:** May it please your ladyships, we have arrived at the River Bend.

**Duchess of Han:** Where is the Prime Minister?

**Attendants:** His Grace has gone to the Vernal Palace where His Majesty is now.

(The three duchesses alight from their carriages.)

**Duchesses:** Behold! It is really beautiful here.

By rivershore,

By rivershore

Red blossoms blush

Amid green leaves so lush

That we adore.

At River Bend,

At River Bend

A row of willow trees stretches without an end.

(The eunuch Gao leading a horse enters with attendants.)

**Gao:** By its jade bit I lead

A crimson-colored steed

For one in butterflied,

Gold-sprinkled dress to ride.

(Greeting the three duchesses) By His Majesty's orders, the Duchesses of Han and Qin shall be feasted in the Second Pavilion, while the Duchess of Guo is to ride to the Vernal Palace to feast with Lady Yang.

**Duchesses** (Kneeling): Long live His Majesty! (Rising)

**Gao** (To the Duchess of Guo): Will Your Ladyship be mounted?

**Guo:** The eunuch hastens me

To leave my sisters and enjoy alone with glee

The vernal breeze with His Majesty.

**Han & Qin:** Be worthy to receive imperial grace

With lightly powdered face!

**Qin:** See how she flicks her whip and rides off!

**Han:** Let her go as she pleases.

**Maid:** Will Your Ladyships come to the pavilion for the feast?

### Epilogue of the Scene

**Maid:** The Vernal Hall's amid peach blossoms and willow trees.

**Qin:** Let us enjoy the happy excursion with the same ease.

**Han:** We would receive imperial favor if we please.

**Together:** Then we may laugh at her who's bathed in sunny breeze.

(Exeunt.)

ACT II

## Scene 1 The Mystery

(Enter the eunuch Gao.)

**Gao sings to the tune of *Thread on Thread of Gold*:**

His Majesty has come back from his trip of pleasure.

How can he be displeased

With Lady Yang, his treasure?

Can it be at the vernal feast

Another gallantry

Overdone by His Majesty?

How can a pleasure change

Into displeasure? O how strange!

The day before yesterday the emperor went with Lady Yang to the River Bend in perfect bliss, but yesterday Lady Yang came back alone, while His Majesty only returned today, looking displeased. I wonder what the reason is. Here comes Ever Fresh. I'll try to ask her.

(Enter Ever Fresh.)

**Ever Fresh sings to the tune of *Thread on Tread of Gold*:**

In inner palace love affair's

Beyond our cares.

One brings fresh shower

For the other's thirsting flower.

Suddenly they upset the bower.

**Gao** (Greeting her): You've come just at the right time. I want to ask you why His Majesty has stopped coming to Lady Yang's Western Palace.

**Ever Fresh:** Ah, don't you know?

> Since they two parted,
>
> They have pretended cold-hearted.

**Gao:** What is the matter?

**Ever Fresh:** By their bedside

> Another beauty would abide.

**Gao:** Who do you mean?

**Ever Fresh:** You are clever enough to guess

> Who is the beauty in fine dress.

**Gao:** How could I know it? Tell me, please.

**Ever Fresh:** Well, it was Lady Yang herself who started the trouble.

**Gao:** How so?

Ever Fresh sings to the tune of *Silver Lantern*:

> Before His Majesty she praised the duchess fair:
>
> Though lightly powdered, her beauty's beyond compare.
>
> That day in the Vernal Palace she asked the emperor to send for the duchess. After three cups of wind.
>
> Without her knowledge, she
>
> Drew them together with high glee.
>
> The duchess' girdle torn apart,
>
> They're tied up heart to heart.

**Gao** (Clapping his hands and laughing): I suspect so. Why then should Lady Yang be angry?

**Ever Fresh:** Then she was afraid that the duchess might take her place in the emperor's affections.

Love turning into hate,

The lovebirds have to separate.

**Gao:** Then the duchess was offended and left?

**Ever Fresh:** Yes, when the duchess took her leave, Lady Yang did not ask her to stay, and the emperor was displeased. He has not been near her today and she is weeping.

**Gao:** I think Lady Yang carries matter too far.

Charming and jealous, she forced Lady Mume Flower

To move reluctantly out to the Eastern Bower

She and the duchess are two branches of one tree.

Why refuse to share royal favor out of jealousy?

**Ever Fresh:** Do not mention that! In the past the emperor never left Lady Yang's side, but now he is staying away from her. What can we do?

**Gao:** What can we do? Why, you and I

Can only watch while standing by.

(A voice offstage summons Gao.)

**Gao:** Coming.

### Epilogue of the Scene

**Gao:** Enjoying vernal feast till it's late, she's afraid.

**Ever Fresh:** Imperial favor lavished too much would soon fade.

**Gao:** She wears a smiling face but is jealous at heart.

**Ever Fresh:** If you ask me, how could I know who stand apart?

(Exeunt.)

## Scene 2 Rivalry

(Enter the Duchess of Guo.)

**Guo** sings to the tune of *Strolling around the Pool*:

> I followed in imperial train to River Bend;
> I did not dream of royal favor in the end.
> How can I not complain
> Of the alluring blue bird?
> I ponder over and again:
> How could my heart not have been stirred?
> How can my slandered sister tolerate
> A rival beauty in the state?
> "The jadelike swallow light
> Plays with snow white;
> She seeks her love in dream
> On painted beam."
> My sister in the palace is a jealous one.
> So do not fly to her bower bathed in the sun!

I am a daughter of Yang married into the Pet family. My husband died early and I would not allow my fragrance be stolen in my green bower. My sister Jade Ring used her influence to have me made Duchess of Guo. In spite of my high rank, I cared nothing for my toilet. Confident in my natural beauty, I dare go into the emperor's presence with unpowdered face. When His Majesty visited the River Bend the other day, we were told to follow in his train. While my two sisters were feasted in the pavilion outside, I was summoned into the vernal palace to attend the emperor. Then I won his favor. Though the emperor is fond of me, I am afraid slanderers may speak against me. So when His Majesty asked me to accompany him to the palace yesterday, I declined the favor and came back. When I think it over, I still feel how fortunate I was.

(Singing to the tune of **Word on Word in Brocade**):

This was a favor sent from high above;

It's surely Fate that destined us to love.

The golden cage was open 'neath the flower;

I was trapped like a phoenix in his bower.

Under the torches red

Wine flowed and cups were passed on tables spread.

With wine cups near,

The emperor whispered in my ear:

"Make haste!

There is no time to waste."

Then I was led

To curtained bed.

In the curtained bed it would seem

Happy as in a dream.

He brought fresh shower

For my thirsting flower;

O We were so near heart to heart

That we would never part.

O We were so close to each other's heart

That we would never part.

But in the morning when my sister came,

When my sister came,

She spoke behind

My back words unkind.

She jeered at me

And sneered at me.

With an injured air she put me into shame.

What could I do but shiver

With fear and quiver

And let her speak ill

Of me and do what she will.

(Enter Guo with attendants in the background.)

(Enter the Duchess of Han with attendants.)

**Han sings to the tune of *Not the Way*:**

If vernal breeze blows on all blooms with equal zest,

Why should one flower outdo all the rest?

The other day the Duchess of Guo was favored by the emperor, and today I asked my other sister, the Duchess of Qin, to come with me to see her. But Qin is sick with envy, so I must pay this visit alone.

**Attendant:** We have reached the Mansion of Guo, my lady.

**Han:** Go in and announce my arrival.

(The attendant goes in to announce her, and the Duchess of Guo comes out.)

(Guo retires with attendants in the background.)

**Guo:** Welcome, my dear sister.

(The attendants, jesting, retire.)

**Han:** I've come to congratulate you, darling.

**Guo:** On what ground?

**Han:** A special favored flower

(Is reddened in imperial sunshine.)

**Guo** (Blushing): What do you mean?

I entered the inner bower

Only to serve the emperor with cups of wine.

As for imperial favor and care,

In and out, we have equal share.

**Han** (Laughing): We all partook of the imperial feast, but what we had outside was not what you had inside the bower.

Do not deceive

Me on imperial favor you did receive!

O who could share with you

The vernal view?

**Guo:** It is not hard for you

To share your due.

**Han:** Let me ask you how is our younger sister Jade Ring?

Guo sings to the tune of *A Garden Full of Spring*:

With vernal river pleased

How happy we were all!

Urged to attend the feast,

I gazed on vernal hall.

Our sister Jade Ring, new-attired

Is more and more admired.

**Han:** How deep does His Majesty love her!

**Guo:** In vernal night,

In vernal night,

They are like flatfish left and right.

> Who knows how one brings shower
> For the other's thirsting flower!

**Han:** Didn't you get an inkling?

**Guo:** My impression is that she has become even more quick-tempered than before.

> I try to guess her mind
> And see through what's behind.
> Charming and spoiled,
> She was embroiled.
> She would find faults with others night and day,
> And she insists on having her own way.

**Han:** That has always been the case. You should try to talk to her about it, sister.

**Guo:** I've lost my patience with her.

**Han:** By nature she is proud
> And will do what is not allowed.
> Relying on inborn address,
> She's full of cleverness.
> We, as her elder sisters, should
> Not speak ill of her as we would.
> In Sunny Bower,
> In Sunny Bower
> Alone on her, imperial favors shower.
> None of three thousand ladies sweet
> With her in beauty could compete.

**Guo:** I have not been competing with her. I'm only afraid that her behavior may make the emperor change his mind.

**Han:** She seems to be hinting at something.

I try to guess her mind

And see through what's behind.

So full of pride,

She chides apart.

What does she hide?

There must be something in her heart.

(An attendant enters.)

**Attendant:** An important thing has happened, my ladies. Lady Yang has offended the emperor and Gao Lishi has been sent to take her back to the Prime Minister's house.

**Han:** Can it be true?

**Guo:** I said her temper would get her into trouble.

**Han:** Even so, we are her sisters, and this may affect us too. I think think we should go to see her.

**Guo:** You are right. Let us go together.

Han sings to the tune of *Epilogue*:

The sudden degradation fills my heart with fear.

**Guo:** Let's drive our cars to hear

What says our sister dear!

What will Lady Mume Flower think of it?

**Together:** Is it better to be the lonely Mume flower?

For she still blooms within the palace bower.

### Epilogue of the Scene

**Guo:** Imperial order changes our sister's fate.

**Han:** We've heard from palace door she comes to premier's gate.

**Guo:** How can she forever in royal favor stay?

**Han:** How sad to see her rise and fall within a day!

(Exeunt.)

# Scene 3  A Lock of Hair

(Prime Minister Yang enters hurriedly.)

**Yang:** The weather fair may turn windy outright;

Weal turns to woe when morning turns to night.

I am Prime Minister Yang. Since my cousin became the emperor's favorite, our power has grown daily. Who could foretell that this morning news would come that she had offended the emperor and has been dismissed from the palace, and that the eunuch Gao is bringing her home in a single carriage. This is a terrible blow! I must go to the gate to meet them. (Exit.)

(Enter Gao leading the way of Lady Yang's carriage.)

Lady Yang sings to the tune of *Gazing on my Homeland*:

Fickle are our sovereign's ways.

Where is his favor of those former days?

His favorite put suddenly apart,

How could he be so hard at heart!

Banished, I feel so desolate

To be severed by the Long Gate.

How deep's the lonely lane!

As I look back, from grief can I refrain?

(The Prime Minister enters.)

**Yang** (Greeting her): Your Ladyship!

**Gao:** After Your Grace has shown Her Ladyship in, I would like to have a word with you.

**Yang:** Attendants, tell the maids to take Her Ladyship to the back hall.
(Maids enter, help Lady Yang out of the carriage and lead her off.)
(Greeting Gao): Be seated, my lord. Would you please tell me
how this happened?

Gao sings to the tune of *A Message*:

Our Lady Yang did win

The greatest favor of our sovereign.

Of inner palace she was at the head;

At night she served alone the imperial bed.

But she offended yesterday the royal heart —

I know not how — and like two stars now they're apart.

If I may speak bluntly, Your Grace,

Her Ladyship's inclined to be self-willed;

With jealousy her heart's unduly filled.

**Yang:** But what can be done now that she is banished?

**Gao:** You had better go to court to apologize for her, and see how this
can be remedied.

**Yang:** I shall depend on you to put a word,

So by our sovereign it will be heard.

**Gao:** You can count on me.

**Together:** Again the palace flower

Must bloom in royal bower.

**Gao:** I will take my leave now.

**Yang:** I am coming with you.

(Calling to an attendant) Tell the maids to look after Her
Ladyship well.

(An attendant's assent can be heard offstage.)

The magpie goes together with crow.

I do not know if it is weal or woe. (They leave.)

(Enter Lady Yang with a maid.)

**Lady Yang sings to the tune of *Incense Burning*:**

Out of the palace gate,

My soul is filled with fears.

My dress is stained with grief, my face with tears.

But how can I express

My heart's distress!

I pity my sad fate

And my pretty face,

And I regret imperial grace.

"Imperial favor goes as water eastward flows.

Whether it's won or lost, you are alike in woes.

Don't sing before wine-cups the song of flower's fall!

The chilly wind is hidden west of palace hall."

Since I went to the palace, I had received such high imperial favor that I thought I could rely on it and enjoy it from year to year. Who would anticipate I was so unlucky as to offend His Majesty and to be sent back in a carriage! Out of the palace, I feel far from him as earth from heaven. (Shedding tears) The bright moon over the palace shall no more see my shadow now; a flower fallen out of the royal garden can never return to the bough. How can I not mourn over my fate! Wiping tears on my sleeves, I still feel an unconsolable grief.

(Singing to the tune of *Weeping Pomegranate Flower*):

When I caress

My silken dress,

I can still tell

Imperial smell.

How can I thank, above

All, the emperor for his love?

I shared his spring delight

From morning to night

(Changing to the tune of **Weeping a Scholar**):

How could I know he'd not bring shower

For my thirsting flower?

In former days the sovereign

To my every whim would give in.

Who knows a sister bough would come athwart

To set entwined branches apart!

(To the maid): Tell me from where can I see the palace!

**Maid:** From the pavilion in front, if you look northwest, Your Ladyship will see the palace wall.

**Lady Yang:** Come with me to the pavilion.

**Maid:** Yes, my lady. (They ascend the pavilion.)

**Lady Yang:** The western palace out of sight,

My heart's broken on the height.

**Maid** (Pointing): Do you see those yellow glazed tiles over there, my lady? Isn't that the palace?

Lady Yang in tears sings to the same tune:

I can't refrain from shedding tears,

While gazing on Celestial Spheres.

They seem so nigh,

But veiled in cloud on high.

Last night I lay in phoenix-curtained bed,

Hoping His Majesty'd relent and turn his head.

But Heaven's cruel as his heart,

Though young, I lost his favor, put apart.

**Maid** (Pointing): There in the distance I can see a eunuch on horseback.

He may be coming to call you back, my lady.

**Lady Yang** (Sighing):

This cannot be good news brought by the phoenix bird,

I fear the crow's ill omen might be heard.

(As she descends the steps, Gao enters.)

**Gao:** I come in secret to tell the lady lovelorn:

His Majesty still pines for her night and morn.

(Greeting her): Your servant, Madame.

**Lady Yang:** What brings you here again, my lord?

**Gao:** Just now when I reported your return to His Majesty, he asked me all that had happened here as if he regretted what had taken place. He is sitting alone, heaving sigh on sigh, and he must be longing for you; so I come to report this to Your Ladyship.

**Lady Yang:** Ah! no, how could he be still longing for me?

**Gao:** Forgive me if I dare advise you, madame, not to be obstinate. Have you anything which you could give me to take back to His Majesty? You never know, but it might move his heart.

**Lady Yang:** What can I send him, my lord?

(Thinking, she sings to the tune of **Happy Fishing Lantern**):

What can I send to show my love and move his heart?

The royal gifts apart,

I have but streams of tears which roll

Like pearls to rend the soul.

How can I string such pearls with golden thread

And send as gift on carved plate red?

Ah, yes, I have got it!

This lock of glossy hair

Once lay on the pillow near his head;

I used to comb it on which he fixed his stare.

(To the maid) Bring me the mirror and the golden scissors from my dressing table!

(The maid brings the scissors, while Lady Yang lets down her hair.)

Lady Yang sings to the tune of *Pride of Fishermen*:

O hair, O hair!

How can I bear

To cut you off which adorn

My head at early morn!

But, if with you I do not part,

How can I show my faithful heart?

(Clipping her hair, holding the lock and weeping)

O hair, O hair! Can I depend on you

To please imperial view? (Curtseying)

Your Majesty, this lock cut from my head

Conveys of broken heart the grievous thread ?

Take it, my Lord, and tell His Majesty (Weeping) I know I deserve a thousand deaths, and as I shall never look upon his celestial countenance again in this life, I present him with this lock of hair as a token of my love.

(Gao takes the lock of hair and places it on his shoulder.)

**Gao:** Take heart, my lady, I shall leave you now.

Depending on this lock of hair like silken thread,

They'll reunite till age snows white hair on their head. (Exit.)

(Lady Yang sits weeping. The Duchesses of Han and of Guo enter.)

Duchesses sing to the tune of *Pomegranate Flower Lantern*:

'Tis said our sister has offended His Majesty;

She has to come back to our family.

We hear our cousin out of favor stay;

We don't know what the eunuch has to say.

(Walking in) Where is Her Ladyship?

(A maid announces the arrival of the two duchesses. Lady Yang, weeping, says nothing.)

**Han:** Don't distress yourself so! (Weeping with her)

**Guo:** That day in the vernal palace His Majesty was in a good humor.

How could this have happened?

(Singing to the tune of *Pride of Fishermen*):

I thought your happiness would not be ended;

I thought you could laugh or sulk all day long,

I thought the emperor'd not be offended

Whatever you might do, right or wrong.

**Han** (To Guo): Sister, do not say such things any more;

(To Lady Yang): Tell us what had happened before.

(Lady Yang pretends not to have heard.)

Guo sings to the tune of *Silver Lantern*:

Sister, excuse me if I frankly speak;

Though in high favor, you'd learn to be meek,

Or favor could to trouble lead.

Do you not know indeed

The emperor's love is like autumn leaves:

If you displease him, his displeasure grieves.

Duchesses sing to the tune of *Wild Geese's Song*:

We come to show our sisterly concern.

Why should you turn

Us a deaf ear

As if you would not hear?

Lady Yang sings the *Epilogue*:

Discarded like a fan in autumn breeze,

I'm grateful for your concern, but ill at ease.

Though preyed on by a thousand griefs, I'll keep

In my heart my sorrow deep. (exit)

**Guo** (To Han): Well, sister! See how she treats us!

**Han:** Yes, indeed. We came to see her, but she has something on her mind and won't listen to us. Next time when you go to vernal palace, sister, be sure not to behave like that!

### Epilogue of the Scene

**Guo** (Blushing): Today we see her come down from celestial gate.

**Hah:** When face to face, how can we not feel desolate!

**Guo:** She's ridiculous to see while we stand by.

**Hah:** Don't thrust out jealous tongue and cast an envious eye!

(Exeunt.)

## Scene 4  The Recall

(The emperor enters.)

**Emperor sings to the tune of _Beautiful Lady Yu_:**

Why should I fall into despair ?

On whom can I lay all the blame?

Such misery is hard enough to bear.

Why should the parrot keep on calling her name?

"On royal roads grass grows;

The garden blooms with flowers.

None of my subjects knows

Why I gaze from the towers."

I was displeased with Lady Yang's jealousy yesterday and sent her away in a fit of anger. But who knows there is no beauty who can take her place! Since her departure, there is no sight but arouses my disgust and no scenery but excites my regret. When the Prime Minister came just now to apologize for his cousin, I was embarrassed to see him.

(Sighing) I want to recall her, yet I find no pretext to give the order. If she is not recalled, how can I spend these lonely hours! I am at a loss what to do.

(Singing to the tune of _Embroidered Girdle_):

The vernal breeze has died away,

The palace curtains are half drawn,

Yet slowly drags the day,

Though birds are singing for joy on the lawn.

All flowers vie in color new,

But I regret at such a view!

(Changing to the tune of **Song Fit for Spring**):

How could I've been so rough

As not to understand her heart enough!

How could I have shown no affectionate regard

For jade-like beauty I discard!

(A eunuch enters and kneels before the emperor.)

**Eunuch:** Here on a plate of jade is well-sliced meat;

There in a golden jug is green wine sweet.

May it please Your Majesty, dinner is served.

(The emperor does not answer, and the eunuch repeats his message.)

**Emperor** (Angrily): Curse you! Who told you to come?

**Eunuch:** Your Majesty has eaten nothing since the morning and the inner palace told me to prepare a meal.

**Emperor:** Who is in the inner palace? Confound you! Attendants! (Two attendants enter.)

Take him away! Give him a hundred lashes and put him in prison!

**Attendants:** As Your Majesty commands. (Taking the eunuch away)

**Emperor:** I was thinking of my dear Lady Yang when this fool came to disturb me.

(Singing to the tune of **Yellow Dragon Conquered**):

How much for her I long!

Even if I had nectar fine,

And food divine,

I'd find them tasteless and wrong.

Without my dear one by my side,

How could my hunger be satisfied?

(Another eunuch enters.)

**Eunuch:** A banquet's spread in royal bowers,

Lutes and pipes played before the flowers.

(Kneeling before the emperor) Will it please Your Majesty to come to feast at Aloes Pavilion and hear the new music composed by the Imperial Music Bureau?

**Emperor:** Who wants to feast at Aloes Pavilion? Do you want to be beaten?

**Eunuch** (Kowtowing): It is not your slave's fault. It was the prince who feared Your Majesty might be unhappy and tried to afford some delightful diversion.

**Emperor:** Who dare say that I am unhappy! Attendants!

(Attendants enter) Take him out and give him a hundred lashes, then send him to be a scullion!

**Attendants:** It shall be done. (Taking the eunuch away)

**Emperor:** Attendants! (Two attendants enter.) Stand at the door and allow no one to enter, or you shall be thrashed.

**Attendants:** As Your Majesty commands. (Stepping to the front of the stage to stand there)

**Emperor:** Alas! What heart have I now to drink and enjoy music?

(Singing to the tune of **Drunk in Peace**):

In the Pavilion the balustrade Is still that one of jade.

But where's the lady fair

Who used to lean together with me there?

Although the music's new,

The connoisseur's out of view.

I hear no more songs from her lute.

How can I play alone my flute?

(Gao enters with Lady Yang's hair on the shoulder.)

Gao sings to the tune of **Silk-Washing Stream**:

Parting grief with lovesickness grows.

They're longing for each other, but who knows?

I who stand by

Understand well their heart.

I'll make the lovebirds fly

Together ne'er to part.

(Greeting the attendants) Where is His Majesty?

**Attendants:** His Majesty is staying alone.

**Gao** (Stopped when he starts to go in): Why do you stop me?

**Attendants:** His Majesty is very angry. He has had two eunuchs thrashed and has forbidden us to admit anyone else.

**Gao:** Very well, I shall wait outside.

**Emperor:** How to spend my leisure? I shall take a stroll outdoors.

(Pacing up and down)

Up to the marble steps has grown spring grass,

But I don't see

The silken skirt and pearl-decked shoes, alas!

That used to follow me.

**Gao** (Watching): Here comes the emperor. I shall hide myself by the door till I have a chance to approach him.

(He goes out, then enters again and listens.)

**Emperor:** As I long for my dear lady, I wonder how much she would be longing for me. This morning Gao Lishi told me she had been weeping ever since she left the palace. It broke my heart

63

to hear it. Many hours have passed and there has been no more news. Why should that scoundrel Gao have been keeping out of my ways!

**Gao** (Bowing): Here is your slave.

**Emperor** (Looking at him): Here you are. What is there on your shoulder?

**Gao:** Her Ladyship's hair.

**Emperor** (Smiling): What hair?

**Gao**: Lady Yang swears that she repents the folly which made her offend Your Majesty, and that she deserves a thousand deaths. As she will not be able to look upon Your Majestic's face again in this life, so she has cut off this lock of hair and asked your slave to present it to Your Majesty as a token of love. (Presenting the hair)

**Emperor** (Holding the hair, looks at it and sheds tears):

Ah! my darling!

(Singing to the tune of **Woodpecker**):

1hair perfumed my pillow but one night ago,

But today it is shorn

And sent me as a token of woe.

My heart is torn

By this symbol of separation late

Of our love, cut by the golden scissors of fate.

**Gao:** Your Majesty, please be not grieved. Since Lady Yang is your favorite, why let her remain outside?

Since the vernal breeze

Blows as you please,

Why not bring the flower

Back to your bower ?

**Emperor** (Reflectively): But I have already dismissed her. How am I to call her back?

**Gao:** To dismiss her because of her fault and call her back because she has repented, this would show the divine mercy of the Son of Heaven. (The emperor nods.) Besides, she was sent out at dawn in a single carriage, and now it is dusk. If we open a side door of Anqing Quarter and let her in from Taihua Hall, who will know of it? (Kowtowing)

Would Your Majesty please, I pray,

Recall her without delay?

Do not wait till tomorrow!

Her laughter would dispel your sorrow.

**Emperor:** Very well, I order you to bring back Her Ladyship.

**Gao:** I will go at once, Sire. (Exit.)

**Emperor:** Ah! How am I going to face her?

(Singing to the tune of **Descending the Tower**):

How happy I will be to see her fair like jade!

And yet I am afraid

She may be angry as to turn her face away.

For if she weeps, what shall I say?

All my excuse is lame,

Because I was to blame.

But now I must do my best to allay

Her sorrow for this separation of half day.

(Gao comes in with attendants and maids holding lanterns and leads in Lady Yang.)

Gao sings to the tune of **Double Melody**:

The fragrant carriage drives;

> The fragrant carriage drives
> Past green trees and arrives
> At royal bowers.
> See lanterns in pairs shine;
> See lanterns in pairs shine
>  On verdant trees in line
> And palace flowers.
> (Attendants and maids withdraw.)
> (Gao advances.) Here arrives Her Ladyship.

**Emperor:** Bring her in at once.

**Gao:** Yes, Your Majesty. (To Lady Yang) His Majesty orders Lady Yang to enter.

**Lady Yang** (Curtseying): Your slave deserves death for her offence.

**Emperor:** You may rise. (Gao kneels and withdraws.)

**Lady Yang** (Kneeling and weeping): I have done wrong and offended Your Majesty. I deserve my punishment. But now I see Your Majesty again and I shall die content.

**Emperor** (Shedding tears): How could you say that, my love?

Lady Yang sings to the tune of *Late Water Clock of Jade*:

> My guilt is heavy as a mountain;
> Your Majesty is mercy's fountain.
> I have repented now.
> In future I shall keep my proper place,
> And never show a jealous brow
> For a beautiful lady so as to lose grace.

**Emperor** (Raising her up): It was my fault. Let bygones be bygones, and don't mention it again.

**Lady Yang** (Rising and weeping): Long live Your Majesty!

**Emperor**, taking her hand and wiping away her tears, sings the *Epilogue*:

> Our sorrow was but half-day old,
> But it's increased our love tenfold
> Now I will tell you how
> Longing all day long has wrinkled my brow.
> (A maid enters.)

**Maid:** A feast is ready in the western palace for Your Majesty and Your Ladyship. (Exit.)

### Epilogue of the Scene

**Emperor:** Our love overbrims like a cup of wine.

**Lady Yang:** How can I show this grateful heart of mine!

**Emperor:** After parting you haunted me night and day.

**Lady Yang:** In our bedroom let's wipe our tears away!

(Exeunt.)

## Scene 5 Prediction

(Enter Guo Ziyi wearing a military uniform and sword.)

**Guo:** Who can appreciate my ideal high?

Wearing a sword in self-defence, I

Wait for the time to set the world aright;

Then I shall show myself a hero bright.

I am Guo Ziyi, a native of Zheng County. I have mastered military arts and strategies in the hope to become a worthy man and help to bring peace to the empire. Now, having passed the military examinations, I come to the capital to wait for my appointment. I find Prime Minister Yang abusing his power and An Lushan favored by the emperor. The government is going wrong, while a man of my capacity still lacks an official post. Who knows when I may have the chance to serve my country? (Singing to the tune of **Good Friends Get Together**):

A hero should carve out his way.

Should I rail at my fate each day?

I laugh at thoughtless swallows in their nest,

Not knowing crows which swarm from east and west.

Can we not guard against caged tiger and bear

But suffer rats and foxes running here and there?

How many times have I risen at cockcrow

To dance alone in woe!

How many ups and downs since olden days!

I mean to win renown to shine always.

I will live if I can,

Not as a woodcutter or fisherman.

**I will walk to the market and drink my fill.**

(Walking, he sings to the tune of *Joy to be Free*):

In royal street slowly I go

To unburden a while my woe

And to divert a stranger's mind.

I see the jostling crowd before and behind

Like drunkards who on foot can't stand

Where is the poet sober in a drunkards' land?

I long to find a companion,

But the fishing marshall's dead and gone;

The tiger-shooting general I adore

And the courageous warriors are no more. (Exit.)

(Enter a waiter of the tavern.)

**Waiter:** I swear our tavern is so fine

That in no time we sell out all our wine.

If you have money, you may drink your fill;

If not, you can't get water as you will.

I am a waiter of Xinfeng Restaurant in the capital. Our restaurant stands between the east and the west market where pass many people. Inhabitants of the capital and travelers beyond, lords and common people, officials and soldiers, all come to our tavern to drink three cups of wine. Some drink only, others have a meal; some take wine home; others feast here. We are kept hard at it. Look, here comes another customer.

(Guo Ziyi enters.)

Guo sings to the tune of **_Riding to the Capital_**:

> From far I see
> A colorful pavilion in the shade
> Of a green willow tree,
> With a blue sign of trade
> Flying in the light breeze.
> I'd find a hero to drink with me as we please.
> (Calling out) **Where is the waiter?**

**Waiter** (Greeting him): Come upstairs, sir.

**Guo** (Going upstairs): This is a fine tavern.

> The breeze through open windows blows in the sunshine;
> The walls are painted with fairies drinking wine.

**Waiter:** Are you drinking alone, sir, or waiting for friends?

**Guo:** I will have a few cups by myself. Bring the best you have.

**Waiter:** We have the best wine here, sir.

> (Bringing the wine) **Here you are, sir,**
> (Someone calls from offstage: "Where is the waiter?" The waiter goes out.)

Guo begins to drink and sings to the tune of **_Plane Leaves_**:

> I am no poet drinking wine at leisure,
> Nor soldier seeking in hard drinking for pleasure.
> While drinking, with wide-open eyes I see
> If in this drunkards' land there's place for me.
> I hear much noise and bustle in the fair,
> But of the sober drinker no one will take care.
> (He gets up to look out of the window. Richly-dressed eunuchs and officials pass with attendants carrying gold, silk, sheep and wine. The waiter brings in more wine.)

**Waiter:** Here is some freshly heated wine for you, sir.

**Guo:** Tell me, waiter, where are those officials going?

**Waiter:** I'll tell you as you drink. The emperor has ordered new mansions to be built for the Prime Minister and the three duchesses. The four mansions will be next door to each other, each like a palace. Every family wants to outdo every other. When one sees the neighbor's house better, one would pull down and rebuild his or her house until it is as splendid. This way, one single hall may cost millions. Today the new buildings are finished, so all the government officials are coming with presents of sheep and wine to offer congratulations. They all pass this way.

**Guo** (Shocked): Is this possible?

**Waiter:** Excuse me, sir. I'll go to warm up some more wine. (Exit)

**Guo**(Sighing): Ah! imperial favor extends as far as to the relatives of the emperor's favorite lady. What will be the end of all this?

(Singing to the tune of **the Gourd of Vinegar**):

> The kinsfolk usurp imperial right;
>
> they vie in luxury at building site.
>
> All courtiers bent their waist
>
> To men in power in all haste
>
> As country folk flock to a fair.
>
> To tell the emperor no one would dare.
>
> Look at the brilliant roofs and tiles overhead!
>
> With people's blood they are stained red. (Rising from his seat)

Anger has made wine go up to my head. Let me look around. (Looking at the wall)

Here is a quatrain written in small characters. Let me read it:

"The hero left the northern town;

The wise on horse would not come down.

The ghost beneath the mountain brings

A silken dress adorned with rings."

What a strange poem!

(Singing to the tune of *the Gourd of Vinegar*):

I read it line by line

And try hard to divine

What's hidden in the verse,

And find things going worse.

Let me see who the author is. (Reading) Li Xiazhou.

(Thinking) The name sounds familiar. Ah! Yes, I've heard there is a fortune-teller named Li Xiazhou, who is good at foretelling the future. This must be the man.

Perhaps the future's in veiled terms foretold,

But where's the riddle-guesser old?

Or can this verse be a poetic line

Written by some drinker of wine?

(A noise is heard offstage.) Waiter!

**Waiter** (Entering): Yes, sir?

**Guo:** What's the noise for?

**Waiter:** Well, sir, just take a look out of the window!

(Guo Ziyi looks out and sees An Lushan riding past, wearing a prince's costume and preceded by attendants.)

**Guo:** Who is that man?

**Waiter** (Laughing as he points at An): Don't you see that big belly, sir? That is An Lushan, a great favorite with the emperor. His Majesty has allowed him to recline on a coach under the golden cock canopy. Today he was made Prince of Eastern Peace, and he is on his way back from the court to his new palace outside the Gate of Eastern Flower.

**Guo** (Looking shocked and angry): So that is An Lushan! What has he done to be so quickly made a prince? He has the face of a rebel; he will certainly bring ruin to the empire.

(Singing to the tune of **Fragrance of Golden Chrysanthemum**):

> Here I see the ambitious bastard in high glee,
>
> With bulging eyes like a bee,
>
> And with a jackal's voice.
>
> How could this cunning rogue rejoice?
>
> What brings this wolf to royal hall?
>
> The verse will come true, written on the wall,
>
> When these imperial kinsmen lord it over all.

**Waiter:** Why do you look so angry, sir?

Guo sings to the tune of **Willow Leaves**:

> Ah! in cold, cold breeze my hair stands on end;
>
> In warm, warm breast my blood and anger blend.
>
> My eyes turn again and again
>
> To my ringing sword in vain.

**Waiter:** Don't look so angry, sir. Let me get you another pot of wine.

**Guo:** A thousand cups, a hundred pots of wine

> Could never wash away this heavy gloom of mine.

(Standing up) I've drunk enough. Here is your money.

**Waiter:** After three cups in peace a drinker goes,

But this official has a thousand woes. (Exit.)

**Guo** (Walking down the stairs and along the road): I'll go back to my room.

(Singing to the tune of **Rising Waves:**)

> These shocking sights and that mysterious line

Show the unfathomable will, human or divine.

I pace along with eyebrows knit and full of gloom,

 And at sunset I reach my lonely room.

(He enters his room and sits down. An attendant comes in.)

**Attendant**: Master, the bulletin has come.

**Guo** (Reading the bulletin): "The Ministry of War announces that by imperial decree Guo Ziyi is appointed military commissioner for Tiande." So the decree has come. I had better pack my things and go at once to my post. Though it is not an important post, at least I shall now be able to serve the state.

(Singing to the high tune of **Epilogue**):

In shallow water still can dart a fish;

In brambles birds can preen their wings as they wish.

At last I have a chance to scale the sky,

To set the world in order far and nigh,

Though dark forces prevail in this land,

I'll prop on my shoulder sun and moon.

I will support with my own hand

The throne which will tatter soon.


### Epilogue of the Scene

My horse has trodden dust for years in vain.

The rich in power still remain;

The poor still suffer a hard fate.

Who will worry about the state?

(Exit.)

ACT III

## Scene 1  Dream Music

(Enter the Goddess of the Moon with her fairy maid Cold Reed.)

**Moon Goddess sings to the tune of *Pacing in the Moon Palace*:**

Alone I shed clear light

Over the lovely night,

Unsallied through ten thousand years.

Dew from my silvery spheres

Is spread in wind o'er the crystalline sky

With fairy music wafting on high.

"Elixir of life drunk, I left the world of woe,

I keep my face with beauty still aglow.

Seeing Celestial fragrance fall amid the cloud,

I lean against the laurel proud."

I am Goddess of the Moon, queen of the night. It was said that I was wife of the Archer, but I have lived within the precious globe for thirty-six thousand years and spread my brilliant light over a thousand leagues. Here the jade hare and golden toad vie in rare splendor, there the white elm and red cassia bloom for all eternity. I have a divine melody called *Rainbow Skirt and Coat of Feather*, long kept in the palace of the moon and unknown to the human world. Now the emperor of the Tang empire below is fond of music and his favorite mistress Yang Yuhuan was a fairy maid on the fairy mountain, who used to visit me during her last life. Why don't I summon her spirit to hear this melody again so that, awakened, she may transcribe it with pipes and strings and carry the divine music to illuminate the human world? Come, Cold Reed!

**Cold Reed:** Yes, my lady.

**Moon Goddess:** Go down to the Tang palace and bring Yang Yuhuan's spirit to hear the divine music. You send her back when the performance is over.

**Cold Reed:** I will, my lady.

**Moon Goddess:** When in the fairy land her soul falls into a trance,

We shall secretly teach her our immortal dance. (Exit)

**Cold Reed:** At my mistress' command, I must leave the moon to go down to the Tang palace.

(Singing to the tune of **Prelude of Liangzhou**):

The Milky Way sprinkles

Star on star which twinkles,

I look down on the dusty world annoyed.

What I see is a fragrant misty void.

I've left the palace of jade with ease,

My pendants quiver in the breeze,

My gown reflects the rosy light

As I tread on clouds bright.

To teach a former palace maid our music divine,

I'll lead her sleeping spirit to the moonshine.

Here I am in the Tang Palace.

(Singing to the tune of **Congratulations to the Bridegroom**):

You see within the locked door the curtained bed,

Where Lady Yang like cherry blossoms red

Lies deep

In sleep,

More beautiful she seems.

Let us awake her from her day-dreams.

(Calling) Wake up, Lady Yang!

**Lady Yang** (Whose spirit enters, sings to the tune of **Fishing Lantern**):

Just now coolness seemed to remain

In clouds and rain;

I slept so deep as to forget the flower

Used in my make-up and face powder.

**Cold Reed:** Your Ladyship!

**Lady Yang:** Who is calling from under the eaves of the inner palace?

How is it that no palace maids announce the guest?

**Cold Reed:** Come quickly, my lady.

**Lady Yang** (Yawning): Still drowsy after rest

I rise and slowly draw aside the screen.

(Seeing Cold Reed,) Oh, it is a maid of honor.

**Cold Reed:** I'm not a palace maid attending the queen.

**Lady Yang:** If not a maid of honor, are you a beauty attending the emperor?

**Cold Reed:** Nor am I an attendant beauty.

**Lady Yang:** Who are you then?

**Cold Reed:** I am a fairy maid of the moon and my name is Cold Reed.

To serve the Goddess of the Moon is my duty.

**Lady Yang** (Startled): Ah! So you are a fairy from the moon.

How did you come here?

**Cold Reed:** Just now my mistress ordered me to invite you

To come to enjoy the laurel flowers' splendid view.

**Lady Yang:** Can it be true?

**Cold Reed:** Don't hesitate, my lady, but let me lead the way and come with me please.

(She leads her along.)

(Together sing to the tune of **Decorated Fishing Lantern**):

> Pointing towards the azure sky,
> We see beneath our feet clouds floating by;
> Stepping into celestial spheres,
> We hear soft breeze whisper into our ears.
> We gaze at stars so near;
> Within the reach of our hands they appear.
> How splendid the Moon Palace's found!
> It is like a reflection in a mirror round.

**Lady Yang:** It is mid-summer now. How is it that I feel so cold!

**Cold Reed:** Here is the moon which people on earth call the Palace of Boundless Cold. Will you please enter now?

**Lady Yang** (Overjoyed): A mortal as I am, how fortunate I am to come to the moon!

(She enters and looks around, and sings to the tune of **Flowers on the Brocade**):

> This blissful journey gives me sweet delight.
> (Thinking) I seem to have visited the scene before.
> The marble steps and emerald eaves in sight
> Look so familiar to me.

> How could the laurel tree bloom so early?

**Cold Reed:** The laurel tree in the moon blooms all the year around with fragrant flowers and leaves.

**Lady Yang:** It is indeed beautiful.

> The longer I look at it, the happier I'll be.

Its blossoms seem of gold,

Its leaves of emerald,

Its heavy fragrance perfume the dress in brocade

Of all within its shade.

(Music is heard offstage.)

Look! There is a group of fairies in white tunics and red skirts coming from under the laurel tree. How sweet is the music they are playing!

**Cold Reed:** This is the song of *Rainbow Skirt and Coat of Feathers.*

(Four, six or eight Fairies in white tunics and red skirts with cloudlike belts and pearled tassels come along, singing and playing music. Lady Yang and Cold Reed stand watching.)

**Fairies sing to the tune of *Beats in the Brocade*:**

We play celestial music among the flowers,

Our rainbow dresses touched with dew.

Far from the human world of dusty bowers,

Our music well expresses the moon's splendid view.

Though our tongues sing and our hands play with grace,

We cannot waken mortals from their dream,

Nor halt celestial palace's fleeting hours.

When the immortal music ends, we halt our pace,

And let the connoisseurs review the theme.

(The Fairies troop off.)

**Lady Yang:** How wonderful is the music, so clear and sweet as to move me heart and soul. It must be a melody of another world.

(Singing to the tune of *Beats after the Brocade*):

These mist-veiled fairies seemed familiar to me.

Listening to their note on note

Which seem to float

In the air, I'm intoxicated

And saturated

To mark each note which lingers

And follows the rhythm with my fingers,

And the beat

With the tip of each of my feet,

I blush to think of my dancing pride

With fairy songstresses by my side.

Tell me, fairy maid, may I see your mistress?

**Cold Reed:** It is not yet time for you to see her. The day will break.

Will Your Ladyship return to your palace?

(Singing the **Epilogue**):

You should remember this trip to the moon.

**Lady Yang:** I won't forget the new tune.

**Cold Reed:** Sorry to have kept you.

Away from the emperor's view. (Exit Lady Yang)

Now Lady Yang has gone back to the Tang Palace, and I'll report to my mistress. (Exit)

### Epilogue of the Scene

From the emerald-tiled, plane-shaded palace divine

You are sent back in the beautiful moonshine.

Mortals may hear celestial music again,

But waterclock hastens you back to the world of men.

## Scene 2  Recording the Music

(Enter the maid Ever Fresh.)

**Ever Fresh sings to the tune of *Drinking Song*:**

> The Western Palace orders me to clean
> And give the lakeside hall a pleasant look.
> Neath rainbow clouds I roll up crystal screen,
> The morning sun seems to hang on jade hook.

I am Ever Fresh waiting on Lady Yang with Mindful Maid in the west palace. Since her return the emperor has shown her greater favor than ever.

> On her alone is lavished royal love and care;
> She has outshone in six palaces all faces fair.

This morning I am ordered to prepare Lotus Bower for use so that music may be composed here. Mindful Maid is helping Her Ladyship at her dressing table and I have come to set out the four writing utensils.

> The brush-stand's bright
> As paper white.
> The inkstone drinks
> The fresh-ground inks.
> What a secluded scene in the shade so green!

**Tune: *End of the Song*:**

> The breeze blowing through the bamboo grove wrinkles
> The fragrant screen;

The lotus sprinkles

Dew and makes quiver

The surface of the river.

I can smell musk and hear the tinkle of jade pendants. Here comes Her Ladyship.

Lady Yang sings to the tune of *New Lotus Leaves*:

I dreamed last night of visiting the moon;

Of *Rainbow Skirt and Feathered Coat* I heard the tune.

Awake, I seem to hear the music and the song;

I'll write it down to pass the summer day so long,

I pencil my slender eyebrows dark or light as I will,

Which spreads out in the mirror like a distant hill.

The morning sun shines on my rouged face

Like a rosy cloud melting into my cheeks with grace.

Since I won back the emperor's love by cutting off a lock of hair, he has lavished more favor on me than before. As I often heard him praise the *Scared Swan's Dance* performed by Lady Mume Blossom, I wish to outdo her by a new one. Last night I dreamed of entering the Moon Palace, where I saw under the laurel tree beautiful fairies in red and white playing delightful music. When I woke up, the melody still lingered in my ears. So I order Ever Fresh to clean the Lotus Bower so that I might compose music for a new dance.

**Ever Fresh:** The four writing utensils are ready for use, my lady.

**Lady Yang:** You and Mindful Maid may stay here.

(Ever Fresh and Mindful Maid wave the fan or burn incense while Lady Yang composes music.)

Lady Yang sings to the tune of *Prelude to the Dance*:

The lotus' scent perfumes the window screen.

I straighten the paper white

And take a brush to write

Down what in the Moon Palace I have heard and seen.

I will reveal

What in my heart I feel.

**But the transition is not natural. How could I rearrange the words to make them harmonious word by word, stanza by stanza?**

How to improve the feet

Lest they are out of beat?

(Orioles sing behind the scene, and Lady Yang listens, brush in hand.) Ah, I've got it.

(She corrects the score and sings to the tune of *Jade Lotus*):

The trilling of the orioles, indeed,

Is just what I need.

(Putting down her brush) Now the music is composed.

What time is it, Ever Fresh?

**Ever Fresh:** It is just noon.

**Lady Yang:** Has His Majesty returned from the court?

**Ever Fresh:** Not yet.

**Lady Yang:** Come with me, Ever Fresh, to help me make my toilet. You wait here, Mindful Maid, and tell me as soon as His Majesty comes.

**Mindful Maid:** Yes, Your Ladyship.

**Lady Yang:** I will repaint my eyebrows and try

To change into a gown fragrant with butterfly.

(Lady Yang goes out with Ever Fresh.)

(The emperor enters and sings to the tune of *Fishing Lantern*):

Having dismissed the courtiers who have done their duty,

I leave the court to see my beauty

To while away

The long, long day.

Having returned to palace rooms,

I'm told she's in the Hall of Lotus Blooms.

So I follow the flowing stream

Along the poolside way

To find the fairy of my dream. (Arrives.)

**Mindful Maid** (Courtesys): Ah, Your Majesty.

**Emperor:** Where is your mistress, Mindful Maid?

Is she at play?

Why on the desk are brush and paper laid?

**Mindful Maid:** Her Ladyship has composed music here and has just left for dressing up.

**Emperor:** My darling, my darling! You have the accomplishments all beautiful ladies crave for. I don't know you are good at composing music, and I would like to have a look.

(He sits down to read the score.)

From the beginning I will read the score.

What delicate notation! How can I not adore?

It is so wonderful that I can never

Find out the faintest dissonance whatever.

How strange it is! I have never heard this tune before. On examining it, the melody seems unearthly. Could it come down from heaven? Such music cannot find its equal on earth. Oh, my darling! You are not only beautiful but also ingenious without a peer.

(Singing to the tune of **Jadelike Lotus**):

Even in intelligence you outshine all

The beauties in imperial palace hall.

**Lady Yang** (Entering in an evening dress, attended by Ever Fresh, sings to the tune of **Universal Joy**):

I've changed into a graceful dress so light

And the silk tunic makes it look more bright.

(Curtseying) Long live Your Majesty!

**Emperor** (Holding her to rise): Sit down, please. (She takes a seat.)

Your evening dress adds to your beauty,

Just like a willow swaying in the breeze,

Or a lotus blooming on the waves with ease.

With a sweet orchid slanting in your hair,

Your face would charm down fairies in the air.

**Lady Yang:** Why has Your Majesty come late from the court today?

**Emperor:** As the important position of governor of Lingwu is vacant and must be filled up, I discussed for long with the courtiers and finally I decided to promote Guo Ziyi to the post. So I was delayed at court.

**Lady Yang:** As I was waiting for Your Majesty alone at Lotus Bower,

I saw the window screen rippled by a breeze light,

Inspiring me with a new tune I tried to write,

But it can't match "*the Swan Leaving no Traces*,"

Brightening at the end of the dance all the faces.

**Emperor:** I have just read your score which is indeed incomparable and leaves the *Scared Swan's Dance* far behind.

**Lady Yang:** It was written in haste and I'm afraid it leaves much to be desired. I hope Your Majesty will kindly check it over.

**Emperor:** All right, I'll go through it carefully with you.

(The maids go out. The emperor sits down with Lady Yang to

read the music. He sings to the tune of **Rosy-faced Maid**):

I caress her long sleeves, we sit shoulder to shoulder,

Turning the music score, hand in hand I hold her.

A tune like this leaves nothing to be desired

How on earth could it not be admired?

Will you please tell me what is the name of this score?

**Lady Yang:** Last night dreamed of going up to the moon, where I saw a group of fairies playing music in rainbow colored dress, so I would like to call it *Dance in Rainbow Dress*.

**Emperor:** This music score does not belie

Its name, as sweet as laurels in the sky.

(Looking at her) You who compose this divine tune

Must once have been a fairy of the moon.

This score should be given to the conservatory at once, but I am afraid our musicians could not fully appreciate its beauty, so I would like to have Ever Fresh and Mindful Maid to copy this script under your personal guidance.Then it may be given to Li Guinian of the imperial orchestra so that his musicians may learn how to play the music.

What do you think of it?

**Lady Yang:** What Your Majesty says shall be done.

**Emperor** (Holding her to rise): The dusk is setting in. Let us go back to the palace.

The evening breeze begins to blow;

The crescent moon is hanging low.

**Lady Yang:** The imperial court is growing cool.

**Emperor:** See the love birds in pair sleep on the pool.

### Epilogue of the Scene

**Emperor:** My beauty's face outshines the lotus flower.

**Lady Yang:** The breeze through willows chills waterside bower.

**Ever Fresh:** A happy song is heard the flowers to caress:

**Together:** Call the musicians to sing *the Rainbow Dress.*

## Scene 3 The Dispute

(Enter Prime Minister Yang with attendants.)

**Yang:** How can I not foresee in the least

The audacious ambition of this beast?

No gratitude for me has he ever shown.

How can a loyal premier not warn the Crown?

I am Prime Minister Yang Guozhong, cousin of the emperor's favorite Lady Yang. There're neither ministers nor generals in the court but bow before me. That fellow An Lushan pretends to be naive, but is insidious at heart. How could the emperor have grown so fond of him and made him a prince? He is so ungrateful as to forget that I have saved his life. How could he become so insolent as to oppose me whenever there was an occasion! Curse him! The other day I warned the emperor against this ambitious wolf, whose face reveals his treacherous heart. I requested His Majesty to take measures to prevent him from making trouble in the future, but my sovereign would not listen to me. Today I should find a chance to renew my request for his dismissal so as to vent my spite against him. Here is the gate to the court. Leave me, attendants! (His attendants retire. Shouts come from offstage: "Clear the way!") Who is making such a noise? I'll, see who it is.

**An** (Entering with attendants):

Since I have won favor divine,

I will hide my secret design.

Leave me, attendants! (His attendants withdraw, and he greets Yang.) Good day, my lord.

**Yang** (Laughing): So it is you, An Lushan.

**An:** Well old Yang, what have you to say to me?

**Yang:** This is the imperial palace. How dare your attendants shout in clearing the way before and after you?

**An** (Insolently): See here, old Yang!

The emperor gives me the robe I wear;

From imperial stable comes the steed I ride.

Consulted at court on frontier affair,

I come out late from our sovereign' side.

Why can't a prince clear his way at court? Could I not do what a prime minister cannot?

**Yang** (Laughing coldly): So none could prevent you from clearing your way. But I would like to ask you, An Lushan, when and how did you win such a high favor?

**An:** I have been so for long.

**Yang:** You should think back a little.

**An:** Of what should I think?

**Yang:** You should think what you looked like when you first came to see me.

**An:** The past is past, but the present is present. Why should I think of the past?

**Yang:** Ah! An Lushan! (Singing to the tune of **Wind Soughing through Pines**):

From the death punishment you were not free,

Then you knelt long, pleading with me.

> If I had not intervened in a subtle way,
>
> How could you live safe and sound to this day?

**An:** It was His Majesty who pardoned me in his mercy and restored me to my post. What had this to do with you?

**Yang:** Well said. It had nothing to do with me.

> Oh! Would your conscience not cry loud?
>
> How could gratitude float away like floating cloud?

**An:** Ah! Don't you know, Yang Guozhong.

> On fortune do depend our rise and fall.
>
> Then do not boast of your power over all!

> You may exaggerate my failure, but how dare you hide the truth of your official's defeat at Nanshao and report it as a victory?

**Yang:** Who would dare to deceive our sovereign? Are you not slandering His Majesty?

**An:** Have you not deceived him?

> How many official posts have you sold?
>
> You squeeze people, to satisfy your greed for gold?

**Yang:** Shut up! You talk about official posts. How could you get yours if it is not sold?

(Laughing cynically.)

**An:** Nor is that all.

> How many times
>
> On your cousin's influence you rely,
>
> Guilty of a thousand crimes.
>
> Can you deny?

**Yang:** How dare you fabricate such slander against me! (Seizing An.) Come with me to His Majesty.

**An:** Do you think I am frightened? I will go with you. I will go with you.

(Gripping each other, they come to the presence of the emperor.)

**Yang:** May it please Your Majesty, —

An Lushan is a brute cool,

Though he pretends to be a fool.

He's like the rebellious leader of long ago,

To the crown prince he would not bow.

The court can't tolerate such a brute,

The evil must be pulled out by the root.

I beg Your Majesty to dismiss him at once.

**An:** I beg Your Majesty to listen to me.

As I'm in royal favor high,

Jealous become one and all.

Simple as I am, where can I fly

If into the snares I would not fall?

Your Majesty knows my loyal heart.

Let me serve you on the frontier far apart.

**Voice Off:** His Majesty decrees that since Minister Yang and General An are at odds, they cannot work together at court. An Lushan is appointed military governor of Fanyang and should proceed to his post at once. Kneel down and bow your thanks for the royal favor!

**An & Yang:** Long live His Majesty! (Rising.)

**An** (Saluting Yang): I am going today, old premier. You will no longer be troubled by my impolite manners.

You may do what you will at court,

But do not interfere

Into the long and short

Of my business on the frontier!

(The Prime Minister laughs bitterly. An starts to go, then turns back again.) **One more word.**

I'm going to take up my appointment new,

Should I bow thanks to you?

(Saluting Yang by bringing both hands together.) Excuse me.

(Aside) **I shall coolly see what he can do with me.** (Exit.)

**Yang** (Watching him go): **How dare he be so insolent!**

How can my anger be allayed?

His insolence can't be outweighed

He is promoted in array instead,

While I become a laughing stock on this head.

**I only hope An Lushan will make trouble when back to the frontier, then the emperor would believe in my foresight, His Majesty!**

What will His Majesty have to say?

Then he would regret what he is doing today.

### Epilogue of the Scene

Make quick decision and don't hesitate,

Or when disaster comes, you will regret too late.

Of the plan unfulfilled it's useless to complain,

Before the beauty cunning tricks are played in vain.

## Scene 4 Stealing the Music

(Enter Ever Fresh and Mindful Maid carrying the musical score.)
(They sing to the tune of **Eight Beats of Ganzhou**):

**Ever Fresh:** The score of *Dance of Rainbow Dress* is made.

**Mindful Maid:** It is copied at the window with gauge screen.

> Our lady with her voice like ringing jade
>
> Has taught us to sing in dress green.

**Ever Fresh:** I am the old maid Ever Fresh.

**Mindful Maid:** I am the young Mindful Maid.

**Ever Fresh:** Since her Ladyship composed the musical score, she has taught us to sing. Today the Emperor is coming to Huaqing Palace to hear the music. We two are ordered to instruct Li Guinian so that he may train his orchestra in Chaoyuan Pavilion.

**Mindful Maid:** They have learned the overture. Today we may teach them the rhythmic prelude.

**Ever Fresh:** Look, the moonlight is water-clear. It is the best time for music. Let us take the score to the pavilion. (They walk forward.)

**Together:** The cool moon rises over the high roof here,

> The warm breeze blows through curtain and screen.
>
> The moonlight is crystal clear,
>
> Just time to play the music taught by Fairy Queen.

(Enter Li Guinian the grey-bearded orchestra leader, singing to the tune of the **Bait to Attract Fish**):

Well-known to musicians old,

I am the leader of orchestra you behold.

I serve the emperor early and late,

Often summoned to cross the royal gate.

**Li Guinian:** I am Li Guinian, formerly a court musician, now made chief of the orchestra by the Emperor. Since Ever Fresh and Mindful Maid are ordered to teach us the music score of *Rainbow Dress* newly composed by her Ladyship, so that we may perform it in the Sunny Palace, we must rehearse it even if it is deep in the night. I have to call my musicians to the performance now. Hallo! Where are my fellow musicians?

(Enter Ma Xianqi , stone-chime player.)

**Ma:** My music will delight fairies on high.

(Enter Lei Haiqing the lutist.)

**Lei:** No lutist on earth with me could vie.

(Enter He Huaizhi the white-bearded pipa player.)

**He:** My fame's widespread, my pipa heard far and wide.

(Enter Huang Fanchuo the clapper-player.)

**Huang:** My clappers will resound from earth to sky.

**All** (Greeting Li): Good evening, sir.

**Li:** Good evening, my fellow musicians.

The royal order's to rehearse

At once the Rainbow Dress's verse.

Ever Fresh and Mindful Maid

Are waiting for the music to be played

With the well-written music score

They're waiting for us at the moonlit palace door.

**All:** Then let us go.

**Li:** Please go with me. (They walk together.)

**All:** As the water clock slowly drips in the cool night,

Let's learn to play the new melody bright. (Exeunt.)

(Enter Li Mo the flutist.)

**Li Mo** (Singing to the tune of **Sober Thrice from Wine**):

Young as I am in spirits high,

I'm deeply drowned in music sweet,

Tonight in fairy land near-by,

New melodies attract my feet.

I'm Li Mo born on the Southern Rivershore and now I'm visiting the capital. Having learned music while young, I am known for my skill in playing the iron flute. It is said that a melody of Rainbow Dance is newly composed in the palace and the chief of orchestra is performing it in the Sunny Palace from night to night. How can I get the music score I like so much? It is said the hall where the rehearsal takes place stands by the palace wall, and the music can be heard from without. Why don't I take my iron flute and go to the summer palace so as to listen to the music under the moon? While walking along the way, I wish the music would be as beautiful as moonlight. (Walking on.)

The evening mist clears over the woods far and nigh;

The hall stands out against the moonlight-spangled sky.

What a sublime scene!

I seem to walk from screen to screen.

(A red curtain hangs in the background in lieu of the palace wall with a tower behind.)

I seem to have come near the palace wall without my knowledge. (Singing to the tune of **Approaching Time**):

I see against the cloud

The palace proud

Magnificent and bright

In the moonlight.

Magnificent and bright

In the moonlight.

Majestic bowers rise

As earthly paradise.

The maids of honor fair as jade

Are leaning on the balustrade.

It is said that the music bower lies at the west end of the royal garden. I will wind my way along the red wall to go there. (Walking on.)

In the shade of flowering trees

I go on the royal path with ease.

I see a building tall

Outside the crimson wall.

It must be the place.

I stretch my eyes and gaze,

I stretch my eyes and gaze.

What have I seen

But painted curtain and window screen?

Which seem hazy like dream,

Just look ahead

Is it not a lantern red?

**Li** (From the other side of the wall): Let us rehearse the first movement today. But we should first learn the overture once more.

**Li Mo:** See lanterns are lit and voices can be dimly heard. It must be here that they rehearse the music. Let me listen without their knowledge. (Listening.)

(Singing to the tune of **Double Crimson Song**):

I'll listen to the music from the hall

Secretly in the shade of palace wall.

(Music is played inside and Li Mo takes out his flute.)

**I'll play my flute to accompany the music so that I may keep the notes in memory.**

After the first watch the moon rises high;

The stringed instruments begin to vie

To give to the forbidden garden delight

In the deep of still night.

How much I like the vibrating string

And the instruments sing!

I'll learn this part of melody by heart.

I'll learn this part of melody by heart.

(Ten instruments play music inside and Li Mo blows through his flute to accompany it. When it stops, the maids sing a chorus and Li Mo plays the flute again.)

**Maids** (Singing to the tune of **Eyebrows Pencilled**):

Like scattered pearls we strike clear notes.

Which waft like cloud on cloud which floats.

We dance like snow in flight,

Whirling in the soft breeze.

We dance like snow in flight,

Whirling in the soft breeze.

With eyebrows painted light

We dance with ease.

**Li Mo:** I've marked this part of music score,

And that part as before.

(Ten instruments play music inside, and Li Guinian and the maids sing the chorus and Li Mo plays on his flute to accompany it.)

**Maids** (Singing to the tune of ***Eyebrows Pencilled***):

    Splendid with emeralds and pearls bright

    As phoenixes soar and then alight

    Atop the enchanted mountain of jade,

    A fairy waves her sleeves to call her maid,

    A fairy waves her sleeves to call her maid,

    The Green Flower turns her head

    To beacon Jasper Red.

**Li Mo:** I've marked this part of music score

    And that part as before.

    (The ten instruments play music inside, while Li Guinian and maids sing the chorus. Li Mo plays on his flute to accompany it.)

**Maids** (Singing to the tune of ***Eyebrows Pencilled***):

    All strings and pipes participate

    In melodies swirl and intricate.

    As floating clouds alight,

    We cease our dance and drop our sleeves light.

    As floating clouds alight,

    We cease our dance and drop our sleeves light.

    Our echoed songs soar high

    Into the azure sky.

**Li Mo:** I've marked this part of music score

    And that part as before.

    (The ten instruments play music inside, and Li Guinian and maids go out.)

**Li Mo:** How wonderful is the music! It is like the breeze whispering in autumn bamboos or snow swirling over vernal ice. Obviously it is music divine and not human. Fortunately I have caught it with my flute. How lucky I am!

(Singing to the tune of **Geese and Duck on Ferry Boat**):

The song of Rainbow Dress comes from the sky

Is heard behind the wall by passers-by.

Its cadence clear and melody please,

Rise and fall with the breeze.

I've captured them all in my flute.

Now why is the palace mute?

Perhaps the musicians will play no more,

They are leaving the palace door.

In the waning moonlight over the wall of the bowers

Are shivering the shadows of the flowers.

**You see the moon is sinking and the Dipper seems to bar the Silver River in the sky. It is time for me to go back now.**

### Tune: *Epilogue*

Turning away

Towards my homeward way,

I hear the rippling river clear

Sing the Rainbow Dance to my ear. (Exit.)

### Epilogue of the Scene

Over sky-scraping palace shines the moon bright;

Songs fly as high as the cloud in the tranquil night.

Having stolen newly-composed music fine,

I'll play it on my flute in the shop of wine.

## Scene 5 The Feast

(Enter the first envoy on horse with a basketful of lychee fruit suspended from a pole.)

**First Envoy** (Singing to the tune of *Fish under Willows*):

For miles and miles I come on horse;

The hard rough journey's spent my force.

To obey orders is not a pleasure,

I don't prefer fortune to leisure.

Arrived after these hard long miles,

Could the fruit win Lady Yang's smiles?

I'm an envoy from the Western District rich in lychee, favorite fruit of Lady Yang. The Emperor has ordered to send it as tribute every year. As the weather is hot and the journey long, I must endure the hardship and speed up all the way to the capital.

(He gallops while singing):

Arrived after these hard long miles,

Could the fruit win Lady Yang's smiles?

(Enter a second envoy on horse, with a basketful of lychee fruit.)

**Second Envoy** (Singing to the tune of *Mountain-shaking Song*):

The lychee's sweetest in the Southern Capital,

And Lady Yang likes it the best of all.

When gathered, it is wrapped in leaves

And sent in a basket by the horse which heaves.

While I gallop all the way night and day

From one station to another without delay.

I am an envoy of the Southern Seaside Capital. Since Lady Yang loves to eat fresh lychee and the fruit grown in the south is even better than that of the west, we are ordered to send it to the capital. But it is a longer journey to go from the south than from the west. As the fruit would lose its flavor seven days after it's picked from the tree, so I have to hurry up.

(Galloping off while singing):

While I gallop all the way night and day

From one station to another without delay.

(Enter an old Peasant.)

**Peasant** (Singing to the tune of ***Ten Drumbeats***):

How hard is a peasant's lot on the plain!

We worry about drought and heavy rain.

From year to year we live on little grain which grows,

But half of our harvest for taxes goes.

How much is left our hunger to stay?

What we can do is but to pray

Heaven to ripen it each day?

I am an old peasant of the eastern village of the Golden County and have to feed a family of eight mouths. It is said that the envoys carrying lychee fruit would take a shortcut across the fields, careless of trampling and damaging the crop under their horses' hooves. So I have come here to guard my crop. (Looking around.) Here are two fortune-tellers coming this way.

(Enter a blind man with clappers in hand and a blind woman with a stringed instrument.)

**Blind Man and Woman Together** (Singing to the tune of ***Young Moth***):

Coming from the west, to the east we go;

Judging by stars, we can foretell how years will flow.

We know how long you'll live and when you'll die;

Our prophesy is well-known far and nigh.

Blind as we are,

We can see from afar.

We're like immortals old.

Would you please have your fortune told?

**Woman:** My old man, we have traveled so long today that my feet are aching now. I can't go any farther. I'm afraid we cannot foretell how long people can live but how soon we'll die.

**Blind Man:** Dear Ma, I hear someone speaking. Let us ask him.

(Speaking to the peasant)

Will you please tell us where we are?

**Peasant:** This is the eastern village of the Golden County, next to the western village of the Riverside Town.

**Blind Man** (Bowing): Thank you very much, sir.

(Bells around the neck of the horse are heard.)

**Peasant** (Looking around): Oh! Here comes a troop of horsemen.

(Calling out) My respectable cavaliers, will you please keep to the highway lest you trample on the grain?

**Blind Man** (to Woman): Dear Ma, it's not far from the capital now.

I'll go ahead to hire a donkey for you. (Singing)

We're like immortals old.

Would you please have your fortune told?

(He walks on while the first envoy comes up, whipping his horse.)

**First Envoy** (Singing): Arrived after these hard long miles,

Could the fruit win Lady Yang's smiles?

(Knocking down the blind man, he gallops off. Immediately after comes the second envoy.)

**Second Envoy** (Singing): While I gallop all the way night and day,

From one station to another without delay.

(Trampling the blind man to death, he gallops off.)

**Peasant** (Stamping and wailing): O Heaven! My paddy field is trampled. How can I get grain enough to eat and to feed my family? What is more, I still have to pay the taxes. How can I afford it!

**Woman** (Crawling on the ground): Alas! I am trampled down and badly hurt. Where are you, my old man? (She gropes for the blind man,) O here is my old man. Why don't you answer me? Have you fainted? (She passes her hand over him.) Why, your head is wet. (She feels him again.) His brain is crushed. (She cries.) O Heaven! O Earth! Who would come to help us?

**Peasant** (Looking around): Oh! A blind fortune-teller is killed.

**Woman** (Getting up): To whom can I appeal? How can I stop the riders to pay my old man's life?

**Peasant:** Ah! The riders are sending lychee fruit for Lady Yang. They have trampled many people without paying any one. How can they pay you a blind woman?

**Woman:** What can I do now? (Crying) Oh! My old man! I fore-told you would die by the roadside. Now you are dead. How can I get you buried?

**Peasant:** How could you find any one in charge to help you? Let me help you to bury him.

**Woman:** Oh! Thank you so much. Could I stay here with you? (Weeping)

(They carry the dead body off.)

(Enter a groom from the posting station.)

**Groom** (Singing the *Prologue*):

The station master's fled,

The station master's fled,

No horse is left but the dead.

No man is left but me the groom,

No money is left in the room,

I'm often whipped;

With curse Tm often tipped

How can I stand their whip?

How can my blood not drip?

I am a groom at the posting station of the Riverside Town. The first day of the sixth moon is the birthday of Lady Yang.She is so fond of eating lychee fruit that the envoys sending it from the west and from the south must reach the capital by that day and they will pass here. But the station master has fled for fear of being beaten by the envoys. He has left the charge to me without money but a lean horse. What can I do when come the envoys? But this can't be helped.

(Enter the first envoy galloping up.)

**First Envoy** (Singing to the tune of *Hastening Song*):

The sun sinks amid dust and cloud;

It seems pecked by mountains proud

Make haste, make haste, make haste,

Before I reach the capital.

I have no time to waste,

No time to waste at all.

(He alights.) Station master, prepare a new horse for me as soon as possible!

(The groom takes his reins while the envoy puts down his basket and dusts his clothes.)

(Enter the second envoy galloping.)

**Second Envoy** (Singing):

My aching limbs are wet

With drenching sweat.

I must gallop with all my force

And race to change my horse.

(He alights.) Station master, change the horse for me at once! (The groom takes his reins while the second envoy puts down his basket and greets the first envoy.) Good day, sir. Are you sending lychee to the capital too?

**First Envoy:** Yes, I am.

**Second Envoy:** Is our meal ready?

**Groom:** Not yet.

**First Envoy:** If not, I won't eat. But bring out the horse for me!

**Groom:** My dear sir, there is only one horse left in the stable.

Either of you may have it as you will.

**Second Envoy:** What! Only one horse in such a big station! Call out your rogue of a station master. Let him tell us where have gone the horses!

**Groom:** Oh! Our horses have been ridden to death by senders of lychee fruit these years. The station master knew not what to do and ran away.

**Second Envoy:** If the station master is not here, we can only demand horses from you.

**Groom** (Pointing to the stable): There is the horse you need.

**First Envoy:** I got here first so I will have it.

**Second Envoy:** I come from the southern seaside farther away than you, so let me have it!

**First Envoy** (Singing to the tune of **Pockmarked Face**):

>I'm going to change my horse.
>
>To argue with you I have no force.

**Second Envoy** (Pulling his back)

>Do not to force appeal,
>
>Or it's my fist you'll feel.

**First Envoy:** How dare you upset my lychee fruit! (He picks up his basket.)

**Second Envoy:** How dare you damage my basket of bamboo!

**Groom** (Pleading): Do not be angry nor use force! Would you ride together this lean horse?

**Second Envoy** (Putting down his basket and beating the groom):

>How dare you say that!
>
>I'll beat you out of breath;
>
>I'll beat you till your death.

**First Envoy** (Putting down his basket to beat the groom too):

>I'll beat you too,
>
>You rascal, you!

**Second Envoy:** How can I not use force!

>You have stolen the horse.

**First Envoy:** O How dare you delay

>The envoy on his way! (They beat the groom.)

**Envoys:** We'll use our whips

>Or kick your hips.
>
>When you go out of force,
>
>You will bring out a horse.

**Groom** (Kowtowing, he sings to the tune of **Pockmarked Face**):

>I beg you not to beat
>
>Nor kick me with your feet!

**Envoys:** If you are afraid of being beaten, bring out the horse at once!

**Groom:** In the stable there is only one horse.

**Envoys:** We need two.

**Groom:** I cannot get two horses though you use force.

**Envoys:** Then we'll beat you again.

**Groom:** Don't beat me, masters,

I'll take off my coat for you to buy wine. (He takes off his coat.)

**First Envoy:** Who needs your dirty coat?

**Second Envoy** (Checking up the coat and putting it on): All right, I
must hurry up to change my horse at the next station.

(He picks up his basket, mounts his horse and rides off.)

Make haste, make haste, make haste,

I have no time to waste.

**First Envoy:** Bring me the new horse at once!

**Groom:** Here it is.

**First Envoy:** I must gallop with all my force,

And race to change my horse. (He rides off.)

**Groom:** Oh! Lady Yang, Lady Yang! This is all for your lychee fruit.

### Epilogue of the Scene

To pass the iron doors and golden gates we're free,

On yellow paper written the royal decree.

Whipping the steed at top of speed forward we go,

O How much weal and woe brings the fruit, do you know?

(Exeunt.)

# Scene 6 The Round Dance

(Enter the emperor accompanied by two attendants and the eunuch Gao Lishi.)

**Emperor** (Singing to the tune of *Spring Coming in Time*):

On long, long day in quiet halls the light breeze blows.

High above the palace hall the fiery cloud glows.

From the east comes the purple light;

Gazing westwards you'll catch the sight

Of the fairy blue birds in flight,

Coming from the Celestial Height.

The first of the sixth moon is the birthday of my dear Lady Yang, who is enjoying the cool with me in the summer palace. I have ordered a feast in the Long-life Hall and the new Rainbow Dance to be performed for the celebration. Lishi, pass on the order to the inner palace requesting Her Ladyship's presence.

**Gao:** Yes, Your Majesty. (He gives the order and is answered.) (Enter Lady Yang in splendid dress accompanied by Ever Fresh and Mindful Maid.)

**Lady Yang** sings to the tune of *More Sugar*:

The sun shines into my sweet-scented bower,

My window screen caressed by twigs of flower.

A yellow silken curtain hangs over the door.

A pair of embroidered phoenixes seem to soar

Above the cloud high and far.

(Curtseying) Long live Your Majesty!

**Emperor:** I'd enjoy my long life together with you. (Lady Yang sits down.)

Deep in the purple clouds shines the Lady Star.

**Lady Yang:** Peach blossoms steeped in dew take splendid hue.

**Maids:** You won't grow old before the flower.

**Together:** Life will be long in Long-Life Bower.

**Emperor:** Today is your birthday and I have prepared a feast to celebrate it and we'll enjoy the pleasure all day long.

**Lady Yang:** How could my humble birthday be worth your royal favor? I would drink to Your Majesty's health and wish you a long life.

**Gao:** The wine is served.

(Lady Yang curtseys and offers wine to the emperor, who then passes her the cup. She kneels to drink so as to show her gratitude and then sits down.)

Emperor sings to the tune of *The Eight Immortals Meeting on the Sea*:

The breeze is warm and the sun bright;

The leaves in the courtyard shiver in burning light.

A splendid feast is opened up.

The Southern Hills infuse long, long life in your cup.

Together sing to the tune *Of Fairy Lanterns*:

With double kernel peaches grow from year to year;

Lotus flowers in pairs for miles and miles appear.

(Changing to the tune of Moonrise over Crabapple)

It pleases all

To enjoy in the Long-life Hall

As in celestial sphere.

(A eunuch enters with a scroll.)

**Eunuch:** With golden-flowered crimson scroll in hand,

Out of the palace all congratulators stand.

I beg to report to Your Majesty and Your Ladyship that the Prime Minister and the three duchesses are waiting outside with their gifts and congratulations for the happy birthday. (Presenting the scroll.)

**Emperor:** Give them our thanks. The Prime Minister need not stand on ceremony. He may withdraw to his office. The three duchesses may wait to feast with us in the palace.

**Eunuch:** Your Majesty's orders shall be obeyed. (Exit.)

**Second Eunuch:** On this happy birthday divine

Comes from the south lychee fruit fine.

May it please Your Majesty that the fresh lychee fruit from the west and the southern seaside has arrived.

**Emperor:** Bring it up.

(Gao Lishi receives the fruit and removes the cover.)

(To Lady Yang): Knowing your love for the fruit, I have ordered local governments to send it by express. It has just arrived in time before your birthday feast begins. Let us drink to your happy birthday, my love.

**Lady Yang:** A million thanks to Your Majesty.

**Emperor:** Fill the cups, maids.

(Ever Fresh and Mindful Maid fill their cups.)

Lady Yang sings to the tune of *Long Life in the Cup*:

A basketful

Of fruit so beautiful,

The yellow-covered lychee blest

Comes afar from south and west.

I love its crimson shell

And crystal fruit so well.

It makes my hand so sweet

And chills my teeth so neat.

**Together sing to the tune of *Prelude to Long Life*:**

It is redder than the date and whiter than the pear,

In royal feast beyond compare,

As good as a nectar divine

Or the Goddess' favorite wine.

**Emperor:** Now Gao Lishi, order Li Guinian and his orchestra to play music in the hall.

**Gao:** As Your Majesty commands. (Giving orders.)

(Enter Li Guinian with other musicians in livery and bright cap.)

**Musicians:** With red clapper and thirteen pegs of string,

In crimson silk we come to dancing feast to sing.

We enter in yellow hats high and new

And halt when royal steps are in view.

**Li Guinian:** Your humble servant Li Guinian and his orchestra salute Your Majesty and Your Ladyship.

**Emperor:** Li Guinian, you played the overture of Rainbow Dance yesterday Are you ready to play the first movement for today?

**Li Guinian:** May it please Your Majesty, we are.

**Emperor:** See it well played.

**Li Guinian:** Yes, Your Majesty. (Exit with his orchestra.)

**Lady Yang:** May I take the liberty to remind Your Majesty that six stanzas of the overture contain no flowing rhythm but pausing beats and that six stanzas of the central movement contain flowing rhythm but no hastening beats, for at that time the music was not made for dancing.

(Singing to the tune of **Eight Immortals Meeting on the Sea**):

The music opens with a flourish loud

To arrest along the rainbow the rosy cloud,

When it comes to the third stanza of "Feathered Coat",

Each dancing motion is hinted at by each note.

It may slow down, linger or roll in sound,

Like a string of pearls clear and round.

It may enter, outspread and go out,

And you see dance on the carpet or thereabout.

There are side beats intermittent;

Hastening or stolen, they are different.

There dance and music blend

To delight us without an end.

**Emperor:** You have well explained the music and dance.

**Lady Yang:** I have had an emerald disk-like carpet made, and I would like to dance on it for Your Majesty's pleasure.

**Emperor:** I have never seen your enchanting dance. I would like to see the performance accompanied by your maids Ever Fresh, Mindful Maid, Zheng Guanyin and Xie Aman.

**Maids:** Yes, Your Majesty.

**Lady Yang:** May I withdraw to change into the dancing costume?

After changing my dress, I'll take my place

On the emerald plate with grace. (Exit with her maids.)

**Emperor:** Gao Lishi, order Li Guinian and his orchestra to play the music according to the score. I myself will beat the rhythm on the drum.

**Gao:** Yes, Your Majesty. (Giving the order.)

(The emperor retires to change his dress. Music is played inside: An emerald plate is placed on the stage. Lady Yang reenters crowned with flowers, in embroidered white dress with tassels and green sleeves, a cap designed with rainbow cloud and a crimson dancing skirt. The four maids in dancing dress and white robe, holding rainbow cloud banners and peacock-embroidered fans to hide Lady Yang from view when she has stepped in the centre of the plate, The music stops, the fans slowly part to disclose Lady Yang dancing on the plate. The four maids begin to sing. Gao Lishi kneels to hold the foreign drum. The emperor reenters, sits in the middle of the stage and begins to beat the drum while musicians play their own instruments to accompany the dance.)

All sing to the tune of the **Second Movement of the Feathered Coat:**

> In silken dress adorned with flowers fair,
> A rosy cloud Seems floating in the air.
> See rainbow banners wave far and nigh,
> And fragrant petals fall from on high.
> Tranquil, the parted fans reveal a beauty still
> Like Moon Goddess come down in a light feathered gown,
> Her rainbow sleeves outspread,
> to To show her skill she's led.
> She flutters in the breeze as lotus sways with ease.
> Like quivering green leaves float her winglike sleeves.
> From side to side she sways;
> O what grace she displays!
> (The music quickens.)
> She whirls, rises and falls like blooming sprays,

Or a quivering willow tree,

Or a phoenix flying with glee.

Beyond description her grace,

The wind blows from on high,

All music echoes far and nigh.

Hear ice crackle with her pace,

And tinkle strings tightened by pegs of jade,

When flutes and pipes are played.

The drum beats out the time so low

That the new melody will clearer grow.

Her gilded skirt would fly on high

If not detained by dancers nearby.

(The emperor stops playing the drum and Gao Lishi carries it off.)

She dances her fill; her rainbow dress is still.

(Lady Yang curtseys to the emperor.)

She lowers her song to wish him a life long.

(The maids help Lady Yang come down from the emerald plate. Gao and others retire.)

**Emperor** (Rising to take her hands): What a wonderful dance! Nothing is so charming and fascinating. It is like snow wafting in the breeze, swallow flying or dragon swimming in the sky that has never been seen before. Maids, bring the wine and I will offer her a cup.

(The Maids bring the wine and the emperor holds the cup.)

Smiling, I hold the golden goblet fine

And hope your sweet lips will sweeten the wine.

(Giving it to her.) Drink the wine up! Leave nothing in the cup!

I thank you for your dance so tender

And the fatigue of your waist so slender.

**Lady Yang** (Receiving the cup and curtseying): Long live Your Majesty!
(Singing to the tune of **Rainbow Dress**):
Your Majesty drink to me this cupful of wine.
How can I be worthy of this favor divine!

**Emperor** (Gazing at her):
Seeing the way you hold your cup, I am all eyes
To find ten thousand bewitching charms arise.

I will give you ten silk rolls embroidered with golden lovebirds and a golden tierce to show my love for your fairy dance. (Taking out a scented pouch) And I give you this jewelled pouch containing ambergris, which I wear myself, for you to dance as with a pendant.

**Lady Yang** (Taking the pouch and curtseying): Long live Your Majesty!

### Tune: *Epilogue*

**Emperor** (Taking Lady Yang by the hand):
As the Rainbow Dance will be loved from year to year,
I wish you forever young, beautiful, my dear.

**Lady Yang:** How fortunate to be steeped in royal dew!
I am perfumed through and through.

### Epilogue of the Scene

**Emperor:** The Long-life Hall stands as high as the azure sky.
**Lady Yang:** My happy birthday wine is distributed far and nigh,
**Emperor:** After drinking, I love your dance with rainbow sleeves,
**Lady Yang:** Five clouds are sweetened as if they were azure leaves.

(Exeunt.)

ACT IV

# Scene 1 The Hunt

(Enter four Tartar Generals Ho, Cui, Gao and Shi.)

**Ho:** My three-foot sword shines bright as snow.

**Cui:** My waist is girt with crescent bow.

**Gao:** I'm fond of drinking my red wine.

**Shi:** My sable cap becomes this suit of mine.

**He:** I am General He of the eastern front.

**Cui:** I am General Cui of the western front.

**Gao:** I am General Gao of the southern front.

**Shi:** I am General Shi of the northern front.

**All** (Greeting each other): Good morning, generals, Ordered
yesterday by the Governor to muster, now we are in his camp.
Here comes His Highness.

(Trumpets blow and all shout.)

(An Lushan enters in military dress with Tartar maids and soldiers.)

An sings to the tune of *Violet Flowers*:

I have the frontier at command:

Tartars and Hans I understand

I'll hold the kingdom in my hand,

First, I'll control the nearby land.

I have been ambitious for long. Appointed at court Lord of the
East, I was an incomparable favorite of the emperor. Though fairly
satisfied, I was at odds with Prime Minister Yang Guozhong. So I
am pleased to be appointed Governor of Fanyang, where I may do

as I will. Formerly I had under me thirty-two generals, on whom I could hardly rely, for there were Hans mingled with Tartars. So I requested to have only Tartar generals under me, and now they were all my tribesmen. (Laughing) I can do what I like without restraint. Yesterday I summoned my generals to come to my camp and they should be here by now.

(The generals bow to him.)

**Generals:** Your thirty-two generals salute Your Highness.

**An:** You may not stand on ceremony.

**Generals:** May we ask why we are summoned to come here?

**An:** Autumn is the best time for us to practise our military arts when horses are strong and sturdy. So I have summoned you to share my pleasure of hunting on the sandy plain.

**Generals:** Yes, we shall do as you will, Your Highness.

**An:** Let us mount our saddled horses and ride forward!

(They mount their horses.)

**All:** Holding the purple reins in hand,

To saddled horses we go,

Our tasselled helmets low.

(Riding forward.)

Our banners flutter like snake or dragon proud,

Twisting and turning like crimson cloud

The nine rings we deploy seem to reach the blue sky;

We belittle the Central Plain before the eye.

How could the Huns withstand our Tartar army grand!

(They gather around An Lushan.)

**An** (Pointing to one general after another):

The first general is brave and bright,

The second dressed in armor tight,

The third with curly hair and a nose high,

The fourth with bristled beard and eagle eye:

The fifth like the full moon can stretch his bow;

The sixth can whirl his mace and make it glow;

The seventh wields his spear with might and main;

The eighth shoots his arrows as thick as rain;

All of them like the tigers leaving mountains high

Could make me heroic khan under the sky.

(They Ride on.)

**All:** We beat the drums to show

Our might and main, and strike fear into the foe.

We blow the horn on steed;

Both man and horse run in array at full speed.

We roar like thunder from the sky,

And run like billows surging high.

There is no stronghold nor iron wall

We cannot conquer at all.

**An:** The sandy plain is wide and flat here. Let us begin our hunt now.

(Standing with Tartar maids oh high ground while generals ride off to hunt.)

They bend the bow,

And twanging its strings they go.

On sandy plain hares and deer try to run away,

But finding no escape, trembling they stay.

(Generals ride in shooting at the games.)

**Unleash the hounds and hawks.**

(Generals ride off while unleashing them.)

120

Above the taloned eagles fly

To scrape the sky;

Below the golden hounds bar the way

To let nor hare nor deer run away.

Soon generals vie

To pile up games mountain-high.

(Generals present the games.)

**Generals:** Will it please Your Highness to see the games?

**An:** Feast on the games with our warriors! Let them rest with their horses on the slope while meat is roasted and wine warmed! Let songstresses sing and dancers dance to the fill!

**Generals:** It shall be done, Your Highness.

(They sit on the ground. Tartar maids offer wine to An. Generals cut meat with sword and drink from the pot. Tartar musicians play their lutes and guitars and beat peace-time tambourines.)

**All:** Let us fill our golden goblets with wine,

And on bleeding meat let us dine!

Let us embrace our beauties' rosy cheeks in laughter,

And play the lute and sing the *Buddhist Dancers' Song* after!

**An** (Rising): We have eaten and drunk our fill. Now the day is growing late. You may go back to your garrisons and keep your men and arms and horses ready for further orders.

**All:** It shall be done as you wish.

(They mount their horses, blow their horns, tilt their caps, wave their hands and ride round.)

Ordered to get ready our forces,

Swiftly we leap to our saddled horses,

With our headdress askew,

We wave our hands to bid adieu.

Back to our posts, with flags and banners in flight,

We'll wait for the summons to fight.

When Heaven makes us brave,

On earth will surge up wave on wave.

The Tang Empire will fall;

We're prompt to answer the call

Of our high-hearted lord

To employ our spear and sword (Exeunt.)

**An:** Now that my Tartar generals are all mighty and ready, you may say I am already fully fledged.

(Laughing) Ah! Tang Emperor, Tang Emperor, what could you do against me?

(Singing to the tune of **Epilogue**):

Without arousing his suspicion at all,

I've got rid of one after another Han General,

And replaced them then

With my own tribesmen.

You may dance to your Rainbow Dress song

All the day long;

I will beat my drum of revolt as high

As a bolt from the sky. (Exit.)

### Epilogue of the Scene

My tribesmen of six states rise in campaign;

Our war steeds neigh on the vast Central Plain.

Like a gust of strong wind our winged troops will spread;

Hills and streams with bloodshed will be dyed red.

## Scene 2  A Night of Grief

(Enter Lady Yang.)

**Lady Yang:** Favored I can't bear to be set apart;

In joy, I still feel sad at heart.

Like a pair of lovebirds which fly,

I fear to lose the emperor's favor high,

The cloud in wind may float away,

To win sunlight all flowers vie,

I feel ill at ease all the day.

(Changing to the tune of **Pure, Serene Music**):

Wordless, I roll up window screen,

Who knows my grief in thousand wreaths unseen?

I fear that time is free

To let spring flee.

My heart in doubt.

How can the imperial trace be found out?

How can his royal cab not yet appear

At sunset in my courtyard drear ?

I have long won the imperial favor and love, but Lady Mume Jiang would still rival with me. Unluckily she offended His Majesty and was moved to the East Bower. I am afraid that she would contrive to win back his love and revive his old passion for her, so I cannot but take care and caution. Oh! Lady Jiang, Lady Jiang! It is not that I am severe with you. If not, I am afraid you would not be lenient with me. My lord has left for the court in the morning, now it is sunset and he has not yet come back. I have to send Ever Fresh and Mindful Maid to find out what has happened. The time drags on. What can I do to while it away? (Singing to the tune of *Wind and Cloud*):

The incense burning low,

The palace seems darkened to grow.

I keep uprolling the window screen

And curtain green.

I've tired my eyes

With watching and sighs.

On other days, he would have come to Palace West,

Holding my hand, we'd stand side by side,

With flowers my bower caressed

With spring my face is beautified

On other days,

He would have shown his love in a hundred ways.

But why tonight

When grass is still fragrant in twilight,

I do not see him from his cab alight?

(Offstage a parrot echoes "his cab alight") Does he alight?

(Startled, she looks around and catches sight of the bird.)

Ah! No, it is the parrot I have heard,

The bird has learned my word.

Alone I linger – but to what avail?

Lost in thoughts, I lean from rail to rail.

(Enter Ever Fresh.)

**Ever Fresh:** Tonight our lord in front palace will remain:

Other ladies need not wait in vain.

Your Ladyship, His Majesty will stay in the Emerald Bower tonight.

**Lady Yang** (Silent for a moment): Can it be true? (Weeping)

How shallow is his love!

Does he not know

Waiting alone, how eager I would grow?

Undressed I'm shy to trim

The candle dim.

How could I not wait for him

To talk with me in laughter,

And feast with me, and feast with me after ?

We may drink to the moon,

Who'll also get drunk soon.

Then we'll go to bed to dream of the shower

Brought for the thirsting flower.

I will enjoy his love undivided

With heart and soul decided

How could I anticipate

A forsaken fate?

**Ever Fresh:** It is by chance that His Majesty happened to pass one night elsewhere. He cannot have done it on purpose.Please be not vexed, my dear lady!

**Lady Yang:** If he had not changed his heart,

Why did he not send a eunuch on his part

To tell me he'd not come tonight?

I think he's never used to a lonely night.

How could he sleep elsewhere

Without a companion bright and fair ?

(Enter Mindful Maid.)

**Mindful Maid:** Hidden behind the snow, the egret white

Cannot be seen unless in flight.

In willow tree a parrot's hard to seek,

If it does not begin to speak.

Your Ladyship, I have found out what is happening in the Emerald Bower.

**Lady Yang:** What is it?

**Mindful Maid:** Will you please let me tell you:

I went quietly to the Emerald Bower,

And waited till an evening hour.

To a eunuch I heard

His Majesty send a word …

**Lady Yang:** Yes?

**Mindful Maid:** To flip the whip upon his steed

To go at highest speed...

**Lady Yang:** To fetch whom?

**Mindful Maid:** To the deserted hall of Eastern Bower

To fetch his former favorite Lady Mume Flower.

**Lady Yang** (Startled): Ah! How can it be she! Has she come?

**Mindful Maid:** In no time came the lady as fair as flower

With the eunuch in the dark to Emerald Bower.

**Ever Fresh:** Are you sure of what you say?

**Mindful Maid:** How can it not be true?

**Lady Yang:** Ah, Heaven! It is Lady Mume Blossoms in favor again.

(Sitting down without a word and weeping again.)

**Maids:** Don't be worried, Your Ladyship.

**Lady Yang:** I tremble at what she reveals.

How can I utter the grief my heart feels!

The love and favor of bygone days

All turn into tears and sprays.

And melt away and fly

Into the sky.

When we first pledged our love,

When we first pledged our love

As the phoenixes above,

My hairpin or its two wings will not part.

How can I know changeable is the royal heart?

If it is I

Who am to blame, he should have told me why.

How could his eastern breeze

Try to warm the mume blossoms which freeze?

How could he stay here while his heart

Flies far away and far apart?

His love is not true — how can I believe?

I am a simpleton easy to deceive.

**Mindful Maid:** Do Your Ladyship know I heard from a eunuch that the emperor secretly sent a pack of pearls to her from the Blooming Blossom Bower yesterday, but she would not accept it and sent it back with a verse:

I have not made up in the deserted Long Gate Hall,

And pearls cannot rid me of my grief at all.

That is the reason why the emperor went to see her tonight.

**Lady Yang:** So that is it. How could I know it?

She wrote to him of her grief in Eastern Bower,

And he sent her pearls in a secret hour.

They cannot forget the past and won't be kept apart.

How bitterly jealousy gnaws my heart!

It's not that narrow is my mind,

But how can my lord be to me unkind,

And leave me far behind?

How can he rekindle his flame of old,

And put a rejected love in a house of gold?

How can I a poor phoenix vie

With orioles and swallows for his vernal eye?

**Ever Fresh:** Since the emperor cannot forget her, why don't you meet his wishes to plead for her return? Then His Majesty would be pleased. I think Lady Mume Blossom dare not be ungrateful.

**Lady Yang:** Ah! No, His Majesty would tie his own love-knot.

As for a go-between, he need not.

If I venture to be so indiscreet,

I am afraid she'll tread me under her feet.

Come with me, both of you, to the Emerald Bower.

**Mindful Maid:** What will Your Ladyship do there?

**Lady Yang:** There I will go

To see how she could charm our monarch so;

What tricks she knows to play

So as to turn night into day;

And to turn upside down

So as to fascinate the Crown.

**Mindful Maid:** I would not dare to tell Your Ladyship to go to the Emerald Bower tonight. For it is nearly midnight now, and His Majesty must have been asleep. It would be inconvenient for Your Ladyship to go there. Better take a rest the leave the matter to tomorrow.

**Lady Yang:** Well said, but how to pass this long, long night! (Singing to the tune of **Epilogue**):

He would be happy to fear time flies too fast.

Turning my back, how can this lonely night be passed!

### Epilogue of the Scene

The far-off royal bower hears water clock sigh;

The cloud will bring no shower in water-blue sky.

Disfavored, can I stop my streaming tears of sorrow?

Leaning on lonely bed alone I sit till the morrow.

## ─── Scene 3  A Visit to the Emerald Bower ───

(Enter Gao Lishi.)

**Gao:** Since she fell in disgrace, spring and autumn have passed.

Her silken dress wet with tears, still more tears fall fast.

The same moon shines on southern and northern palace ground.

The south rings with songs while the north in grief is drowned.

I am Gao Lishi who brought Lady Jiang from the south and she won the royal favor and was called Lady Mume Blossom for it is the flower she loves best. But since Lady Yang arrived, she fell from favor and was removed to the east bower of the Sunny Palace. However, last night the emperor slept in the Emerald Bower under one pretext or another, and sent a eunuch secretly to summon Lady Mume Blossom. All the maids were warned against the leakage of the secret to Lady Yang, and I have been ordered to stand guard outside the door to forbid free entrance. Now it is dawn and I had better wait here till Lady Mume Blossom returns to her bower. (Exit.)

(Enter Lady Yang.)

Lady Yang sings to the tune of *Tipsy in the Shade of Flowers*:

Sleepless with grief all night,

I come here on tiptoe before daylight.

I used to sleep in my vernal bower

Till the rising sun reddened the flower,

And I would not toss my pillow away.

But why should I leave my bed early today?

Because I can't forget that matter anyway.

**Gao** (Reentering and seeing her): Ah! Is it not Lady Yang coming? How can the secret have leaked out? Lady Mume Blossom is still in the bower. What shall I do?

(Lady Yang comes near and Gao bows.)

Your servant Gao Lishi is bowing to Your Ladyship.

**Lady Yang:** Where is His Majesty?

**Gao:** In the bower.

**Lady Yang:** Who else is with him?

**Gao:** No one else.

**Lady Yang** (Laughing coldly): Open the door and let me see for myself.

**Gao** (Embarrassed): Please take a seat, Your Ladyship.

(Lady Yang sits down.)

I beg to inform Your Ladyship

His Majesty, tired would take a rest

Last night in the Bower of the West.

**Lady Yang:** If His Majesty felt tired, why should he sleep here?

**Gao:** Longing for a quiet hour,

He'd rest in Western Bower

**Lady Yang:** What was he doing here?

**Gao:** Reclining on the imperial bed,

He would rest his weary head.

**Lady Yang:** And what are you doing here?

**Gao:** I am guarding the door so that no intruder would enter.

**Lady Yang:** Dare you bar my entrance?

**Gao** (Kowtowing, embarrassed): Do not be angry, Your Ladyship.

I'm carrying out the order of our lord.

How dare I disobey his word?

**Lady Yang:** How dare you pretend to be true!

To play the false how dare you!

**Gao:** How dare I deceive Your Ladyship!

**Lady Yang**: Anxiety gnaws at my heart,

I know how you dare to keep me apart,

For you have another in your eye,

Who is now in favor high.

You think me in disgrace,

And dare to insult me to my face.

(Rising) Well, I'll knock at the door myself.

**Gao:** Will you please take a seat and let me ask them to open the door?

(Calling out) Will you open the door? Lady Yang is coming.

(Lady Yang sits down again.)

(Enter the emperor not fully dressed, followed by an attendant.)

**Emperor:** Who is calling loud in palace deep

To wake me from my sleep?

**Gao** (To the attendant): Will you please open the door for Lady Yang?

**Attendant:** Will Your Majesty allow me to open the door for Lady Yang's coming?

**Emperor:** What shall we speak

If she finds spring light leak?

**Attendant:** Shall I open the door or not?

**Emperor:** Wait a minute! (Turning his back.)

What can I do but let Lady Mume Flower

Hide behind the screen in the bower ? (Exit.)

**Attendant** (Laughing): How can the imperial crown

Fear his golden house turned upside down?

**Emperor** (Resting his head on the desk after his reentrance):

> I may pretend to take a rest.
>
> You may unlock the door of Bower West.

**Attendant:** Yes, Your Majesty.

> (The door opened, Lady Yang comes in.)

**Lady Yang:** I was told that Your Majesty felt indisposed, so I come to inquire after you.

**Emperor:** I just felt a little ill at ease, so I did not go to your bower. Why should you come so early in the morning?

**Lady Yang:** I have more or less guessed why Your Majesty felt ill at ease.

**Emperor** (Laughing): What have you guessed?

**Lady Yang:** You were longing for someone kept apart,

> So it was lovesickness that gnawed your heart.

**Emperor:** How can I be lovesick of anyone other than you?

**Lady Yang:** As Your Majesty has favored none so frequently as Lady Mume Flower, why not summon her here to get rid of your longing for her?

**Emperor** (Startled): Ah! Lady Mume Flower!

> Long ago I sent her away to Eastern Bower.
>
> Why should I call her back now?

**Lady Yang:** When spring steals on the Mume bough,

> You may long to eat its fruit first
>
> So as to quench your thirst.

**Emperor:** How could I?

**Lady Yang:** If not, why should you send her a pack of pearls? Why?

**Emperor:** You need not be so suspicious.

> I was in a sorry plight,
>
> So I needed a rest last night.

How could you give free rein to your fanciful heart

And make fun with me on your part?

(Yearning) I'm still so tired,

Wordless, I wish to be retired,

Would you go back to your bower deep

So that I may continue my sleep?

**Lady Yang** (Looking around): Why is there a pair of woman's slippers under the bed?

**Emperor** (Rising in haste and trying to hide them): Where?

(As he stands up, an emerald trinket falls from his lap.)

**Lady Yang** (Picking it up and looking at it): Ah! A trinket too, a woman's ornament! Where did these things come from if Your Majesty were sleeping alone?

**Emperor** (Ashamed): Strange! Where could they have come from? It is beyond my understanding.

**Lady Yang:** How can it go beyond Your Majesty's understanding?

**Gao** (Turning in anxiety to the attendants): It goes from bad to worse. Seeing the trinket and slippers, how could Lady Yang not inquire into the matter? You must escort Lady Mume Flower back to the Eastern Bower without the knowledge of Her Ladyship.

**Attendants:** Yes, it shall be done. (Exeunt.)

**Lady Yang:** The royal bedroom is forbidden at night.

Could it be a goddess coming in flight?

Or how could the slippers and trinket be left here?

(She throws the slippers and trinket on the ground, and Gao picks them up unperceived.)

Who did last night in royal bower appear?

My lord enjoyed so much with his mate

That at sunrise he did not leave the palace gate.

Those who know not would blame me for keeping him late,

But I was not the thirsting flower

For whom my lord did bring fresh shower.

Will Your Majesty please go to the court?

I shall wait here whether the time be long or short.

**Emperor:** Indisposed, I shall not go to the court today.

**Lady Yang:** Though you dreamed of the butterfly

Or love-birds on waves high

Bewitching you with amorous eye,

Though drowsy for a moment short,

Could you keep ministers waiting in the court?

(She goes forward and turns back her back to the emperor.)

**Gao** (Advancing unnoticed and whispering to the emperor):

Lady Mume Flower has gone back. Will Your Majesty please go to the court?

**Emperor** (Nodding): Since Lady Yang urges on me to go to the court, I'll try. Gao Lishi, stay here till her ladyship goes back!

**Gao:** Yes, Sire. (Looking offstage) Get the carriage ready for His Majesty!

(An answer is heard offstage.)

**Emperor:** From love all troubles rise,

Known but to lovers' eyes, (Exit.)

**Lady Yang** (Sitting down): What have you done behind me, Gao Lishi? Now tell me to whom belong the slippers and the trinket!

**Gao:** Your Ladyship need not worry about trifles new;

Beyond compare is His Majesty's love for you,

These slippers and trinket you'd pretend to ignore

If they belong to his love of yore,

Even if they belong to some beauty new,

It should bring no worry to you.

Why should you spend time to investigate?

Need I tell you out of the royal gate

High officials have concubines they treasure?

How could you deny the emperor one night's pleasure?

**Lady Yang:** It is not that I have a narrow mind,

Which won't allow another to share his bed,

But that I'm hurt to find

That he deceives me on this head.

**Gao:** If His Majesty did not want Your Ladyship to know, it was only because he was afraid it would make you unhappy.

**Lady Yang:** If he's afraid of hurting me,

To send for her he'd not be free.

How could he float like wanton cloud

To another mountain peak proud?

He pretends to forsake her and then

Summons her back again. (Shedding tears.)

(Enter Ever Fresh.)

**Ever Fresh:** When I got up this morning, I found Her Ladyship not there. She must have come to this bower.

(Entering and curtseying)

Why are you, my lady, sitting here, shedding tears?

Why silent and depressed your face appears?

(To Gao Lishi) Who has offended Her Ladyship?

**Gao:** Do not mention it. (Showing her slippers and trinket) She is angry at finding these.

**Ever Fresh** (In a low voice): Where is that lady?

**Gao:** She's gone back.

**Ever Fresh:** Where is His Majesty?

**Gao:** Gone to the court. You've come in time, Ever Fresh, you may persuade Her Ladyship to go back now.

**Ever Fresh:** Yes. (Turning to Lady Yang)

> You need not frown, my lady dear,
>
> Nor shed a tear,
>
> Nor troubled need you feel,
>
> Without taking the morning meal,
>
> Why should you harm your health and annoy
>
> Yourself? Why not go back to find some joy?
>
> (An attendant outside announces the emperor's return. Lady Yang rises, and the emperor enters.)

**Emperor:** She is charming to weep;

> Jealousy reveals her love deep.
>
> I have suffered more from half a night's pleasure than enjoyed it. If I should lay blame on her, she might say I have given favor to Lady Mume Flower. So I had better be tolerate. Gao Lishi, where is Her Ladyship?

**Gao:** Still in the bower. (Going out with Ever Fresh.)

> (The emperor greets Lady Yang, who turns her back on him and wipes her tears silently.)

**Emperor:** Ah! my darling, why are you covering your face without saying a word?

> (Lady Yang remains wordless. The emperor smiles.) Why are you annoyed like that?
>
> Let us go to enjoy flowers in the Blooming Bower!

**Lady Yang:** Ask, ask, ask the Blooming Flower

    If, if, if it's as fair as that in Eastern Bower!

    Since, since, since spring mume blossoms please,

    Do, do, do you still need green willow trees ?

**Emperor:** How can you not know where my true love lies?

**Lady Yang:** Be, be, be true to your first flame!

    Or, or, or I would be to blame,

    (Kneeling) May I ask Your Majesty a favor?

**Emperor** (Raising her): Why don't you rise and speak?

**Lady Yang** (Sobbing): I know I do not deserve your royal favor. If I do not withdraw in time, I would bring rumor and woe to harm Your Majesty. So I beg to withdraw from your favor. Would you please confer it to other favorites than poor me?

    Bye, bye, bye, bye to royal favor heaven-high! (Taking out the hairpin in the box)

    The hairpin and box were your royal gifts to show

    Your favor for your servant in weal and woe.

    Now I return my ever, ever, everlasting love on my part.

**Emperor:** What do you mean?

**Lady Yang:** I'll keep, keep, keep my undeserved favor in my heart. (Weeping)

**Emperor** (Helping her to rise): Why should you speak like that?

    We're so deep in love, so deep in love,

    Even a hundred years will not be enough.

    Why should you say to part from me?

    It's all my fault. Be not angry! (Smiling at her.)

    Seeing your frowning brows and tearful eyes,

    Could any lover not utter sighs?

Keep the box and hairpin! If you don't like flowers,

Let us go to the Western Bowers!

**Lady Yang:** If Your Majesty wants me to stay,

How dare I this royal favor disobey?

I'll keep this hairpin of phoenix in flight.

When we share our bed together tonight,

I'll retell to Heaven above

Our first night pledged with love. (Exeunt.)

**Gao** (Reentering): Now that His Majesty and Lady Yang have gone, I may return the trinket and slippers to Lady Mume Blossom.

### Epilogue of the Scene

See the green bower in willows' shade

Where stays the royal cab of jade!

But beauties are jealous without cease.

How can they not annoy the eastern breeze?

## Scene 4 The Scout's Report

(Enter General Guo Ziyi with his lieutenant and armed attendants.)

**Guo:** Guarding the border

And cities under my order,

How often have I heard

From the frontier alarming word.

How can my hair not turn more white

To worry for the empire's plight!

I, Guo Ziyi, governor of Lingwu Province appointed by His Majesty, have foreseen, judging by his behavior, that An Lushan must be a rebel and that he would plot against the empire. But, unexpectedly he was appointed governor of Fanyang, which amounts to a tiger released to the mountains. Then he was allowed to replace Chinese generals by Tartar chiefs, which would mean the tiger added with two wings. Since my promotion from the Jiande District, I have been worrying about this day and night. Lingwu is an important strategic point which must be well guarded. I have sent scouts to Fanyang to gather more information from there. I am waiting for their return so that I may make a better decision.

(A scout enters with a small red flag in hand.)

**Scout** (Singing to the tune of **Night Sailing Boat**):

Swift as a shooting star

Or lightning flash my two legs are.

I've learned what's happening on the frontier,

And left the Northern Mountain to come here.

(Kneeling on one knee to salute the general.)

I should report in Yellow Hall as loud

As thunder from the cloud

**Guo:** So you are back.

**Scout** (Bowing): On my shoulder a small flag red,

As swift as wind night and day I hurried ahead.

Knowing what's happening on the frontier,

I hasten to report for you to hear.

**Guo:** Close the gate.

(The attendants go out to close the gate.)

Now tell me, scout, what An Lushan is doing in Fanyang.

How strong is his army? Come forward and tell me in full.

**Scout:** I beg your lordship to listen what happened in Fanyang when

I reached there.

(Singing to the tune of **the Brushwood**):

I saw but snow-bright swords and spears

And tent on tent Full of armed cavaliers.

At his military order

Would tremble all the border.

Who would listen to the crown ?

All would obey him up and down.

**Guo:** What is An Lushan doing there now?

**Scout:** He has replaced Han generals by

His Tartarian chiefs low and high.

They hunt and bend their bows from day to day,

And put their skill on full display.

**Guo:** What else?

**Scout** (Singing to the tune of ***Fallen Mume Blossoms***):

> What they have done's beyond belief;
> What they plot against would bring grief.
> They gathered together men in force
> And rallied outlaws on horse,
> Like those who plot and hide
> In their lair side by side.

**Guo:** Why is there none to inform the court?

**Scout:** It was said in the capital one month ago that An Lushan was accused of plotting rebellion and the emperor sent secretly an envoy to Fanyang to watch what happened there. On seeing the envoy,

> An Lushan pretended to know nothing and tried
> To be polite and bribe him to hide
> The fact so that the envoy came back in time
> To clear An Lushan of any crime.
> The emperor believed
> The envoy deceived
> While the informer was sent
> To An's camp for punishment,
> He can do what he pleases with his men.
> Who dare inform the court of anything since then?

**Guo:** What should and could be done?

**Scout:** The Prime Minister has recently made a proposal to the emperor to put An Lushan to death for it is evident that he will revolt one day. On hearing of this,

> An Lushan would stumble and sigh,
> Afraid his end was nigh,

But the emperor believed him sincere

And told the minister not to fear.

An Lushan burst into laughter:

What could the minister do after ?

He swore with clenched teeth

To put the Prime Minister underneath.

To take revenge is his desire,

Which bursts out into fire.

**Guo:** Would it not be rebellion to plot to put down the Prime Minister? How could I know nothing of the Prime Minister's proposal?

**Scout:** The proposal should be kept as a top secret. Since the Prime Minister would excite An Lushan to rebellion, he had a copy sent to him on purpose.

**Guo** (Angrily): A rebellious general without and a treacherous prime minister within. How could my hair not stand on end!

**Scout:** What is more, An Lushan had a scheme of presenting horses to the court.

(Singing to the tune of **Leaving the Pavilion**):

Under the pretext of presenting horses

He plots to attack the capital with armed, forces.

**Guo:** How so? Explain clearly.

**Scout:** He sent General He Qiannian with a proposal to present to the throne three thousand horses, each accompanied with two armed guards, two horsemen and one groom so that there would be fifteen thousand armed men sent to the capital.

With armed forces and strong horses, they

Would make great trouble all the way.

How to refrain those soldiers in disorder

And the intractable horses from the border ?
Who could bar their way to the capital
And stop their horses under the city wall?
When they arrive at the imperial town,
They would turn all things upside down.

**Guo** (Startled): Ah, if his plan were carried out, the capital would be in danger.

**Scout:** An's proposal has just been submitted and not yet approved. But it is clear that An Lushan plots to deceive the emperor.
Even if the horse plan failed to be carried out,
There would be a wolf's plot he's thinking about.
Do not wait till he beats the war drum
To announce his army's come.
My lord may make preparations beforehand
So that I may report your victory through the land.

**Guo:** Well, you will be rewarded with a jar of wine, one sheep and fifty taels of silver and granted one month's leave. You may go now.

**Scout** (Bowing): Thank you, my lord.

**Guo:** Open the gate, attendants.
(The attendants come in to open the gate and let the scout withdraw.) Lieutenant!

**Lieutenant:** Here, my lord.

**Guo:** Give orders to hold manoeuvres tomorrow and feast our men with wine and meat.

**Lieutenant:** Yes, my lord, your order shall be executed.

## Epilogue of the Scene

**Guo:** My scouts come back from the frontier on horse:

Like wind and thunder fight my men in force.

Having my plan to pacify the border,

I'll drink to men in arms under my order.

(Exeunt.)

## Scene 5 The Bath

(A maid of honor enters.)

**Funny Maid:** I was born with natural grace,
Though with a pockmarked face.
I am the first maid of honor, first of all,
To sweep the palace hall.
I try to flirt with a eunuch above,
But he cannot make love.
I put into his pants my hand,
But find him not a husband.
I am the first maid of honor on duty;
No other maids can rival me in beauty.
My cheeks are smeared with powder white,
My lips with rouge too bright.
As two bronze balls my eyes are fine;
My arched brows form a straight line.
Each of my fingers looks like a drumstick,
My skin like coarse varnish thick,
My willowy waist is too heavy to take a seat,
As big as boats are my lotus-like feet.
Lady Yang who loved my wit
Chose me to dance a bit,
But my voice is as loud
As thunder from the cloud

In dance I turned the table upside down,

Which annoyed the imperial crown,

Who forbade me to dance and sing,

And sent me to the palace in Warm Spring.

The emperor came with Lady Yang yesterday,

And by the Flower-Clear Pool they would stay.

They are going to take a bath today,

And I am ordered to sweep the pathway.

**Here comes another maid.**

(Another maid enters.)

**Second Maid** (Singing to the tune of **Swan Dance**):

Who knows the grief

Of palace maid lonely beyond belief?

What is the use even if we beat

The breast and stamp the feet!

Oh, who would care

For a lonely swan dancing there?

(Greeting the first maid.)

**Maid:** Dear sister, what dancing swan are you singing about? Now the emperor would enjoy Lady Yang's Rainbow Dance, caring not at all for the Swan Dance of Lady Mume Blossom.

**Second Maid:** It is true. I used to wait on Lady Mume Blossom who, angered after coming back from the Emerald Pavilion, fell ill and died. And I was sent to do service here.

**Maid:** If that is the case, I am afraid the jealous Lady Yang would not let us have any chance with the emperor.

**Second Maid:** But I won't care.

**Maid:** His Majesty will soon be here. It would be better for us to wait outside. (Exeunt.)

(A eunuch leads in the emperor and Lady Yang with her two maids.)

**Emperor** (Singing to the tune of **Flowers of Four Seasons**):

> Look! The pleasure palace has cloudlike beam,
>
> And like raindrops is uprolled the pearl screen.
>
> Red railings wind along the picturesque stream,
>
> And corridor on corridor leads to mountains green.
>
> They stretch along the crimson wall
>
> To the jade gate of palace hall.

**Eunuch:** May it please Your Majesty, here is the Warm Spring.

**Emperor:** Leave us. (The eunuch withdraws.) See:

> In the pool ripples water clear
>
> So fragrant, soft and soothing to the skin, my dear.
>
> Let us take a bath.
>
> (The maids help them to take off their garments.)
>
> When you take off your cloudlike dress,
>
> I see your beauty bright as jade.
>
> How can I not love you, caress
>
> And cherish you lest it should fade.
>
> (The emperor goes out with Lady Yang.)

**Ever Fresh:** Dear sister, you see how much our lord loves our lady. Don't you feel enviously?

**Mindful Maid:** Yes, I do.

**Ever Fresh** (Singing to the tune of **Phoenix Hairpin**):

> Hand in hand by day, cheek to cheek by night,
>
> They have enjoyed love's delight.

**Mindful Maid** (Singing to the tune of **Surpassing Flowers**):

> She follows him like a shadow true;

They can't be parted as water can't be cut in two,

Each thinks of the other's part;

They seem to have only one heart.

No tongue can tell with how much love they're fed;

No word can describe their lovebirds' bed,

Where they'd enjoy their fill

And their love blazes still.

**Ever Fresh:** Dear sister, we have waited on Lady Yang for years, yet we have never seen her Ladyship's naked beauty. Why not take a peep through the curtain today?

**Mindful Maid:** Yes, just take a peep.

(They peep through the curtain.)

**Both** (Singing to the tune of Red *Flowers on Water*):

We take a peep on her body slender,

Floating like lotus flower tender

With sweet impearled dew

Shining in fascinating hue.

She moves her arms like a fairy queen,

And her willowy waist in water green,

And her breast blooming like double flower.

**Ever Fresh:** See her private vernal bower!

**Mindful Maid:** Spring hides there where our lord would bring fresh shower.

Bewitched, he fixes on her his smiling eyes

As if crazy for her he sighs.

**Both** (Singing to the tune of *A Billet Doux*):

Not only maids of honor would lose their soul.

But even our lord would his self-control.

**Ever Fresh:** They would bathe till the spring goes dry.

**Mindful Maid:** Or till they've washed clean Jade Mountain high.

**Ever Fresh:** He never stops kissing her shoulder.

**Mindful Maid:** In long embrace he would hold her.

**Ever Fresh:** Our lady, silent, smiles with ease.

**Mindful Maid:** Our lord seems drunk with vernal breeze.

**Ever Fresh:** They frolic in warm water bright

Like two love-birds in warm sunlight.

**Both:** Until the lover's drunk in moonlit bower

And the beloved comes back after the vernal shower.

(Two other maids come in and laugh.)

**Maids:** Dear sisters, you are happy in having fun. Why not let us take a look?

**Both:** We are waiting on Lady Yang as she takes her bath.

What is funny to see?

**Maids:** You are not just waiting on Lady Yang, we are afraid, but also taking a good look on the emperor.

**Both:** Silence! Here come His Majesty and Lady Yang,

(The maids go out. The emperor and Lady Yang enter.)

**Emperor:** Coming out of the pool, we feel so tired and cool,

I see your jadelike face with still more grace.

Your look more fair with disheveled hair,

Which is so clean as evening cloud is green.

(Ever Fresh and Mindful Maid dress them.)

(Lady Yang looks tired and the two maids support her.)

**Emperor:** Like drooping willow in the breeze,

You stand as a flower in fear of dew.

You look so tired and cannot walk with ease;

You need your maids to support you.

(Two eunuchs enter with a pleasure carriage and its driver.)

**Eunuchs:** May it please Your Majesty, the carriage is ready to take you back to the Palace.

**Emperor:** Let the carriage follow us.

**Eunuchs:** Yes, Your Majesty.

**Emperor:** Let us go side by side and hand in hand with ease.

We need no carriage in the balmy breeze.

(Singing together with Lady Yang):

I am in love with you

And you in love with me.

Even the love-birds in view

Are lovesick of the blooming tree.

### Epilogue of the Scene

**Emperor:** Flowers exhale their fragrance cool.

**Lady Yang:** We've come out of the Warm Spring Pool.

**Emperor:** You are too tired to raise your head.

**Lady Yang:** We laugh to lean on royal bed.

(Exeunt.)

## Scene 6 The Secret Vow

(Enter the Celestial Weaving Maid followed by two fairies.)

**Weaving Maid** (Singing to the tune of **Sand-Sifting Stream**):

Weaving With cloud-adorned shuttle of jade,

I'm busy all the year until silk-cloth is made.

No one should be lovesick in heaven.

Now comes the Day of Double Seven.

How can I forget

Last time when we met?

(Singing to the tune of **Magpie Bridge**):

Clouds weave a work of art:

Shooting stars bring word to the heart,

Across the Silver River my Cowherd meets his Maid,

When Autumn's golden breeze embraces Dew of Jade,

All the love scenes on earth, however many, fade.

Our tender love flows like a stream;

Our happy date seems but a dream.

Before us lies each homeward way,

If love between us can last for aye,

Why need we stay together night and day?

I am the Celestial Weaving Maid. By order of the Celestial Emperor, I am married to the Celestial Cowherd, and we are allowed to meet once a year across the River of Silver Stars on the Double Seventh Day. It is the seventh day of the seventh moon on earth now. Behold! The Silver River is calm and the magpies are busy building a celestial bridge. I should stop weaving, dress up and get ready for the crossing.

(Musicians playing the role of magpies flying around stop at the two ends of the bridge.)

**Fairies:** The magpies have built the bridge. Will it please your ladyship to cross the Silver River?

**Weaving Maid** (Singing to the tune of **Red Peach Blossoms**):

I'll leave my loom and mount my carriage with ease,

When cloudless is the sky and cool the breeze.

(Mounting the bridge,)

The bridge casts its shadow on the stream,

Where I see ripples gleam.

I like the crescent new

Still bathed in dew.

The magpies circle in the air,

Never before is autumn sky so fair.

(Crossing the bridge)

**Fairies:** Here we are on the other side of the bridge.

**Weaving Maid:** Below the Silver River I see smoke rise.

From where has it come to my eyes?

**Fairies:** It is Lady Yang of the Tang dynasty praying for blessing and skill of weaving.

**Weaving Maid:** So pious she looks that I would like to go down with my Cowherd to see her.

**All:** We meet in heaven from year to year.

How transient does love in human world appear! (Exeunt.)

(Two eunuchs holding lanterns usher in the emperor.)

**Emperor** (Singing to the tune of *the Young God*):

>Tranquil is autumn light;
>
>Mist melts in the sky with twilight.
>
>After a shower the plane trees shiver;
>
>Light clouds adorn the twin stars by the Silver River.
>
>(Laughter is heard and the emperor listens.)
>
>Attendants, who is laughing and talking there?

**Eunuchs:** His Majesty asks who is laughing and talking there.

**Voice off:** Lady Yang is praying for blessing and art of weaving in the Long-life Hall.

**Eunuchs:** Lady Yang is praying for blessing and art of weaving. So they talk and laugh.

**Emperor:** Do not announce me, attendants. I will go there quietly.

>Without the lanterns red,
>
>To Long-life Hall I'll go ahead.
>
>(Lady Yang comes in, followed by Ever Fresh and Mindful Maid and two other maids, holding a box of incense, a round fan, a vase of flowers and a golden basin.)

**Lady Yang:** Smoke rises in the hall from golden censer bright,

>With gleaming candlelight.
>
>See the webs spiders spin,
>
>And budding peas drowned in the golden basin.
>
>How flowers wave with grace
>
>In silver vase!

**Ever Fresh:** Here we are at the Long-life Hall. The offering is ready. Will it please Your Ladyship to offer incense?

>(The maids place the vase of flowers and the golden basin on the table. Ever Fresh takes the box of incense and gives it to

Lady Yang who picks out three sticks of incense.)

**Lady Yang:** Piously I offer incense to the twin stars above and pray for blessing from heaven.

May our love pledged by hairpin last for long!

May I not be like the fan chilled by an autumn song!

**Emperor** (Coming in quietly and watching her pray.):

With how much grace

She kneels on marble steps and prays!

**Maids** (Seeing the emperor): Ah, His Majesty is here.

(Lady Yang turns hastily to bow to the emperor, who helps her up.)

**Emperor:** What are you doing here, my dear?

**Lady Yang:** On the eve of the Double Seventh Day, I offer melon and fruit to heaven and pray for blessings, grace and skill.

**Emperor** (Laughing): You are so graceful and skilful. What more is there to pray for?

**Lady Yang:** I am afraid I do not deserve your royal praise.

(They take their seats. The maids withdraw.)

**Emperor:** Look, my dear! The Cowherd Star and the Celestial Weaving Maid, separated by the Silver River, could meet only once a year. How much they must long for each other?

(Singing to the tune of **Gathering of Talents**):

The autumn night is still

And the blue sky is chill.

The time has come for the twin stars to meet,

But how short is their time so sweet!

The cock's crow will soon reach their ear.

In cold clouds and chilly dew clear

They must be lonely in waiting a long year.

**Lady Yang:** You speak of their grief at parting which grieves me. What do we know about things in heaven? On enquiry, we may be told that they are lovesick too.

(Wiping tears away.)

**Emperor:** Why are you, my dear, shedding tears?

**Lady Yang:** Though the Cowherd Star and the Celestial Weaving Maid meet only once a year, yet their love will last forever, while ours, I am afraid, may not last as long.

**Emperor:** Why should you say that, my dear?

(Singing to the tune of **Golden Oriole**):

Though the immortals may live long,

Yet can their love as ours be strong?

Who in a hundred years knows more of love's delight

Than we on such a scene and such a night?

Why should you complain on your part,

And weep and sigh to break your heart?

(Moving closer to her and whispering to her ear):

Ask Weaving Maid and Cowherd Star,

Could they be lovers day and night as we are?

**Lady Yang:** It is true that Your Majesty has lavished favor on me, but, if I am allowed, I still have something to say.

**Emperor:** You are allowed to say what you will.

**Lady Yang** (Sobbing): Though I have received more imperial favor than any other lady of the palace, yet I am afraid I might lose your favor when age wrinkles my face.

(Singing to the tune of **Golden Oriole**):

To think of this would break my heart.

Of humble birth, I've played an unrivaled part

To serve at Your Majesty's side.

I am more honored than any royal bride.

But I'm afraid,

Imperial favor might fade.

Flowers will fall one day

When spring has passed away.

How can I on imperial favor rely?

(Clinging to the imperial robe and weeping)

If our love can last long, I'd be content to die.

How many sovereigns love dance and song!

Why could not royal love last long?

When left lonely at the palace gate,

The disfavored could only weep her fate

With a broken heart, desolate!

**Emperor** (Wiping away her tears with his sleeves): Do not be grieved, my dear! How could common love compare with ours?

(Singing to the tune of **Royal Forest**):

Do not be worried nor shed tears!

Fear not our love will change with years. (Taking her hand)

As honey sticks to cake,

I cannot leave you, asleep or awake.

Together as flowers bathed in moonbeams,

We can't be parted in light or shade, even in dreams.

**Lady Yang:** Since your love is so dear, Sire, may I beg you to vow under the twin stars that our love will last as long as our life?

**Emperor:** Let us offer incense and make a vow together.

(They walk together.)

**Together** (Singing to the tune of **Arbor Song**):

We go down the marble steps hand in hand.

The Silver River brightens all our land.

**Lady Yang:** My silken dress feels night grow chill.

**Emperor:** It is so still

That I may whisper to your ear

Our vow so dear that seas and mountains would hear.

(The emperor offers incense. They both bow to the stars.)

**Both:** May the twin stars be our witness. We, Li Longji and Yang Yuhuan, love each other so dearly that we would be husband and wife from life to life, and will never be parted. May the twin stars witness our vow.

**Emperor** (Bowing): On high we'd be two love-birds flying wing to wing.

**Lady Yang** (Bowing): On earth two branches twined from spring to spring.

**Together:** The boundless sky and earth may have an end.

Our hearts in love will ever blend.

**Lady Yang** (Curtseying): Thank Your Majesty for your love. I'll be true to this vow in life and in death.

**Emperor** (Taking her arm): We have made a secret vow in Long-life Hall.

**Lady Yang:** May I ask who the witnesses are?

**Emperor** (Pointing overhead): The Celestial Weaving Maid

and the Cowherd Star.

Beside the Silver River in the fall. (Exeunt.)

(Enter the Cowherd crowned with cloud in fairy garment and the Weaving Maid with other fairies.)

**Together:** They have prayed and made a vow never to part. Pure with one heart.

**Cowherd:** See, my dear, how deep in love the Tang emperor and Lady Yang are!

Shoulder to shoulder they stand

And hand in hand.

**We lovers in heaven who should take care of lovers on earth are**

**requested to witness their secret vow, so we should help them to be**

Two love-birds flying wing to wing

And two branches entwined from spring to spring.

**Weaving Maid:** But a sad fate awaits them and they will be separated

by death. If they remain true to the vow, we should bring them

together again.

**Cowherd:** You are right. Let us go back to heaven.

(Walking forward together.)

**Together:** From year to year in heaven shall we meet,

And laugh how transient human love is, though sweet.

(Exeunt.)

### Epilogue of the Scene

From year to year we're hastened, why?

See across the bridge magpies fly!

Say not it's hard to meet on high.

Who can on earth say no goodbye?

ACT V

## Scene 1  The Fall of the Pass

(Enter An Lushan with two Tartar generals and four soldiers carrying flags.)

**An** (Singing to the tune of **A Skyful of Apricots**):

As wolf or tiger I can do no wrong.

From Yuyang my army of a million strong

To Western Pass drives along.

When victory is won, we'll sing our triumphant song.

I, An Lushan, have contrived with Northern tribes and rallied all rebels on the frontier since I came to Yuyang. Now I have an army of a million strong and may start my great career. But since the emperor has done me high favor, I could not start it until his death. Then what could I do when the Prime Minister warned the emperor again and again that my intention to revolt was evident and he proposed to put me to death? Though his proposal was rejected, yet he is in the court while I am far away on the frontier. If I do not start before his proposal is adopted, I may suffer great harm. So I cannot but forge a secret imperial decree, ordering my army to march in secret to the capital to rid of the treacherous prime minister. How can I not take the advantage to seize the capital and overthrow the empire so as to fulfill my life-long ambition? Today will bring me good fortune. My dear generals, let us start the march!

(They march with trumpets blowing.)

**An** (Singing to the tune of ***the Leopard's Song***):

> When in the court a treacherous premier appears,
>
> How can we not rise in arms on the frontiers!

**All:** We'll sweep the towns and kill the foe,

> Let the dead piled up and blood flow.
>
> We'd burn and rape along the way we go.
>
> (Marching off with war cries.)
>
> (Enter old General Geshu Han with two soldiers.)

**Geshu:** I am not old,

> Just eighty and no more.
>
> From Yuyang come the rebels bold,
>
> But I am still to the fore.
>
> I am old General Geshu Ham in charge of the defence of the Western Pass. Now An Lushan with his army in revolt is marching against us. I planned to strengthen our defence, but the army inspector from the court insisted that we should come out of the Pass to fight them. What can I do but give in to him? Now soldiers, let us fight with might and main!

**Soldiers:** Yes, sir, we will. (Marching forward.)

> (An Lushan comes in with his army. They fight. Geshu Han is defeated and captured.)

**An:** Bring the old general here. (To Geshu) I will spare your life if you surrender the Pass.

**Geshu:** Things being so, what can I do but surrender?

> (Pushed off with his men.)

**An:** Now the Pass is in my hands. Having defeated the old general as easily as splitting the bamboo, now we may drive on to the capital.

> (Marching on to while shouting.)

**All:** Galloping forward, we brandish our spears
　　　　With a million soldiers and cavaliers.
　　　　How can mountain and river
　　　　Under our feet not shiver!

(Exeunt.)

### Epilogue of the Scene

From dawn to dusk we fight all day long,
The sky trembles at drum beats and war song.
Tartars rejoice to win the Pass,
They drink, golden whip in hand, alas!

## Scene 2  The Alarm

(Enter Gao Lishi)

**Gao:** Music and flute songs come from jade palace in mid-air.

Interwoven with laughter of maidens fair.

From moonlit bower waterclock can be heard clear;

Pearl screen uprolled, the Silver River seems so near.

I am Gao Lishi. By the emperor's order I have prepared an intimate feast in the imperial garden for His Majesty and Her Ladyship, and I am waiting here.

(Enter the emperor and Lady Yang in a carriage, followed by Ever Fresh and Mindful Maid. Two eunuchs usher them in.)

**Emperor** (Singing to the tune of **Pink Butterflies**):

Free clouds float in the azure sky,

In rows the new-coming wild geese fly.

In royal garden the golden autumn grieves

And yellows willow leaves.

The duckweed's lost its green

And red lotus its sheen.

Beyond the painted balustrade

No fragrant laurel flowers will fade.

**Gao:** May it please Your Majesty to alight with Your Ladyship.

(The emperor descends from the carriage with Lady Yang. Gao retires with other eunuchs.)

**Emperor:** Let us take a stroll here, my dear.

**Lady Yang:** Yes, Sire. (The emperor takes her hand.)

> Hand in hand we stroll among flowers
>
> To while away leisurely hours.
>
> The pavilion turns cool,
>
> When the breeze blows over lotus blooms in the pool.
>
> I love the calm in the shade of plane trees,
>
> Winding along the green corridor with ease.
>
> The autumn swallows love their fragrant nest;
>
> The love-birds on silver waves take their rest.

**Emperor:** Gao Lishi, bring wine here. I will drink a few cups with her ladyship.

**Gao:** The feast is spread in the pavilion. Will it please Your Majesty to step over there.

(Lady Yang starts to pour out wine, but the emperor stops her.)

**Emperor:** Sit down, my dear. (Singing to the tune of **Pomegranate Flower**):

> On ceremony you need not stand,
>
> Nor present wine with your own hand.
>
> Let us drink two or three cups face to face,
>
> To while away the time with grace.

Though a simple meal, it is more agreeable than a sumptuous feast prepared by the imperial kitchen. I prefer fresh vegetables more suitable for a beauty than a table piled up with dainty food and accompaniment by palace music. I would not hear the old tunes played by palace musicians in our intimate meal. Do you still remember the three stanzas written by Li Bai and set to music by Li Guinian while we were enjoying peony flowers in Fragrant Pavilion? The poem is well written.

**Lady Yang:** Yes, I do.

**Emperor:** Will you sing it for me while I play an accompaniment on my jade flute?

**Lady Yang:** With great pleasure, Your Majesty.

(Ever Fresh brings the jade flute to the emperor who starts to play on it.)

In flower's grace

We see her face,

And in the rainbow cloud

The dress of which she's proud

Who can with her compare?

Only the new-dressed Lady Swallow fair.

A flower which beguiles

The monarch with her smiles.

If you ask why his love won't fade?

See them lean on the pavilion's balustrade.

**Emperor:** Beautiful. The poet's beautiful verse can only be matched by your beautiful voice.

Maids, bring a large cup. (The maids pour wine.)

(Singing to the tune of **Fighting Quails**):

How happy she is ending her song!

How happy she is ending her song!

How happy I am offering her wine along!

Drink this cup, my dear. (Drinking a cup with her.)

We need no help from drinking merriment,

Nor from musical instrument.

(Drinking to her again) Now another cup.

**Lady Yang:** I cannot drink any more.

**Emperor:** Maids, come and offer wine.

**Ever Fresh and Mindful Maid:** Yes, Your Majesty.

(Kneeling to Lady Yang)

Will it please Your Ladyship to drink another cup?

(Lady Yang forces herself to drink and the maids urge her again.)

**Emperor:** I watch her, cup in hand, with silent eyes,

And see rosy cloud on her cheeks rise.

**Lady Yang** (Tipsy): I am really drunk.

**Emperor:** She is now tender as flower or willow tree,

Now tender as flower or willow tree,

Now weary as a swallow or oriole free.

Her Ladyship is drunk. Maids, help her to the carriage and go back to the palace.

**Ever Fresh and Mindful Maid:** Yes, Your Majesty.

**Lady Yang** (Drunkenly): Oh, Your Majesty. (The maids help her up.)

(Singing to the tune of **Moth in a Candle Flame**):

I feel my limbs as soft as clouds are white,

And my eyes dazzled by shade and light.

My willowy waist is limp, though full of charm;

I am too tired to raise my arm.

The ground slips away where my feet are led,

My hair in disorder outspread,

I seek my pillow to lay down my head;

Slowly my maids help me to my curtained bed.

(Exit with the support of Ever Fresh and Mindful Maid.)

(Enter Gao Lishi with other eunuchs. Drums heard in the distance.)

**Emperor** (Startled): From where come the drumbeats?

(Enter Prime Minister Yang Guozong hastily.)

**Yang:** The rebels beat their war drums making the earth quake,

And dance and songs of Rainbow Dress break.

(To Gao) Where is His Majesty?

**Gao:** In the imperial garden.

**Yang:** The situation is urgent. I must go in at once.

(Seeing the emperor) Your Majesty, urgent news! An Lushan rising in revolt has taken the Western Pass. His army is marching on to the capital.

**Emperor** (Alarmed): What about the garrison of the Western Pass?

**Yang:** General Geshu Han, defeated, has surrendered.

**Emperor** (Singing to the tune of *Mounting the Attic*):

You say Geshu Han's wrong,

He has surrendered to An's army strong.

They've left Yuyang, alas!

And broken through the Western Pass.

How can I not tremble with broken heart!

How can I not tremble with broken heart!

What is to be done on our part?

The moon's no longer bright,

The flowers in sad plight.

What would you do to beat back the rebels?

**Yang:** I have warned Your Majesty again and again that An Lushan would revolt sooner or later, but Your Majesty would not believe. Now my prediction has come true. But what could we do without preparations at all! I would advise Your Majesty to withdraw to the west and wait till loyal forces come to restore the royalty.

**Emperor:** Do as you suggest, and give orders for princes and ministers to be ready for the western withdrawal.

**Yang:** Yes, Your Majesty. (Hurrying out.)

**Emperor:** Gao Lishi, get horses ready and give orders to General Chen Yuanli in command of the Imperial Guards to despatch three thousand men as royal escort.

**Gao:** Yes, Your Majesty. (Exit.)

**Eunuchs:** May it please Your Majesty to return to the palace?

**Emperor** (Turning back, sighing): What surprise in such a happy moment! What else can be done?

(Singing to the tune of **Moth in a Candle Flame**):

A happy feast in palace hall is broken by a bolt

From the blue, rebels on the frontier come in revolt.

We hear the drumbeats loud,

And see the beacon fire rise to the cloud.

People are fleeing from the town,

The empire is turned upside down,

The devastated country looks desolate far and near,

At dusk the west wind soughs and sighs sad and drear.

The sun sets at nightfall;

Dark and cold grows the capital.

(Calling to the maids) Has Lady Yang retired?

**Ever Fresh and Mindful Maid** (offstage): Yes, she is asleep.

**Emperor:** Do not wake her. We'll leave tomorrow at dawn. (weeping) Ah, Heaven! What misfortune befalls us! What a distress for a flowerlike beauty to suffer a hard journey! (Singing to the tune of **Southern Epilogue**):

Used to indulgent life in palace deep.

How could she bear the hard journey in mountains steep!

(Weeping) Ah, my darling!

Tender as a flower in May,
How could you suffer the hardship all the way!

### Epilogue of the Scene

The setting sun shines on palaces high and low;
The Western pass is lit with beacon fire aglow.
Her song is lost when moaning wind is loud.
Where are the Western mountains veiled by yellow cloud?

# Scene 3 Death of Lady Yang

(Enter General Chen Yuanli with troops.)

**Chen** (Singing to the tune of *Golden Flowers*):

> With flags and spears,
>
> We march ahead with cavaliers.
>
> We are vanguard
>
> Of the Imperial Guard
>
> To protect His Majesty
>
> From the revolting enemy.
>
> In haste we go on rugged way
>
> To escape from the foe without delay.
>
> When can we reach the West
>
> To have a rest?

I am General Chen Yuanli, commander of the right wing of the Imperial Guards. As An Lushan's revolting army has taken the Western Pass, the emperor is going to Chengdu in the West so as not to be endangered by the disaster. Ordered to escort the imperial convoy, we have had a hard journey and here we are at the Horse-Halting Slope.

(Shouting is heard offstage.) Where comes the uproar?

**Voice off:** An Lushan in revolt has forced His Majesty to leave the capital. Who should take the blame but the Prime Minister Yang Guozhong? If he were not put to death, how could we obey his order to protect His Majesty?

**Chen:** Do not make such a hue and cry but pitch your camp at once. I shall report to His Majesty, and we should wait for the imperial decision. (A shout of assent is heard.)

In haste we go on rugged way

To escape from the foe without delay.

When can we reach the West

To have a rest? (Exeunt.)

(Enter the emperor and Lady Yang on horse, followed by her two maids and Gao Lishi.)

**Emperor** (Singing to the tune of **Rosy-faced Child**):

In haste we left the capital in tears,

With only half of our equipage and cavaliers.

How sad and drear

Do we appear!

Chengdu seems to our eyes

As far as the blue skies.

We go farther and farther away

From the capital each day.

In front lie scattered hills and lonely streams

And two or three empty houses with broken beams.

**Gao:** Here we are at the Horse-Halting Slope. May it please Your Majesty to alight?

(The emperor and Lady Yang alight, enter the station and sit down.)

**Emperor:** I was unwise to trust that rebellious general. But it is now too late to regret.

(To Lady Yang) What can I do to have involved you in this trouble, my dear?

**Lady Yang:** I will follow Your Majesty wherever you go.

How dare I shrink from any hardship? I only hope that the rebels will soon be beaten so that Your Majesty may return to the capital with me.

**Voices off** (Shouting): It is Yang Guozhong who has got us into trouble. How can we serve one who has secretly schemed with the Western tribesmen? How can we live under such a treacherous minister! Come with us if you want to put him to death!

(Yang Guozhong runs in, pursued by guards armed with swords. Running around, the Prime Minister is caught and put to death at last. Soldiers go off with a shout of triumph.)

**Emperor** (Startled): Why are the soldiers shouting? Call General Chen Yuanli at once!

**Gao:** Yes, Your Majesty.

(Hearing the order, General Chen enters.)

**Chen** (Saluting the emperor): General Chen pays homage to Your Majesty.

**Emperor:** Why are the soldiers shouting?

**Chen:** Would Your Majesty allow me to report? On discovering the Prime Minister was to blame for An Lushan's revolt, soldiers rose against him; on learning his intrigue with the Western tribesmen, they put him to death.

**Emperor** (Startled): How could this have happened!

(Lady Yang turns her head to wipe away tears.)

**Emperor** (After a moment's reflection): This is done against my will. Give order that the army should go on pursuing the journey.

**Chen:** His Majesty pardons the guards to have put the prime minister to death, and orders the army to go on the journey.

**Shouts off:** Lady Yang is still at the emperor's side after the death of

Yang Guozhong. How could we allow her to revenge on us! We demand her death at once.

**Chen** (To the emperor): Soldiers say that they would not go on until Lady Yang is put to death. I beg Your Majesty to consider their demand.

**Emperor** (Greatly alarmed): How can they make such a rebellious demand!

(Lady Yang, frightened, takes hold of the emperor's sleeves.)

**Emperor** (Singing to the tune of Red Peony):

If the Prime Minister is guilty at all,

He's punished with his death.

But Lady Yang serves me in inner palace hall,

Why should the army take away her breath?

**Chen:** Your Majesty is fair and square. But what to do with a furious army beyond reason!

**Emperor:** Dear General, go at once to tell the throng

What is right above what is wrong! (Shouts off.)

**Chen:** Your Majesty,

The army rise in disorder,

How could they listen to my order!

**Lady Yang** (Weeping): Your Majesty.

(Singing to the tune of ***Playing a Child***):

What a surprise

To know my cousin dies!

Even I'm implicated;

To suffer I seem fated.

I beg Your Majesty

To abandon poor me.

I have only a word to say on my part,

Though it should break my heart.

**Emperor:** Wait a moment, my dear. Let me think it over.

**Shouts off:** If Lady Yang is still protected, how could we protect His Majesty?

**Chen:** Though Lady Yang is blameless, Your Majesty, yet the Prime Minister is her cousin. How could the army feel secure with her at Your Majesty's side? How could Your Majesty feel secure if the army feel not? I beg Your Majesty to consider it again.

**Emperor** (Reflecting and singing):

I meditate, wordless,

With my mind in a mess.

**Lady Yang** (Clinging to the emperor's robe and crying):

Dry sorrow gnaws my heart.

How can I from you part?

**Together:** Like a pair of love-birds in stormy turbulence,

How can we suffer such violence!

(An uproar of threatening shouts is heard again.)

**Lady Yang:** They threaten me with death.

**Emperor** (Catching hold of her and bursting in tears.): What can I do against their violence, my darling!

(Soldiers burst in shouting, walk around to show the station besieged and then withdraw.)

**Gao:** Your Majesty, the station is besieged. If no action is taken, things may turn worse. What could be done?

**Emperor:** General Chen, go and try to dissuade the army while I'll think of a way out.

**Chen:** Yes, Your Majesty. (Exit.)

(The emperor and lady Yang clinging to each other in tears.)

**Lady Yang** (Singing to the tune of **Golden Wreath**):

> My soul has fled
> While tears are shed.

**Emperor:** High as Imperial Majesty,

> From grief I am not free.

**Together** (In tears): How can I forget

> In love I owe you a debt!

**Lady Yang** (Kneeling): I have received so much imperial favor that it cannot be repaid with my life. Now the danger is imminent, I beg Your Majesty to allow me to commit suicide so that the army may be pacified. When Your Majesty has arrived safely at the Western capital, I would feel more comforted to be dead than alive. (Singing):

> There's no way to satisfy their demand
> But to sacrifice my life at your command,
> But to sacrifice my life at your command.

(Crying with her head in his lap.)

**Emperor:** How could you say that, my love! Without you by my side, what is the use of the throne? I would lose the empire rather than you. (Singing to the tune of **Embroidered Carpet**):

> Their shout and clamour I won't hear,
> But only turn them a deaf ear.
> It is all my fault, how can I bear a flower
> To be destroyed by roaring wind and shower!
> If the army should still rebellious stand,
> Instead of you, I would be buried in the sand.

**Lady Yang:** Your Majesty is lavish with your love and favor, but the situation is desperate, you cannot sacrifice a jade for a stone, or a greater blame would lie on me. Please give me up for the empire's sake.

**Gao** (Wiping tears away and kneeling): Since Her Ladyship is so gracious as to sacrifice her own life, I beg Your Majesty to grant her request for the empire's sake. (Shouts off.)

**Emperor** (Stamping his feet in tears): What could I do if she insists? Gao Lishi, let Her Ladyship do what she wishes. (Sobbing, he covers his face and withdraws.)

**Lady Yang** (Sobbing and bowing): Long live Your Majesty! (Falling down in tears.)

**Gao** (Calling to the soldiers outside): Listen! His Majesty has ordered Lady Yang's death.

**Shouts off:** Long, long live the emperor! (Gao helps Lady Yang to rise.)

**Gao:** Please come this way, Your Ladyship. (Helping her along.)

**Lady Yang** (Singing in tears to the tune of Lovesickness):
In a moment I'll bid an eternal adieu
To my lord for whom I'd lose my rosy hue. (They halt.)

**Gao:** Here is a shrine.

**Lady Yang** (Standing before the shrine): Wait! Let me worship the Buddha! (Bowing.)
O Great Buddha, so sinful am I,
Would you pardon me after I die?

**Gao** (Bowing): May Your Ladyship go up to Heaven! (Lady Yang rises weeping, and Gao kneels in tears)
Have Your Ladyship anything to confide to me?

**Lady Yang:** Gao Lishi, His Majesty is growing old. You are the only one after me who can understand His Majesty. Would you take good care of him and tell him to forget me?

**Gao** (Weeping): I know what I should do.

**Lady Yang:** I have something else to tell you. (Unfastening the hairpin from her hair and taking out a jewel box) The twin hairpin and the jewel box are given to pledge His Majesty's love for me. Be sure to bury them with me and do not forget it!

**Gao** (Taking them): Yes, it shall be done as Your Ladyship wishes.

**Lady Yang** (Singing in tears): Heart-broken in distress,
My grief is too deep to express.

**Chen** (Hurrying in with soldiers): By imperial decree, Lady Yang should commit suicide.
How could she still be here to delay His Majesty's journey?
(Soldiers shout and Gao tries to stop them.)

**Gao:** Keep back! Lady Yang is going to return to Heaven.

**Lady Yang:** Ah! Chen Yuanli, Chen Yuanli!
Why should you bring no rebels' death,
But take away my breath?
(Soldiers shout again in uproar.)

**Gao:** Alas! The soldiers are breaking in.

**Lady Yang** (Looking around): What can I do but end my life on this pear tree!
(Taking off her white silk girdle and curtseying to the distance)
I kowtow in thanks for the royal favor conferred on his humble maid. I'm afraid we'll never see each other again in this life.
(Gao weeps.)

**Lady Yang** (Preparing in tears to hang herself): Your Majesty,

I'll end my life and go to underground stream.

My soul will never leave Your Majesty's dream. (Exit.)

**Gao** (To soldiers): Don't break in now! Lady Yang is gone!

(Soldiers withdraw.)

**Gao** (in tears): Alas! His Majesty! (Exit.)

(The emperor enters.)

**Emperor:** Six armies—what could be done?—would not march with speed

Unless my Lady Yang be killed before their steed

(Gao re-enters with the white silk girdle and presents it to the emperor.)

**Gao:** Your Majesty, Lady Yang is gone.

(The emperor, terror-stricken, remains wordless.)

Lady Yang is gone. Here is the silk girdle with which she hanged herself.

**Emperor** (Looking at the girdle and crying bitterly): Alas! My love, my love! How can my heart not be broken! (Staggering, supported by Gao)

(Singing to the tune of **Embroidered Red Shoes**):

Then fair as peach blossom was she,

As peach blossom was she!

**Gao:** Now she is dead under a pear tree,

Dead under a pear tree.

(Showing the hairpin and the jewel box)

The hairpin and the jewel box, Her Ladyship told me to bury them together with her remains.

**Emperor** (Looking at them in tears):

The hairpin and jewel box are root of evils all.

How much joy we knew in the Long-life Hall!

Now at Horse-Halting Slope,

Our love ends without any hope.

**Gao:** How could we prepare in such a hurry a coffin fit for Her Ladyship?

**Emperor:** Since it is impossible to do anything fit, you may wrap her up in a silk quilt and mark the burial place so that her remains may be removed later. The hairpin and the jewel box may be put into her clothes.

**Gao:** Yes. Your Majesty's order shall be executed.

(Exit.)

**Emperor** (Singing to the tune of the ***Epilogue in tears***):

Her warm fragrance and jade-white beauty have passed away.

Where could I find her in the world of today?

(General Chen enters and kneels to the emperor.)

**Chen:** Will it please Your Majesty to go on the journey to the West?

**Emperor:** What do I care for the Western journey!

(Trumpets blow and the guards march in.)

(Gao Lishi re-enters to lead the emperor to his horse.)

**All** (Singing to the tune of ***Paying the Homage***):

Mist veils the sky,

The cold wind blows and flags and banners fly.

The way is long,

And dust-covered the throng.

Who could anticipate the emperor

Should brave the danger with his minister ?

We hate the rebels putting the country in fire

With flames rising higher and higher.

When will end the times hard?

When shall we quell rebellious tiger and pard?
Far, far away the Western Mountain towers,
Looking back, we can't find the palace bowers
But floating clouds so white
With the capital lost to sight,
And the capital lost to sight.

### Epilogue of the Scene

With royal banners sweeping west clouds westwards fly;
The capital in danger darkens earth and sky.
The lord can't find the rosy face of his fair bride;
In vain he sighs for love-birds swimming side by side.

许译中国经典诗文集

# 长生殿

【清】洪升 著

许渊冲 许明 译

五洲传播出版社　中华书局

# 序

　　"七月七日长生殿，夜半无人私语时：在天愿作比翼鸟，在地愿为连理枝。"这是唐代白居易《长恨歌》中写唐明皇和杨贵妃海誓山盟的名句。唐皇和杨妃轻歌曼舞、生离死别的爱情故事，在中国流传了一千多年，最著名的剧本是这部清代洪升著的《长生殿》。林语堂认为洪升的生花妙笔才能使"此恨绵绵"，"天长地久"。陈寅恪却认为唐皇对杨妃的爱情，朝欢暮乐，"从此君王不早朝"，是中国黄金时代由盛转衰的关键，因为"玉颜自古关兴废"。不但中国如此，西方也有例证，法国哲学家巴斯加就说过：埃及女王克柳葩的鼻子假如高了一公分，世界历史就要改写，因为假如她不是那么美艳，古罗马的凯撒大帝就不会坠入爱河，大将安东尼也不会"不爱江山爱美人"，那西方的古代史就要重写了。

　　埃及女王克柳葩比杨贵妃要早几百年，和克柳葩同时的中国美人有汉武帝的李夫人，她的哥哥李延年为她写了一首诗：

　　　　北方有佳人，绝世而独立。

　　　　一顾倾人城，再顾倾人国。

　　　　宁不知倾城与倾国？佳人难再得。

　　但汉武帝并没有像罗马大将那样让美人倾国倾城，而是为了江山牺牲了美人。但是在她死后，他却写了一首哀悼她的《落叶哀蝉曲》：

　　　　罗袂兮无声，玉墀兮尘生。

　　　　虚房冷而寂寞，落叶依于重扃。

　　　　望彼美之女兮安得？感余心之未宁。

　　汉武帝思念李夫人，看见她穿过的罗衣，却听不到她穿衣的窸窣之声；看见她走过的台阶，却盖满了尘埃，看不到她的脚印；卧房里空荡荡的，身体感到寒冷，心里觉得寂寞，看到门槛上一片孤零零的落叶，仿佛是李夫人的幽灵，依依不舍地留恋着寝宫的房门。这首诗没有描写李夫人的外形，只写看到的、听到的、感到的环境，用景语来写情，再通过武帝之情来想象李夫人之美，这是一种通过外部世界来写内心世界，又通过内心世界来想象外部世界的写法。

　　关于杨贵妃的描写，中国古诗也用景语来作情语，这在《诗经》中叫作"比兴"之法。如李白著名的《清平调》："云想衣裳花想容，春风拂槛露华浓。若非群玉山头见，会向瑶台月下逢。"就是先把杨妃比作花，又把她比作月中仙子。但在白居易的《长恨歌》中，却是先用一个特写镜头："回头一笑百媚生"，再用反比来作衬托："六宫粉黛无颜色。"到了洪升的《长生殿》，描写就更含蓄细致：

　　"看了这粉容嫩，只怕风儿弹破。"

　　"袅临风百种娇娆，还对镜千般婀娜。"

　　这是含蓄地把杨妃比作临风玉树，显示了深厚的文化底蕴。

　　而在西方，莎士比亚是如何描写埃及女王的呢？我们来看一段安东尼和克柳葩的对话：

　　克：你对我到底有多少爱情？

　　安：对乞丐的施舍才算得清。

　　克：我要摸一摸你爱情的底。

安：那你就需要开辟新天地。

莎士比亚用对乞丐施舍的具体金钱，来比抽象的算不清的爱情，又用具体的看得见、摸得着的高天低地来比爱情的无底深渊，这和洪升用袅袅秋风来形容美人的身材，又用风可吹破来形容美人的嫩脸，可以说是各有巧妙。洪升是如何描写美人内心感情的呢？在第七出中他写杨贵妃：

她情性多骄纵，恃天生百样玲珑，

一人独占三千宠，问阿谁能与竞雌雄？

这和白居易写"六宫粉黛"一样。在第六出中写她对梅妃的妒忌心理：

娇痴心天生忒利害。

前时逼得个梅娘娘，直迁置楼东无奈。

这是用叙事来写情。总的看来，比较简单；而莎士比亚笔下的埃及女王却心情复杂，丰富多姿。如第一幕第三场她要侍女去看安东尼，

"瞧瞧他在什么地方，跟什么人在一起，

在干些什么事；不要说是我叫你去的。

要是你看见他在发恼，就说我在跳舞；

要是他样子很高兴，就说我突然病了。"

看来简单的几句话，却把女王挑动安东尼的心理，写得淋漓尽致了。

在唐明皇和杨贵妃生离死别的时候，景语情语也很简单。

妃：魂飞颤，泪交加。

皇：堂堂天子尊，不及莫愁家。

合：难道把恩和义，霎时抛下！

皇：你若捐生，朕虽有九重之尊，四海之富，要他则甚！

宁可国破家亡，决不肯抛舍你也。

这时的唐明皇和安东尼一样"不爱江山爱美人"，但是安东尼的死却更英雄，似乎爱情是他的不死药：

安：不是凯撒战胜了安东尼，是安东尼战胜了自己。

我要死了，女王，让我的嘴唇带走你最后一个吻！

而埃及女王在死前却说：

克：我是火，我是风，我身上其他的东西，

让它们和我的皮囊同归于尽吧！我要

死得像香膏一样甜蜜，像清风一样温柔！

《长生殿》留下来的只是"此恨绵绵无绝期"，莎剧的英雄主义却似乎战胜了死亡。这也是中西文化一个不同之点吧。

许渊冲

2009年3月

第一本

# 第一出 传 概[1]

【南吕 引子】【满江红】（末上）今古情场，问谁个真心到底？但果有精诚不散[2]，终成连理。万里何愁南共北，两心那论生和死。笑人间儿女怅缘悭，无情耳。　感金石，回天地。昭白日，垂青史。看臣忠子孝，总由情至[3]。先圣不曾删《郑》《卫》[4]，吾侪取义翻宫徵[5]。借太真外传谱新词，情而已。

【中吕 慢词】【沁园春】天宝明皇，玉环妃子，宿缘正当。自华清赐浴，初承恩泽。长生乞巧，永订盟香。妙舞新成，清歌未了，鼙鼓喧阗起范阳[6]。马嵬驿，六军不发[7]，断送红妆[8]。　西川巡幸堪伤[9]，奈地下人间两渺茫。幸游魂悔罪，已登仙籍，回鸾改葬，只剩香囊。证合天孙[10]，情传羽客[11]，钿盒金钗重寄将。月宫会，霓裳遗事，流播词场。

> 唐明皇欢好霓裳宴，　杨贵妃魂断渔阳变[12]。
>
> 鸿都客引会广寒宫[13]，　织女星盟证长生殿[14]。

注释

[1]传概：传奇的第一出，一般称作"家门引子"。家门引子用来说明：一、创作缘起（如本出的《满江红》）；二、剧情梗概（如本出的《沁园春》）。

[2]但：只要。

[3]"感金石"至"总由情至"：即"情之所至，金石为开"的意思。

[4]先圣不曾删《郑》《卫》：《诗经》中的《郑风》《卫风》有不少

热情活泼的情歌，旧时被贬斥为"淫奔之诗"。孔子也曾说"郑声淫"，但他整理《诗经》时，并没有删去《郑风》《卫风》。

[5]吾侪取义翻宫徵（zhǐ）：吾侪，我辈；侪，同辈、同类的人。翻宫徵，作曲；古代音乐以宫、商、角、徵、羽为音阶名，宫徵泛指乐曲。

[6]鼙鼓喧阗起范阳：指安禄山在范阳（今北京大兴）起兵叛乱。鼙鼓，战鼓。

[7]马嵬驿，六军不发：安禄山乱起，唐明皇逃出长安，至马嵬驿（在今陕西兴平），随驾的军队不肯前进，要求处死杨国忠、杨贵妃。

[8]断送红妆：断送，葬送；红妆，指杨贵妃。

[9]西川巡幸：字面意思是说唐明皇到四川西部巡幸游历，其实是讳言其逃难。

[10]证合天孙：本剧最后部分有这样的情节，织女让唐明皇、杨贵妃在月宫相会，为他们的爱情作证。本书未录这段剧情。天孙，天帝的孙女儿，即神话传说中的织女。

[11]情传羽客：道士杨通幽为唐明皇、杨贵妃传情达意，终使他们在月宫团圆。这段情节本书亦未收录。羽客，道士。

[12]渔阳变：指安禄山在范阳起兵叛变。渔阳，即范阳。

[13]鸿都客：神仙中人，指道士杨通幽。鸿都，仙府。

[14]在形式上，第一出结尾四句与其他出一样也是下场诗，但就内容而论，它们是全剧剧情的概括。

# 第二出 定 情

【大石 引子】【东风第一枝】（生扮唐明皇引二内侍上）
端冕中天，垂衣南面[1]，山河一统皇唐。层霄雨露回春，深宫草
木齐芳。《升平》早奏[2]，韶华好，行乐何妨。愿此生终老温
柔，白云不羡仙乡[3]。

"韶华入禁闱，宫树发春晖。天喜时相合，人和事不
违。《九歌》扬政要[4]，《六舞》散朝衣[5]。别赏阳台
乐[6]，前旬暮雨飞[7]。"朕乃大唐天宝皇帝是也。起自
潜邸[8]，入缵皇图[9]。任人不二，委姚、宋于朝堂[10]；
从谏如流，列张、韩于省闼[11]。且喜塞外风清万里，民
间粟贱三钱。真个太平致治，庶几贞观之年[12]；刑措成
风[13]，不减汉文之世。近来机务余闲，寄情声色。昨见
宫女杨玉环[14]，德性温和，丰姿秀丽。卜兹吉日，册为
贵妃。已曾传旨，在华清池赐浴，命永新、念奴伏侍更
衣。即着高力士引来朝见，想必就到也。

【玉楼春】（丑扮高力士，二宫女执扇引，旦扮杨贵妃上）恩
波自喜从天降，浴罢妆成趋彩仗。（宫女）六宫未见一时愁[15]，
齐立金阶偷眼望。

（到介，丑进见生跪介）奴婢高力士见驾。册封贵妃杨
氏，已到殿门候旨。（生）宣进来。（丑出介）万岁爷
有旨，宣贵妃杨娘娘上殿。（旦进，拜介）臣妾贵妃
杨玉环见驾，愿吾皇万岁！（内侍）平身。（旦）臣妾

寒门陋质，充选掖庭[16]，忽闻宠命之加，不胜陨越之惧。（生）妃子世胄名家，德容兼备。取供内职[17]，深惬朕心。（旦）万岁。（丑）平身。（旦起介，生）传旨排宴。（丑传介）（内奏乐。旦送生酒，宫女送旦酒。生正坐，旦傍坐介）

【大石 过曲】【念奴娇序】（生）寰区万里，遍征求窈窕[18]，谁堪领袖嫔墙？佳丽今朝，天付与，端的绝世无双[19]。思想，擅宠瑶宫，褒封玉册[20]，三千粉黛总甘让。（合）惟愿取，恩情美满，地久天长。

【前腔】【换头】[21]（旦）蒙奖。沉吟半晌，怕庸姿下体，不堪陪从椒房[22]。受宠承恩，一霎里身判人间天上。须仿，冯嫙当熊，班姬辞辇，永持彤管侍君傍。（合）惟愿取，恩情美满，地久天长。

【前腔】【换头】（宫女）欢赏，借问从此宫中，阿谁第一？似赵家飞燕在昭阳[23]。宠爱处，应是一身承当。休让，金屋妆成，玉楼歌彻，千秋万岁捧霞觞。（合）惟愿取，恩情美满，地久天长。

【前腔】【换头】（内侍）瞻仰，日绕龙鳞，云移雉尾[24]，天颜有喜对新妆。频进酒，合殿春风飘香。堪赏，圆月摇金，余霞散绮，五云多处易昏黄[25]。（合）惟愿取恩情美满，地久天长。

（丑）月上了。启万岁爷撤宴。（生）朕与妃子同步阶前，玩月一回。（内作乐。生携旦前立，众退后，齐立介）

【中吕 过曲】【古轮台】（生）下金堂，笼灯就月细端相，庭花不及娇模样。轻偎低傍，这鬓影衣光，掩映出丰姿千状。（低笑，向旦介）此夕欢娱，风清月朗，笑他梦雨暗高唐。（旦）追游宴赏，幸从今得侍君王。瑶阶小立，春生天语，香萦仙仗[26]，玉露冷沾裳。还凝望，重重金殿宿鸳鸯。

（生）掌灯往西宫去。（丑应介，内侍、宫女各执灯引
　　生、旦行介）（合）

**【前腔】【换头】**辉煌，簇拥银烛影千行。回看处珠箔斜
开[27]，银河微亮。复道回廊，到处有香尘飘扬。夜色如何？月
高仙掌[28]。今宵占断好风光[29]，红遮翠障，锦云中一对鸾凰。
《琼花》《玉树》，《春江夜月》[30]，声声齐唱，月影过宫墙。
褰罗幌[31]，好扶残醉入兰房。

（丑）启万岁爷，到西宫了。（生）内侍回避。（丑）
　　"春风开紫殿，（内侍）天乐下珠楼。"（同下）

**【余文】**（生）花摇烛，月映窗，把良夜欢情细讲。（合）莫
问他别院离宫玉漏长。

（宫女与生、旦更衣，暗下，生、旦坐介，生）"银烛回
　　光散绮罗，（旦）御香深处奉恩多。（生）六宫此夜含
　　颦望，（合）明日争传《得宝歌》。"（生）朕与妃子
　　偕老之盟，今夕伊始。（袖出钗、盒介）特携得金钗、
　　钿盒在此，与卿定情。

**【越调　近词】【绵搭絮】**（生）这金钗钿盒百宝翠花攒。我
紧护怀中，珍重奇擎有万般[32]。今夜把这钗呵，与你助云盘[33]，
斜插双鸾；这盒呵，早晚深藏锦袖，密裹香纨。愿似他并翅交
飞，牢扣同心结合欢。（付旦介，旦接钗、盒谢介）

**【前腔】【换头】**谢金钗钿盒赐予奉君欢。只恐寒姿，消不
得天家雨露团。（作背看介）恰偷观，凤翥龙蟠，爱杀这双头旖
旎，两扇团圞[34]。惟愿取情似坚金，钗不单分盒永完。

（生）胧明春月照花枝，元　稹

（旦）始是新承恩泽时。白居易

（生）长倚玉人心自醉，雍　　陶

（合）年年岁岁乐于斯。赵彦昭[35]

注 释 ────────────────────────

[1] 端冕中天，垂衣南面：天下太平，无为而治。中天，喻盛世；南面，帝王的座位朝南，作统治解；端冕，帝王的冠服。垂衣，表示无为之治。

[2] 《升平》：歌颂太平的曲调。

[3] 愿此生终老温柔，白云不羡仙乡：温柔即温柔乡，这里指和杨妃在一起。白云不羡仙乡，即不羡白云仙乡。

[4] 《九歌》：夏代庙堂乐曲。

[5] 《六舞》：周代舞乐，即武王的《大武》。

[6][7] 阳台、暮雨：指男女欢会。

[8] 潜邸：皇帝在即位以前所住的府第。"潜"字从《易经•乾卦》"初九，潜龙勿用"而来，潜龙指未做皇帝之前。

[9] 缵（zuǎn）：继承。

[10] 姚、宋：姚崇、宋璟，唐开元时贤相。

[11] 列张、韩于省闱：张说、韩休，或指张九龄、韩休，唐开元时贤相。省闱，中央政府。

[12] 贞观：唐太宗年号（627—649），这时期是历史上著名的太平盛世，号称"贞观之治"。

[13] 刑措：不动用刑法。措，废置。据载西汉文帝时刑法宽缓，人民生活安定。

[14] 杨玉环：本是李隆基之子寿王李瑁的妃子，后被唐明皇占为己有，册封贵妃。剧中所述与历史不同。

[15] 六宫未见一时愁：王建《宫词》百首中的诗句。

[16]掖庭：皇宫里妃嫔所住的地方。

[17]内职：宫内妇女的职务，这里指贵妃。

[18]窈窕：形容体态美好。这里作名词用，指美女。

[19]端的：正是。

[20]玉册：刻在玉版上的文书，这里指册封贵妃的证书。

[21]前腔：南曲中指和前面一个乐调曲牌相同。

[22]椒房：花椒果实繁多，象征多生男子，又性质温暖，气味芳香，古
　　　时用来涂抹后妃居室的墙壁，所以称后妃居室为椒房。

[23]赵家飞燕在昭阳：赵飞燕，汉成帝的皇后，她和妹妹昭仪受到成帝的
　　　宠幸，这里用来比杨贵妃。昭阳，赵昭仪居昭阳舍，这里指代后宫。

[24]日绕龙鳞，云移雉尾：龙，指皇帝；雉尾，雉尾扇，皇帝仪仗队所用。

[25]五云多处：相传天子所在的地方有五色的云彩。

[26]仙仗：指皇帝的仪仗。

[27]珠箔：珠帘。

[28]仙掌：即仙人掌，汉宫中的一种装置，作仙人以手掌举盘接天上甘
　　　露的样子。

[29]占断：占尽。

[30]《琼花》《玉树》，《春江夜月》：都是古代歌曲名称。

[31]罗幌：即罗帷，门幕一类的东西。

[32]奇擎：即擎。

[33]云盘：云，形容头发像乌云那样黑；盘，盘髻。

[34]双头旖旎，两扇团圞：双头，指两股金钗；两扇，指钿盒。

[35]以上四句是本出结尾的下场诗，用来概括本出戏的大意。下场诗有
　　　的是剧作家自己写的，有的是集句。

# 第三出 贿 权[1]

【正宫 引子】【破阵子】（净扮安禄山箭衣、毡帽上）失意空悲头角[2]，伤心更陷罗罝[3]。异志十分难屈伏，悍气千寻怎蔽遮[4]？权时宁耐些[5]。

"腹垂过膝力千钧，足智多谋胆绝伦。谁道孽龙甘蠖屈[6]，翻江搅海便惊人。"自家安禄山，营州柳城人也。俺母亲阿史德，求子轧荦山中，归家生俺，因名禄山。那时光满帐房，鸟兽尽都鸣窜。后随母改嫁安延偃[7]，遂冒姓安氏。在节度使张守珪帐下投军。他道我生有异相，养为义子。授我讨击使之职，去征讨奚契丹。一时恃勇轻进，杀得大败逃回。幸得张节度宽恩不杀，解京请旨。昨日到京，吉凶未保。且喜有个结义兄弟，唤作张千，原是杨丞相府中干办。昨已买嘱解官，暂时松放。寻他通个关节[8]，把礼物收去了。着我今日到彼候复，不免前去走遭。（行介）唉，俺安禄山，也是个好汉，难道便这般结果了么？想起来好恨也！

【正宫 过曲】【锦缠道】莽龙蛇，本待将河翻海决，反做了失水瓮中鳖，恨樊笼霎时困了豪杰。早知道失军机要遭斧钺，倒不如丧沙场免受缧绁，蓦地里脚双跌。全凭仗金投暮夜[9]，把一身离阱穴。算有意天生吾也，不争待半路枉摧折[10]。

来此已是相府门首，且待张兄弟出来。（丑扮张千上）
"君王舅子三公位，宰相家人七品官。"（见介）安大
哥来了。丞相爷已将礼物全收，着你进府相见。（净
揖介）多谢兄弟周旋。（丑）丞相爷尚未出堂，且到班
房少待。"全凭内阁调元手[11]，（净）救取边关失利
人。"（同下）

【仙吕 引子】【鹊桥仙】（副净扮杨国忠引祗从上）荣夸
帝里，恩连戚畹[12]，兄妹都承天眷。中书独坐揽朝权[13]，看炙手
威风赫烜[14]。

"国政归吾掌握中，三台八座极尊崇[15]。退朝日晏归私
第，无数官僚拜下风。"下官杨国忠，乃西宫贵妃之兄
也。官居右相，秩晋司空。分日月之光华，掌风雷之号
令。（冷笑介）穷奢极欲，无非行乐及时；纳贿招权，
真个回天有力。左右回避。（从应下）（副净）适才张
千禀说，有个边将安禄山，为因临阵失机，解京正法。
特献礼物到府，要求免死发落。我想胜败乃兵家常事，
临阵偶然失利，情有可原。（笑介）就将他免死，也是
为朝廷爱惜人才。已曾分付令他进见，再作道理。（丑
暗上，见介）张千禀事：安禄山在外伺候。（副净）着
他进来。（丑）领钧旨。（虚下，引净青衣、小帽上，
丑）这里来。（净膝行进见介）犯弁安禄山[16]，叩见丞
相爷。（副净）起来。（净）犯弁是应死囚徒，理当跪
禀。（副净）你的来意，张千已讲过了。且把犯罪情
由，细说一番。（净）丞相爷听禀：犯弁遵奉军令，去
征讨奚契丹呵，（副净）起来讲。（净起介）

【仙吕 过曲】【解三醒】恃勇锐冲锋出战，指征途所向无

前。不提防番兵夜来围合转，临白刃剩空拳<sup>[17]</sup>。（副净）后来怎生得脱？（净）那时犯弁杀杀血路，奔出重围。单枪匹马身幸免，只指望鉴录微功折罪愆。谁想今日呵，当刑宪！（叩首介）望高抬贵手，曲赐矜怜。

**【前腔】【换头】**（副净起介）论失律丧师关巨典，我虽总朝纲敢擅专？况刑书已定难更变，恐无力可回天。（净跪哭介）丞相爷若肯救援，犯弁就得生了。（副净笑介）便道我言从计听微有权，这就里机关不易言。（净叩头介）全仗丞相爷做主！（副净）也罢。待我明日进朝，相机而行便了。乘其便，便好开罗撤网，保汝生全。

（净叩头介）蒙丞相爷大恩，容犯弁犬马图报。就此告辞。（副净）张千引他出去。（丑应，同净出介）"眼望捷旌旗，耳听好消息<sup>[18]</sup>。"（同下）（副净想介）我想安禄山乃边方末弁，从未著有劳绩。今日犯了死罪，我若特地救他，必动圣上之疑。（笑介）哦，有了。前日张节度疏内<sup>[19]</sup>，曾说他通晓六番言语，精熟诸般武艺，可当边将之任。我就授意兵部，以此为辞，奏请圣上，召他御前试验。于中乘机取旨，却不是好。

| | | |
|---|---|---|
| 专权意气本豪雄，卢照邻 | | 万态千端一瞬中。吴　融 |
| 多积黄金买刑戮，李咸用 | | 不妨私荐也成公。杜荀鹤 |

## 注释

[1]幽州节度使张守珪派安禄山去攻打奚契丹部落，安禄山轻敌落败，依法应该被处死。张守珪是安的义父，把他解到京师。丞相张九龄主张把安杀了。李隆基却宽赦了他，只解除他的官职，仍旧叫他带兵。这是唐玄宗开元二十四年（736）的事。据史实，这时杨玉环还是寿王的妃子，杨国忠也没有在朝做官。

[2]头角：指高贵的相貌。

[3]罗置：罗网，陷罗置指解京问罪。

[4]千寻：古代八尺为一寻。千寻高，形容悍气之高涨。

[5]权时：暂时。

[6]蠖屈：不得志。蠖，尺蠖，虫名，行动时一屈一伸。

[7]安延偃：突厥族一个部落的酋长。

[8]通个关节：买通官员。

[9]金投暮夜：东汉时王密以金十斤送给杨震，杨震不收，王密说不会有人知道，杨震说："天知地知，我知你知，怎么没有人知道呢？"

[10]不争：不曾，不至于。

[11]调元：调和阴阳，指宰相治理国家。

[12]戚畹：即戚里，外戚所居的地方。

[13]中书：唐中书省的长官中书令，是最高执政官员。

[14]炙手：炙手可热，形容气焰很盛，权势很大。

[15]三台八座：指封建王朝的最高政权机关。汉以尚书、御史、谒者为三台，唐以左右仆射及左右相、六尚书为八座。

[16]弁：下级武官，也用作一般武将的自称。

[17]临白刃剩空眷：奋勇不屈，战至最后。空眷，箭射完了，只剩一张弓。眷（quān），弓弦，指代弓。

[18]眼望捷旌旗，耳听好消息：等待好消息之意。

[19]疏：奏章。

# 第四出　春　睡

【越调 引子】【祝英台近】（旦引老旦扮永新、贴旦扮念奴上）梦回初，春透了，人倦懒梳裹。欲傍妆台，羞被粉脂涴[1]。（老旦、贴旦）趁他迟日房栊，好风帘幕，且消受熏香闲坐。

　　永新、念奴叩头。（旦）起来。[海棠春]"流莺窗外啼声巧，睡未足，把人惊觉。（老）翠被晓寒轻，（贴）宝篆沉烟袅[2]。（旦）宿醒未醒宫娥报[3]，（老、贴）道别院笙歌会早。（旦）试问海棠花，（合）昨夜开多少？"（旦）奴家杨氏，弘农人也。父亲元琰，官为蜀中司户。早失怙恃[4]，养在叔父之家。生有玉环，在于左臂，上隐"太真"二字。因名玉环，小字太真。性格温柔，姿容艳丽。漫揩罗袂，泪滴红冰；薄试霞绡，汗流香玉。荷蒙圣眷，拔自宫嫔。位列贵妃，礼同皇后。有兄国忠，拜为右相，三姊尽封夫人，一门荣宠极矣。昨宵侍寝西宫，（低介）未免云娇雨怯。今日晌午时分，才得起来。（老、贴）镜奁齐备，请娘娘理妆。（旦行介）绮疏晓日珠帘映[5]，红粉春妆宝镜催。

【越调 过曲】【祝英台】（坐对镜介）把鬓轻撩，鬓细整，临镜眼频睃[6]。（老）请娘娘贴上这花钿。（旦）贴了翠钿，（贴）再点上这胭脂。（旦）注了红脂，（老）请娘娘画眉。（旦画眉介）着意再描双蛾。（旦立起介）延俄[7]，慢支持杨柳腰身。（贴）呀，娘娘花儿也忘戴了。（代旦插花介）好

添上樱桃花朵。（老、贴作看旦介）看了这粉容嫩，只怕风儿弹破。（老、贴）请娘娘更衣。（与旦更衣介）

**【前腔】【换头】**飘堕，麝兰香，金绣影，更了杏衫罗。（旦步介）（老、贴看介）你看小颤步摇[8]，轻荡湘裙。（旦兜鞋介）低蹴半弯凌波[9]，停妥。（旦顾影介）（老、贴）袅临风百种娇娆。（旦回身临镜介）（老，贴）还对镜千般婀娜。（旦作倦态，欠伸介）（老、贴扶介）娘娘，恹恹恹，何妨重就衾窝。

　　（旦）也罢，身子困倦，且自略睡片时。永新、念奴，与我放下帐儿。正是："无端春色熏人困，才起梳头又欲眠。"（睡介）（老、贴放帐介）（老）万岁爷此时不进宫来，敢是到梅娘娘那边去么[10]？（贴）姐姐，你还不知道，梅娘娘已迁置上阳楼东了！（老）哦，有这等事！（贴）永新姐姐，这几日万岁爷专爱杨娘娘，不时来往西宫，连内侍也不教随驾了。我与你须要小心伺候。（生行上）

**【前腔】【换头】**欣可[11]，后宫新得娇娃，一日几摩挲！（生作进，老、贴见介）万岁爷驾到。娘娘刚才睡哩。（生）不要惊他。（作揭帐介）试把绡帐慢开，龙脑微闻[12]，一片美人香和[13]。（瞧科）爱他红玉一团，压着鸳衾侧卧。（老、贴背介）这温存，怎不占了风流高座！

**【前腔】【换头】**（旦作惊醒，低介）谁个？蓦然揭起鸳帏，星眼倦还挼。（作坐起，摩眼、撩鬓介）（生）早则浅淡粉容[14]，消褪唇朱，掠削鬓儿欹斜[15]。（老、贴作扶旦起，旦作开眼复闭，立起又坐倒介）（生）怜他，侍儿扶起腰肢，娇怯怯难存难坐[16]。（老、贴扶旦坐介）（生扶住介）恁朦腾，且索消详停和[17]。

（旦）万岁！（生）春昼晴和，正好及时游赏，为何当午睡眠？（旦低介）夜来承宠，雨露恩浓，不觉花枝力弱。强起梳头，却又朦胧睡去。因此失迎圣驾。（生笑介）这等说，倒是寡人唐突了。（旦娇羞不语介）（生）妃子，看你神思困倦，且同到前殿去，消遣片时。（旦）领旨。（生、旦同行，老、贴随行介）（生）"落日留王母，（旦）微风倚少儿。（老、贴合）宫中行乐秘，少有外人知[18]。"（生、旦转坐介）（丑上）"昼漏稀闻高阁报，天颜有喜近臣知。"启万岁爷：国舅杨丞相，遵旨试验安禄山，在宫门外回奏。（生）宣奏来。（丑宣介）杨丞相有宣。（副净上）"天下表章经院过，宫中笑语隔墙闻。"（拜见介）臣杨国忠见驾。愿吾皇万岁，娘娘千岁！（丑）平身。（副）臣启陛下：蒙委试验安禄山，果系人才壮健，弓马熟娴，特此复旨。（生）朕昨见张守珪奏称：禄山通晓六番言语，精熟诸般武艺，可当边将之任。今失机当斩，是以委卿验之。既然所奏不诬，卿可传旨禄山，赦其前罪。明日早朝引见，授职在京，以观后效。（副）领旨。（下）（丑）启万岁爷：沉香亭牡丹盛开，请万岁爷同娘娘赏玩。（生）今日对妃子，赏名花。高力士，可宣翰林李白，到沉香亭上，立草新词供奉。（丑）领旨。（下）（生）妃子，和你赏花去来。

（生）倚槛繁花带露开，罗　虬

（旦）相将游戏绕池台。孟浩然

（生）新歌一曲令人艳，万　楚

（合）只待相如奉诏来。李商隐

## 注 释

[1]羞被粉脂浼：嫌脂粉沾污了天然的肤色。浼（wò），沾污。

[2]宝篆沉烟袅：点起珍贵的沉水香，上升起袅袅的烟缕。篆，形容烟缕在空中蜿蜒飘扬好像篆字。

[3]宿醒：宿醉。

[4]怙（hù）恃：指父母。

[5]绮疏：纱窗。

[6]睃（suō）：斜视。

[7]延俄：即俄延，待会儿。

[8]步摇：插在鬓后的一种首饰，人行走时它会摇动。

[9]半弯凌波：指纤小的脚；凌波，形容行走时好像仙女洛神在水波上行走一样。

[10]梅娘娘：梅妃江采苹。

[11]欣可：表示满意。

[12]龙脑：即冰片，一种香料。

[13]美人香和：形容贵妃一身清香。

[14]早则：早是、原来是。

[15]掠削：梳理。

[16]难存难坐：行动不得。

[17]恁朦腾，且索消详停和：这样睡昏昏的，还得休息一会儿。消详停和，消停，休息。

[18]"落日留王母，微风倚少儿。宫中行乐秘，少有外人知"：杜甫五律《宿昔》的后四句。王母，指杨贵妃；少儿，即卫少儿，汉武帝皇后卫子夫的姐姐；"微风倚少儿"，指杨氏姊妹因贵妃而得宠。

## 第五出 禊 游

【双调 引子】【贺圣朝】（丑上）崇班内殿称尊，天颜亲奉朝昏。金貂玉带蟒袍新，出入荷殊恩。

咱家高力士是也，官拜骠骑将军[1]。职掌六宫之中，权压百僚之上。迎机导窾[2]，摸揣圣情；曲意小心，荷承天宠。今乃三月三日，万岁爷与贵妃娘娘游幸曲江[3]，命咱召杨丞相并秦、韩、虢三国夫人，一同随驾。不免前去传旨与他。"传声报戚里，今日幸长杨[4]。"（下）

【前腔】（净冠带引从上）一从请托权门，天家雨露重新。累臣今喜作亲臣[5]，壮怀会当伸。

俺安禄山，自蒙圣恩复官之后，十分宠眷。所喜俺生的一个大肚皮，直垂过膝。一日圣上见了，笑问此中何有？俺就对说，惟有一片赤心。天颜大喜，自此愈加亲信，许俺不日封王。岂不是非常之遇！左右，回避。（从应下）（净）今乃三月三日，皇上与贵妃游幸曲江。三国夫人随驾。倾城士女，无不往观。俺不免换了便服，单骑前往，游玩一番。（作更衣、上马行介）出得门来，你看香尘满路，车马如云，好不热闹也。正是："当路游丝萦醉客，隔花啼鸟唤行人。"（下）

（副净、外扮王孙，末扮公子；各丽服，同行上）（合）

【仙吕入双调】【夜行船序】春色撩人，爱花风如扇，柳烟成阵。行过处，辨不出紫陌红尘[6]。（见介）请了。（副净、外）今日修禊之辰[7]，我每同往曲江游玩。（末、小生）便是，那边簇拥着一队车儿，敢是三国夫人来了。我每快些前去。（行介）纷纭，绣幕雕轩，珠绕翠围，争妍夺俊。氤氲，兰麝逐风来，衣彩佩光遥认。（同下）

> （老旦绣衣扮韩国，贴白衣扮虢国，杂绯衣扮秦国，引院子、梅香各乘车行上[8]）（合）

【前腔】【换头】安顿，罗绮如云，斗妖娆，各逞黛娥蝉鬓。蒙天宠，特敕共探江春。（老旦）奴家韩国夫人，（贴）奴家虢国夫人，（杂）奴家秦国夫人，（合）奉旨召游曲江。院子把车儿趱行前去。（院）晓得。（行介）（合）朱轮，碾破芳堤，遗珥坠簪，落花相衬。荣分，戚里从宸游[9]，几队宫妆前进。（同下）

【黑蟆序】【换头】（净策马上，目视三国下介）妙啊，回瞬，绝代丰神，猛令咱一见，半晌销魂。恨车中马上，杳难亲近。俺安禄山，前往曲江，恰好遇着三国夫人，一个个天姿国色。唉，唐天子，唐天子！你有了一位贵妃，又添上这几个阿姨，好不风流也！评论，群花归一人，方知天子尊。且赶上前去，饱看一回。望前尘，馋眼迷奚，不免挥策频频。

> （作鞭马前奔，杂扮从人上，拦介）咄，丞相爷在此，什么人这等乱撞！（副净骑马上）为何喧嚷？（净、副净作打照面，净回马急下）（从）小的方才见一人，骑马乱撞过来，向前拦阻。（副净笑介）那去的是安禄山。怎么见了下官，就疾忙躲避了。（作沉吟介）三位夫人的车儿在那里？（从）就在前面。（副净）呀，安禄山那厮怎敢这般无礼！

【前腔】【换头】堪恨，藐视皇亲，傍香车行处，无礼厮混。

陡冲冲怒起，心下难忍。叫左右，紧紧跟随着车儿行走，把闲人
打开。（众应行介）（副净）忙奔，把金鞭辟路尘[10]，将雕鞍逐
画轮。（合）语行人，慎莫来前，怕惹丞相生嗔。（同下）

【锦衣香】（净扮村妇，丑扮丑女，老旦扮卖花娘子，小生扮舍
人，行上[11]）（合）妆扮新，添淹润[12]；身段村[13]，乔丰韵[14]。
更堪怜芳草沾裾，野花堆鬓。（见介）（净）列位都是去游曲江
的么？（众）正是。今日皇帝、娘娘，都在那里，我每同去看一
看。（丑）听得皇帝把娘娘爱的似宝贝一般，不知比奴家容貌
如何？（老旦笑介）（小生作看丑介）（丑）你怎么只管看我？
（小生）我看大姐的脸上，倒有几件宝贝。（净）什么宝贝？
（小生）你看眼嵌猫睛石，额雕玛瑙纹，蜜蜡装牙齿，珊瑚镶
嘴唇。（净笑介）（丑将扇打小生介）小油嘴，偏你没有宝贝。
（小生）你说来。（丑）你后庭像银矿，掘过几多人！（净笑
介）休得取笑。闻得三国夫人的车儿过去，一路上有东西遗下，
我每赶上寻看。（丑）如此快走。（行介）（丑作娇态与小生
诨介）（合）和风徐起荡晴云，钿车一过，草木皆春。（小生）
且在这草里寻一寻，可有什么？（老旦）我先去了。向朱门绣
阁，卖花声叫的殷勤。（叫卖花下）（众作寻、各拾介）（丑问
净介）你拾的什么？（净）是一枝簪子。（丑看介）是金的，上
面一粒绯红的宝石。好造化！（净问丑介）你呢？（丑）一只凤
鞋套儿。（净）好好，你就穿了何如？（丑作伸脚比介）啐，一
个脚指头也着不下。鞋尖上这粒真珠，摘下来罢。（作摘珠、丢
鞋介）（小生）待我袖了去[15]。（丑）你倒会作揽收拾！你拾的
东西，也拿出来瞧瞧。（小生）一幅鲛绡帕儿，裹着个金盒子。
（净接作开看介）咦，黑黑的黄黄的薄片儿，闻着又有些香，莫
不是耍药么[16]？（小生笑介）是香茶。（丑）待我尝一尝。（净

争吃，各吐介）呸，稀苦的，吃他怎么！（小生作收介）罢了，大家再往前去。（行介）（合）蜂蝶闲相趁，柳迎花引，望龙楼倒泻，曲江将近。

（小生、净先下，丑吊场[17]，叫介）你们等我一等。阿呀，尿急了，且在这里打个沙窝儿去[18]。（下）（老旦、贴、杂引院子、梅香行上）

【浆水令】扑衣香花香乱熏，杂莺声笑声细闻。看杨花雪落覆白蘋，双双青鸟，衔堕红巾。春光好，过二分[19]，迟迟丽日催车进。（院）禀夫人，到曲江了。（老旦）丞相爷在那里？（院）万岁爷在望春宫，丞相爷先到那边去了。（老旦、杂、贴作下车介）你看果然好风景也！环曲岸，环曲岸，红酣绿匀。临曲水，临曲水，柳细蒲新。

（丑引小内侍、控马上）"敕传玉勒桃花马，骑坐金泥蛱蝶裙[20]。"（见介）皇上口敕：韩、秦二国夫人，赐宴别殿。虢国夫人，即令乘马入宫，陪杨娘娘饮宴。

（老旦、杂、贴跪介）万岁！（起介）（丑向贴介）就请夫人上马。（贴）

【尾声】内家官[21]，催何紧。姐姐妹妹，偏背了春风独近[22]。（老旦、杂）不枉你淡扫蛾眉朝至尊。

（贴乘马，丑引下）（杂）你看裴家姐姐，竟自扬鞭去了。（老旦）且自由他。（梅香）请夫人别殿里上宴。

　　　　红桃碧柳禊堂春，沈佺期

（老旦）一种佳游事也均。张　谔

（杂）　愿奉圣情欢不极，武平一

（合）　向风偏笑艳阳人。杜　牧

注 释 ————————————————————————————

[1]高力士：宦官，原为左监门大将军知内侍省事，天宝七载加骠骑大将
　　军，从一品，是唐明皇的宠臣。

[2]导窾（kuǎn）：窾，骨节中空处，杀牛时刀可以比较方便地从这里过
　　去。导窾，在这里作看人眼色、见机行事讲。

[3]曲江：曲江池，在长安东南，唐时皇家园林所在地。

[4]长杨：秦、汉宫殿名，代指皇家宫苑。"今日幸长杨"，指游曲江
　　池。

[5]累臣：被囚的臣子，指他曾解京问罪。

[6]辨不出紫陌红尘：形容夹道花、柳很盛。紫陌，都城的道路；红
　　尘，指闹市。

[7]修禊：古代三月上巳在水边袚除邪祟的一种祭礼。上巳，阴历三月上
　　旬的巳日，魏以后，以三月三日为上巳。

[8]院子、梅香：院子指仆人，梅香指丫环。

[9]宸：皇帝的住处，这里指皇帝。

[10]辟（pì）路尘：开路。辟，叫行人走开。

[11]舍人：公子、少爷。

[12]淹润：丰韵。

[13]村：土气。

[14]乔丰韵：怪模样。

[15]袖：这里作动词用，把东西放在袖子里。

[16]耍药：疑指春药。

[17]吊场：其他角色先下场，留下一、二人独唱下场诗或打诨，称为吊
　　场。后面转到另一场戏了。

[18]打个沙窝儿：俗语，指女性就地小便。

[19]过二分：美好的风光过了三分之二，指春光灿烂的时候。

[20]金泥：金屑做成的颜料。

[21]内家官：宫内官，这里指传旨的小内侍。

[22]偏背了：意即独自去了。

# 第一出 傍 讶

【中吕 过曲】【缕缕金】（丑上）欢游罢，驾归来。西宫因个甚，恼君怀？敢为春筵畔，风流尴尬。怎一场乐事陡成乖[1]？教人好疑怪，教人好疑怪。

前日万岁爷同杨娘娘游幸曲江，欢天喜地。不想昨日娘娘忽然先自回宫，万岁爷今日才回，圣情十分不悦。未知何故？远远望见永新姐来了，咱试问他。（老旦上）

【前腔】宫帏事[2]，费安排。云翻和雨覆，蓦地闹阳台。（丑见介）永新姐，来得恰好。我问你，万岁爷为何不到杨娘娘宫中去？（老）唉，公公，你还不知么！两下参商后[3]，装幺作态。（丑）为着甚来？（老）只为并头莲傍有一枝开。（丑）是那一枝呢？（老笑介）公公，你聪明人自参解，聪明人自参解。

（丑笑介）咱那里得知！永新姐，你可说与我听。

（老）若说此事，原是我娘娘自己惹下的。（丑）为何？（老）只为娘娘把那虢国夫人呵，

【剔银灯】常则向君前喝采，妆梳淡天然无赛。那日在望春宫，教万岁召他侍宴。三杯之后，便暗中筑座连环寨[4]，哄结上同心罗带。（丑拍手笑介）阿呀，咱也疑心有此。却为何烦恼哩？（老）后来娘娘恐怕夺了恩宠，因此上嫌猜。恩情顿乖，热打对鸳鸯散开。

（丑）原来虢国夫人，在望春宫有了言语，才回去的。

（老）便是。那虢国夫人去时，我娘娘不曾留得。万岁

爷好生不快[5]，今日竟不进西宫去了。娘娘在那里只是
哭哩。（丑）咱想杨娘娘呵，

【前腔】娇痴性天生忒利害。前时逼得个梅娘娘，直迁置楼东
无奈。如今这虢国夫人，是自家的妹子，须知道连枝同气情非
外，怎这点儿也难分爱。（老）这且休提。只是往常，万岁爷与
娘娘行坐不离，如今两下不相见面，怎生是好？（丑）吾侪，如
何布摆，且和你从旁看来。

  （内）有旨宣高公公。（丑）来了。

    狎宴临春日正迟[6]， 韩 偓
（老旦）宠深还恐宠先衰。  罗 虬
（丑）  外头笑语中猜忌，  陆龟蒙
（老旦）若问傍人那得知！  崔 颢

---

注 释

[1]陡成乖：突然闹别扭。

[2]宫帏事：指皇帝和后妃之间的事。宫帏，即宫闱，后妃所居的地
  方。

[3]两下参商：两人意见不合，闹别扭。

[4]筑座连环寨：军队分兵屯扎，以便互相呼应。这里比喻两相勾结。

[5]好生：非常。

[6]临春：南朝陈后主的宫殿名。

# 第二出 幸 恩

【商调 引子】【绕池游】（贴上）瑶池陪从[1]，何意承新宠？怪青鸾把人和哄[2]。寻思万种。这其间无端嗾动[3]，奈谣诼蛾眉未容[4]。

"玉燕轻盈弄雪辉，杏梁偷宿影双依。赵家姊妹多相妒[5]，莫向昭阳殿里飞。"奴家杨氏，幼适裴门。琴断朱弦[6]，不幸文君早寡[7]；香含青琐，肯容韩掾轻偷[8]？以妹玉环之宠，叨膺虢国之封。虽居富贵，不爱铅华[9]。敢夸绝世佳人，自许朝天素面[10]。不想前日驾幸曲江，敕陪游赏。诸姊妹俱赐宴于外，独召奴家，到望春宫侍宴。遂蒙天眷，勉尔承恩。圣意虽浓，人言可畏。昨日要奴同进大内[11]，再四辞归。仔细想来，好侥幸人也。

【商调 过曲】【字字锦】恩从天上浓，缘向生前种。金笼花下开，巧赚娟娟凤[12]。烛花红，只见弄盏传杯。传杯处，蓦自里话儿唧哝。匆匆，不容宛转[13]，把人央入帐中。思量帐中，帐中欢如梦。绸缪处两心同。绸缪处两心暗同。奈朝来背地，有人在那里，人在那里，装模作样，言言语语，讥讥讽讽，咱这里羞羞涩涩，惊惊恐恐，直恁被他抟弄。

【不是路】（末扮院子、副净扮梅香暗上）（老旦引外扮院子、丑扮梅香上）吹透春风，戚畹花开别样秾[14]。前日裴家妹子独承恩幸。我约柳家妹子，同去打觑一番[15]。不料他气的病了，因此独自前去。（外）禀夫人到虢府了。（老旦）通报去。（外报介）（末传介）韩国夫人到。（贴）道有请。（副净请介）

（外、末暗下）（贴出，迎老旦进介）（贴）**姊姊请。**（副净、丑诨下）<sup>[16]</sup>（老旦）**妹妹喜也。**（贴）**有何喜来？**（老旦）邀殊宠，一枝已傍日边红<sup>[17]</sup>。（贴作羞介）**姊姊，说那里话！我进离宫，也不过杯酒相陪奉，湛露君恩内外同。**（老旦笑介）虽则一般赐宴，外边怎及里边。休调哄，九重春色偏知重<sup>[18]</sup>，有谁能共？（贴）**有何难共？**

（老旦）我且问你，看见玉环妹妹，在宫光景如何？

**【满园春】**（贴）春江上景融融。催侍宴望春宫。那玉环妹妹呵，新来倚贵添尊重。（老旦）不知皇上与他怎生恩爱？（贴）春宵里，春宵里，比目儿和同。谁知得雨云踪<sup>[19]</sup>？（老旦）难道一些不觉？（贴）只见玉环妹妹的性儿，越发骄纵了些。细窥他个中<sup>[20]</sup>，漫参他意中，使惯娇憨。惯使娇憨，寻瘢索绽<sup>[21]</sup>，一谜儿自逞心胸<sup>[22]</sup>。

（老旦）他自小性儿是这般的，妹妹，你还该劝他才是。（贴）那个耐烦劝他？

**【前腔】【换头】**（老旦）他情性多骄纵，恃天生百样玲珑，姊妹行且休傍作诵<sup>[23]</sup>。况他近日呵，昭阳内，昭阳内，一人独占三千宠<sup>[24]</sup>，问阿谁能与竞雌雄？（贴）**谁与他争！只是他如此性儿，恐怕君心不测！**（老旦起，背介）细听裴家妹子之言，必有缘故。细窥他个中，漫参他意中，使恁骄嗔。恁使骄嗔，藏头露尾，敢别有一段心胸<sup>[25]</sup>！

（末上）"意外闻严旨，堂前报贵人。"（见介）禀夫人，不好了。贵妃娘娘忤旨，圣上大怒，命高公公送归丞相府中了。（老旦惊介）有这等事！（贴）我说这般心性，定然惹下事来。（老旦）虽然如此，我与你姊妹之情，且是关系大家荣辱，须索前去看他才是<sup>[26]</sup>！（贴）正是，就请同行。（老旦）

【尾声】忽闻严谴心惊恐，（贴）整香车同探吉凶。姊姊，那玉环妹妹，可不被梅妃笑杀也！（合）倒不如冷淡梅花仍开紫禁中！

（贴）　传闻阙下降丝纶[27]，　刘长卿

（老旦）出得朱门入戟门[28]。　贾　岛

（贴）　何必君恩能独久，　　乔知之

（老旦）可怜荣落在朝昏。　　李商隐

## 注 释

[1]瑶池：相传是西王母所住的地方。瑶池陪从，指曲江池侍宴。

[2]青鸾：即青鸟。传说西王母来看汉武帝，有青鸟先飞来报信。

[3]噷（xīn）动：一作"歆动"，动情。

[4]奈谣诼蛾眉未容：无奈有人造谣说坏话，使我不能容身。蛾眉，代指美女，这里是虢国夫人自称。

[5]赵家姊妹多相妒：汉代赵飞燕、赵昭仪姊妹都受汉成帝宠幸，两人相互妒忌。这里借指杨贵妃和虢国夫人自己。

[6]琴断朱弦：比喻丧偶。

[7]文君早寡：卓文君遇到司马相如之前，寡居在家。虢国夫人借此说明自己寡居。

[8]香含青琐，肯容韩掾轻偷：这句说自己行为规矩，不会轻易与人偷情。

[9]不爱铅华：不爱打扮。铅华，古代女子用的化妆粉。

[10]朝天素面：虢国夫人以美貌自许，不加修饰就去朝见天子。

[11]大内：皇宫。

[12]金笼花下开，巧赚娟娟凤：在花下打开金笼，巧妙地把美丽的凤鸟骗了进去。

[13]宛转：这里作迟疑讲。

[14]戚畹花开别样秾：花，指虢国夫人。秾（nóng），花木盛，喻女子美艳。

[15]打觑：探看。

[16]副净、丑诨下：两家婢女打诨着下场。

[17]一枝已傍日边红：你这朵花已经开到皇帝身边了。日，喻皇帝。

[18]九重春色偏知重：在许多美女中，皇帝只看重你。九重，本指天子住处，这里指天子。

[19]谁知得雨云踪：谁知道他们怎样欢爱？

[20]个中：就里，其中底细。

[21]寻瘢索绽：挑剔人，找不是。

[22]一谜儿自逞心胸：一味任性。

[23]姊妹行且休傍作诵：我们姊妹且不要在一边说她。

[24]一人独占三千宠：皇帝对后宫三千美人的宠爱集中在她一个人身上。

[25]敢别有一段心胸：怕是她别有用心吧。

[26]须索：须要。

[27]丝纶：圣旨。

[28]朱门、戟门：都指显贵之家。这里是说杨贵妃出了宫门，又进了丞相府门。

# 第三出　献　发

（副净急上）"天有不测风云，人有旦夕祸福。"下官杨国忠，自从妹子册立贵妃，权势日盛。不想今早忽传贵妃忤旨，被谪出宫，命高内监单车送到门来。未知何故，好生惊骇！且到门前迎接去。（暂下）

【仙吕　过曲】【望吾乡】（丑引旦乘车上）无定君心，恩光那处寻？蛾眉忽地遭撅窖[1]，思量就里知他怎？弃掷何偏甚！长门隔，永巷深[2]。回首处愁难禁。

　　（副净上，跪接介）臣杨国忠迎接娘娘。（丑）丞相，快请娘娘进府，咱家还有话说。（副）院子，分付丫鬟每，迎接娘娘到后堂去。（丫鬟上，扶旦下车，拥下）（副净揖丑介）老公公请坐，不知此事因何而起？

　　（丑）娘娘呵，

【一封书】君王宠最深，冠椒房专侍寝。昨日呵，无端忤圣心，骤然间商与参。丞相不要怪咱家多口，娘娘呵，生性娇痴多习惯，未免嫌疑生抱衾[3]。（副净）如今谪遣出来，怎生是好？（丑）丞相且到朝门谢罪，相机而行。（副净）老公公，全仗你进规箴，悟当今[4]。（丑）这个自然。（合）管重取宫花入上林[5]。

　　（丑）就此告别。（副净）下官同行。（向内介）分付丫鬟，好生伺候娘娘。（内应介）（副净）"乌鸦与喜鹊同行，吉凶事全然未保。"（同丑下）

【中吕 引子】【行香子】（旦引梅香上）乍出宫门，未定惊魂，渍愁妆满面啼痕。其间心事，多少难论。但惜芳容，怜薄命，忆深恩。

"君恩如水付东流，得宠忧移失宠愁。莫向樽前奏《花落》[6]，凉风只在殿西头。"我杨玉环，自入宫闱，过蒙宠眷。只道君心可托，百岁为欢。谁想妾命不犹[7]，一朝逢怒。遂致促驾宫车，放归私第。金门一出，如隔九天[8]。（泪介）天那，禁中明月，永无照影之期；苑外飞花，已绝上枝之望。抚躬自悼，掩袂徒嗟。好生伤感人也！

【中吕 过曲】【榴花泣】【石榴花】罗衣拂拭犹是御香熏，向何处谢前恩？想春游春从晓和昏，【泣颜回】岂知有断雨残云。我含娇带嗔，往常间他百样相依顺，不提防为着横枝[19]，陡然把连理轻分。

丫鬟，此间可有那里望见宫中？（梅）前面御书楼上，西北望去，便是宫墙了。（旦）你随我楼上去来。（梅）晓得。（旦登楼介）"西宫渺不见，肠断一登楼。"（梅指介）娘娘，这一带黄设设的琉璃瓦，不是九重宫殿么？（旦作泪介）

【前腔】凭高洒泪遥望九重阊，咫尺里隔红云。叹昨宵还是凤帏人，冀回心重与温存。天乎太忍，未白头先使君恩尽。（梅指介）呀，远远望见一个公公，骑马而来，敢是召娘娘哩！（旦叹介）料非他丹凤衔书[10]，多又恐乌鸦传信。

（旦下楼介）（丑上）"暗将怀旧意，报与失欢人。"（见介）高力士叩见娘娘。（旦）高力士，你来怎么？（丑）奴婢恰才复旨，万岁爷细问娘娘回府光景，似有悔心。现今独坐宫中，长吁短叹，一定是思想娘娘。因此特来报知。（旦）唉，那里还想着我！（丑）奴婢愚不谏贤，娘娘未可太执意了。倘有什么东西，付与奴婢，乘间进上，或者感动圣心，也未可知。（旦）高力士，你教我进什么东西去好？（想介）

【喜渔灯犯】【喜渔灯】思将何物传情悃，可感动君？我想一身之外，皆君所赐，算只有愁泪千行，作珍珠乱滚；又难穿成金缕，把雕盘进。哦，有了，【剔银灯】这一缕青丝香润，曾共君枕上并头相偎衬，曾对君镜里撩云。丫鬟，取镜台金剪过来。（梅应取上介）（旦解发介）哎，头发，头发！【渔家傲】可惜你伴我芳年，**剪去**心儿未忍。只为欲表我衷肠，（作剪发介）剪去心儿自悯。（作执发起，哭介）头发，头发！【喜渔灯】全仗你寄我殷勤[11]。（拜介）我那圣上呵，奴身，止鬖鬖发数根，这便是我的残丝断魂。

（起介）高力士，你将去与我转奏圣上。（哭介）说妾罪该万死，此生此世，不能再睹天颜！谨献此发，以表依恋。（丑跪接发搭肩上介）娘娘请免愁烦，奴婢就此去了。"好凭缕缕青丝发，重结双双白首缘。"（下）

（旦坐哭介）（老旦、贴上）

【榴花灯犯】【剔银灯】听说是贵妃妹忤君，【石榴花】听说是返家门，【普天乐】听说是失势兄忧悯，听说是中官至[12]，未审何云？（进介）贵妃娘娘那里？（梅）韩、虢二国夫人到了。（旦作哭不语介）（老旦、贴见介）（老旦）贵妃请免愁烦。（同哭介）（贴）前日在望春宫，皇上十分欢喜，为何忽有此变？【渔家傲】我只道万岁千秋欢无尽，【尾犯序】我只道任伊行笑鼚[13]，【石榴花】我只道纵差池[14]，谁和你评论！（老旦）裴家妹子，【锦缠道】休只管闲言絮陈。贵妃，你逢

薄怒其中有甚根因？（旦作不理介）（贴）贵妃，你莫怪我说，

【剔银灯】自来宠多生嫌衅，可知道秋叶君恩？恁为人，怎趋承至尊？（老旦合）【雁过声】妹妹每情切来相问，为什么耳畔啾啾，总似不闻！（旦）

【尾声】秋风团扇原吾分，多谢连枝特过存[15]。总有万语千言只在心上忖。

  （竟下）（贴）姊姊，你看这个样子，如何使得？（老旦）正是，我每特来看他，他心上有事，竟自进房去了。妹子，你再到望春宫时，休要学他。（贴羞介）啐！

    今朝忽见下天门，　张　籍
  （老旦）相对那能不怆神。廖匡图
  （贴） 冷眼静看真好笑，徐　夤
  （老旦）中含芒刺欲伤人。陆龟蒙

---

注　释

[1]撅窨（diān yìn）：挫折，指被遣送回家。

[2]长门隔，永巷深：长门宫，失宠的后妃所居的地方；永巷，禁闭有罪的宫女之处。

[3]嫌疑生抱衾：因抱衾而生嫌疑。

[4]当今：指称当下在位的皇帝。

[5]上林：上林苑，御花园。这里以宫花喻贵妃。

[6]《花落》：即《梅花落》，乐曲名。

[7]不犹：不同平常，变坏。

[8]九天：九重天，喻相隔之远。

[9]横枝：枝杈，喻虢国夫人。

[10]丹凤衔书：指赦免的圣旨。

[11]全仗你寄我殷勤：全要靠你把我的殷勤之意寄去。

[12]中官：太监。

[13]伊行：她。行，用在人称之后。

[14]纵差池：纵然有了过失。差池，即参差、不齐，这里义为过失。

[15]多谢连枝特过存：多谢姐姐们特地来慰问我。

# 第四出 复 召

【南吕 引子】【虞美人】（生上）无端惹起闲烦恼，有话将谁告？此情已自费支持，怪杀鹦哥不住向人提。

"辇路生春草，上林花满枝。凭高何限意，无复侍臣知。"寡人昨因杨妃娇妒，心中不忿[1]，一时失计，将他遣出。谁想佳人难得，自他去后，触目总是生憎，对景无非惹恨。那杨国忠入朝谢罪，寡人也无颜见他。（叹介）咳，欲待召取回宫，却又难于出口，若是不召他来，教朕怎生消遣，好刬划不下也[2]！

【南吕 过曲】【十样锦】【绣带儿】春风静宫帘半启，难消日影迟迟。听好鸟犹作欢声[3]，睹新花似斗容辉。追悔，【宜春令】悔杀咱一划儿粗疏[4]，不解他十分的娇殢[5]。枉负了怜香惜玉，那些情致。（副净扮内监甲上）"脍下玉盘红缕细[6]，酒开金瓮绿醅浓。"（跪见介）请万岁爷上膳。（生不应介）（副净又请介）（生恼介）咦，谁着你请来！（副净）万岁爷自清晨不曾进膳，后宫传催排膳伺候。（生）咦，什么后宫！叫内侍。（二内侍应上）（生）搇这厮去，打一百，发入净军所去[7]。（内侍）领旨。（同搇副净下）（生）哎，朕在此想念妃子，却被这厮来搅乱一番。好烦恼也！【降黄龙换头】思伊，纵有天上琼浆，海外珍馐，知他甚般滋味！除非可意[8]，立向跟前，方慰调饥[9]。（净扮内监乙上）"尊前绮席陈歌舞[10]，花外红楼列管弦。"（见跪介）请万岁爷沉香亭上饮宴，听赏梨园新乐。（生）咦，说甚沉香亭，好打！（净叩头介）非

223

干奴婢之事，是太子诸王，说万岁爷心绪不快，特请消遣。（生）嗐，我心绪有何不快！叫内侍。（内侍应上）（生）揣这厮去，打一百，发入惜薪司当火者去[11]。（内侍）领旨。（同揣净下）（生）内侍过来。（内侍应上）（生）着你二人看守宫门，不许一人擅入，违者重打。（内侍）领旨。（作立前场介）（生）唉，朕此时有甚心情，还去听歌饮酒。【醉太平】想亭际，凭阑仍是玉阑干，问新妆有谁同倚？就有新声呵，知音人逝，他鹍弦绝响[12]，我玉笛羞吹。（丑肩搭发上）【浣溪纱】离别悲，相思意，两下里抹媚谁知[13]！我从旁参透个中机，要打合鸾凤在一处飞。（见内侍介）万岁爷在那里？（内侍）独自坐在宫中。（丑欲入，内侍拦介）（丑）你怎么拦阻咱家？（内侍）万岁爷十分着恼，把进膳的连打了两个，特着我每看守宫门，不许一人擅入。（丑）原来如此，咱家且候着。（生）朕委无聊赖，且到宫门外闲步片时。（行介）看一带瑶阶依然芳草齐，不见蹴裙裾珠履追随。（丑望介）万岁爷出来了，咱且闪在门外[14]，觑个机会。（虚下，即上，听介）（生）寡人在此思念妃子，不知妃子又怎生思念寡人哩！早间问高力士，他说妃子出去，泪眼不干，教朕寸心如割。这半日间，无从再知消息。高力士这厮，也竟不到朕跟前，好生可恶！（丑见介）奴婢在这里。（生）（作看丑介）（生）高力士，你肩上搭的什么东西？（丑）是杨娘娘的头发。（生笑介）什么头发？（丑）娘娘说道：自恨愚昧，上忤圣心，罪应万死。今生今世，不能够再睹天颜，特剪下这头发，着奴婢献上万岁爷，以表依恋之意。（献发介）（生执发看，哭介）哎哟，我那妃子呵！【啄木儿】记前宵枕边闻香气，到今朝剪却和愁寄。觑青丝肠断魂迷。想寡人与妃子，恩情中断，就似这头发也。一霎里落金刀长辞云鬓。（丑）万岁爷！【鲍老催】请休惨凄，奴婢想杨娘娘既蒙恩幸，万岁爷何惜宫中片席之地，乃使沦落外边！春风肯教天上回，名花便从苑外移[15]。（生作想介）只是寡人已经放出，怎好召还？（丑）有罪放出，悔过召还，正是圣主如天之度。（生点头介）（丑）况今早单车送出，才是黎明，此时天色已暮，开了安庆坊，从太华宅而入，外人谁得知之。（叩头介）乞鉴原，赐迎归，无淹滞[16]。稳情取一笑愁城自解围[17]。（生）高力士，就着你迎取贵妃回宫便了。（丑）领旨。（下）（生）咳，妃子来时，教寡人怎生相见也！【下小楼】喜得玉人归矣，又愁他惯娇嗔，背面啼，那时将何言语饰前非！罢，罢，这原是寡人不是，拚把百般亲媚[18]，酬他半日分离。（丑同内侍、宫女纱灯引旦上）【双声子】香车曳，香车曳，穿过了宫槐翠。纱笼对，纱笼对，掩映着宫花丽。（内侍、宫女下）（丑进报介）杨娘娘到了。（生）快宣进来。（丑）领旨。杨娘娘有宣。（旦进见介）臣妾杨氏见驾，死罪，死罪！（俯伏介）（生）平身。（丑暗下）（旦跪泣介）臣妾无状[19]，上干天谴。今得重睹圣颜，死亦瞑目。（生同泣介）妃子何出此言？（旦）【玉漏迟序】念臣妾如山罪累，荷皇恩如天容庇。今自艾[20]，愿承鱼贯敢妒蛾眉[21]？

　　（生扶旦起介）寡人一时错见，从前的话，不必再提了。（旦泣起介）万岁！（生携旦手与旦拭泪介）

【尾声】从今识破愁滋味，这恩情更添十倍。妃子，我且把这一日相思诉与伊[22]！

　　（宫娥上）西宫宴备，请万岁爷、娘娘上宴。

　　（生）陶出真情酒满尊，　李　中

　　（旦）此心从此更何言。　罗　隐

　　（生）别离不惯无穷忆，　苏　颋

　　（旦）重入椒房拭泪痕。　柳公权

## 注 释

[1]不忿：不满。

[2]刬（bǎi）划：即摆划，这里作决断解。

[3]欢：鸟鸣声，双关所欢，即情人。

[4]一刬（chàn）儿：一味。

[5]娇殢（dì）：撒娇。殢，纠缠。

[6]红缕：指脍，细切的肉。

[7]净军所：监禁太监的地方。

[8]可意：中意，引申为心上人。

[9]调（chōu）饥：朝饥，早上没吃东西时的饥饿状态，意义双关。

[10]尊前：即樽前，筵前。

[11]惜薪司：明朝设置的一个太监服役机关，专管供应柴炭之类事情。

[12]鸲弦：鸲鸡筋做的琵琶弦，这里指代琵琶。

[13]抹媚：形容害相思的痴迷状态。

[14]闪：躲。

[15]春风肯教天上回，名花便从苑外移：意谓只要皇帝回心转意，贵妃
　　就可以从宫外回来。

[16]淹滞：停留。

[17]稳情取一笑愁城自解围：包管她一笑就使您消愁。

[18]拚：甘愿。

[19]无状：即无善状，一无是处。

[20]自艾：自怨。

[21]愿承鱼贯：愿意依次而进，不再嫉妒。

[22]伊：这里作"你"解。

# 第五出　疑　谶[1]

（外扮郭子仪将巾、佩剑上）"壮怀磊落有谁知，一剑防身且自随。整顿乾坤济时了，那回方表是男儿。"自家姓郭名子仪，本贯华州郑县人氏。学成韬略，腹满经纶。要思量做一个顶天立地的男儿，干一桩定国安邦的事业。今以武举出身，到京谒选[2]。正值杨国忠窃弄威权，安禄山滥膺宠眷。把一个朝纲，看看弄得不成模样了。似俺郭子仪，未得一官半职，不知何时，才得替朝廷出力也呵！

【商调】【集贤宾】论男儿壮怀须自吐，肯空向杞天呼[3]？笑他每似堂间处燕[4]，有谁曾屋上瞻乌[5]！不提防柙虎樊熊，任纵横社鼠城狐[6]。几回家听鸡鸣起身独夜舞[7]。想古来多少乘除[8]，显得个勋名垂宇宙，不争便姓字老樵渔！

且到长安市上，买醉一回。（行科）

【逍遥乐】向天街徐步，暂遣牢骚，聊宽逆旅。俺则见来往纷如，闹昏昏似醉汉难扶，那里有独醒行吟楚大夫[9]！俺郭子仪呵，待觅个同心伴侣，怅钓鱼人去，射虎人遥，屠狗人无[10]。

（下）（丑扮酒保上）"我家酒铺十分高，罚誓无赊挂酒标。只要有钱凭你饮，无钱滴水也难消。"小子是这长安市上，新丰馆大酒楼，一个小二哥的便是。俺这酒楼，在东、西两市中间，往来十分热闹。凡是京城内外，王孙公子，官员市户，军民百姓，没一个不到俺楼上来吃三杯。也有吃寡酒的，吃案酒的[11]，买酒去的，

包酒来的，打发个不了。道犹未了，又一个吃酒的来也。（外行上）

【上京马】遥望见绿杨斜靠画楼隅，滴溜溜一片青帘风外舞[12]，怎得个燕市酒人来共沽[13]！（唤科）酒家有么？（丑迎科）客官，请楼上坐。（外作上楼科）是好一座酒楼也。敞轩窗，日朗风疏。见四周遭粉壁上，都画着醉仙图。

（丑）客官自饮，还是待客？（外）独饮三杯，有好酒呵取来。（丑）有好酒。（取酒上科）酒在此。（内叫科）小二哥，这里来。（丑应忙下）（外饮酒科）

【梧叶儿】俺非是爱酒的闲陶令[14]，也不学使酒的莽灌夫[15]，一谜价痛饮兴豪粗。撑着这醒眼儿谁偢睬？问醉乡深可容得吾？听街市恁喧呼，偏冷落高阳酒徒[16]。

（作起看科）（老旦扮内监，副净、末、净扮官，各吉服，杂捧金币、牵羊担酒随行上，绕场下）（丑捧酒上）客官，热酒在此。（外）酒保，我问你咱[17]，这楼前那些官员，是往何处去来？（丑）客官，你一面吃酒，我一面告诉你波。只为国舅杨丞相，并韩国、虢国、秦国三位夫人，万岁爷各赐造新第。在这宣阳里中，四家府门相连[18]，俱照大内一般造法。这一家造来，要胜似那一家的；那一家造来，又要赛过这一家的。若见那家造得华丽，这家便拆毁了，重新再造。定要与那家一样，方才住手。一座厅堂，足费上千万贯钱钞。今日完工，因此合朝大小官员，都备了羊酒礼物，前往各家称贺，打从这里过去。（外惊科）哦，有这等事！（丑）待我再去看热酒来波。（下）（外叹科）呀，外戚宠盛，到这个地位[19]，如何是了也！

【醋葫芦】怪私家恁僭窃[20]，竞豪奢夸土木。一班儿公卿甘作折腰趋[21]，争向权门如市附[22]。再没有一个人呵，把舆情向九重分诉[23]。可知他朱甍碧瓦总是血膏涂！

（起科）心中一时忿懑，不觉酒涌上来，且向四壁闲看一回。（作看科）这壁厢细字数行，有人题的诗句。我试觑波。（作看念科）"燕市人皆去，函关马不归。若逢山下鬼，环上系罗衣。"呀，这诗是好奇怪也！

【幺篇】[24]我这里停睛一直看，从头儿逐句读。细端详诗意少祯符[25]。且看是什么人题的？（又看念科）李遐周题[26]。（作想科）李遐周，这名字好生识熟！哦，是了，我闻得有个术士李遐周，能知过去未来，必定就是他了。多则是就里难言藏谶语[27]，猜诗谜杜家何处[28]？早难道醉来墙上信笔乱鸦涂[29]！

（内作喧闹科）（外唤科）酒保那里？（丑上）客官，做什么？（外）楼下为何又这般喧闹？（丑）客官，你靠着这窗儿，往下看去就是。（外看科）（净王服、骑马，头踏职事前导引上[30]，绕场行下科）（外）那是何人？（丑笑指科）客官，你不见他那个大肚皮么？这人姓安名禄山。万岁爷十分宠爱他，把御座的金鸡步障都赐与他坐过，今日又封他做东平郡王。方才谢恩出朝，赐归东华门外新第，打从这里经过。（外惊怒科）呀，这、这就是安禄山么？有何功劳，遽封王爵？唉，我看这厮面有反相，乱天下者，必此人也！

【金菊香】见了这野心杂种牧羊的奴[31]，料蜂目豺声定是狡徒。怎把个野狼引来屋里居？怕不将题壁诗符？更和那私门贵戚一例逗妖狐。

（丑）客官，为甚事这般着恼来？（外）

【柳叶儿】哎，不由人冷飕飕冲冠发竖，热烘烘气夯胸脯[32]，咕嘟嘟把腰间宝剑频频觑。（丑）客官，请息怒，再与我消一壶

229

波。（外）呀，便教俺倾千盏，饮尽了百壶，怎把这重沉沉一个愁担儿消除！

  （作起身科）不吃酒了，收了这酒钱去者。（丑作收科）别人来"三杯和万事"，这客官"一气惹千愁"。

  （下）（外作下楼、转行科）我且回到寓中去波。

【浪来里】见着那一桩桩伤心的时事迍[33]，凑着那一句句感时的诗谶伏，怕天心人意两难摸，好教俺费沉吟、跅踱地将眉对蹙[34]。看满地斜阳欲暮，到萧条客馆兀自意踌蹰。

  （作到寓进坐科）（副净扮家将上）（见科）禀爷，朝报到来。（外看科）"兵部一本：为除授官员事奉圣旨，郭子仪授为天德军使。钦此。"原来旨意已下，索早收拾行李，即日上任去者。（副净应科）（外）俺郭子仪虽则官卑职小，便可从此报效朝廷也呵！

【高过随调煞】赤紧似尺水中展鬣鳞，枳棘中拂毛羽[35]。且喜奋云霄有分上天衢，直待的把乾坤重整顿，将百千秋第一等勋业图。纵有妖氛孽蛊[36]，少不得肩担日月[37]，手把大唐扶。

马蹄空踏几年尘，  胡 宿
长是豪家据要津[38]。 司空图
卑散自应霄汉隔[39]， 王 建
不知忧国是何人？ 吕 温

## 注 释

[1]本出所涉史事：一、天宝九载，安禄山封东平郡王，唐代以将帅而封王的，他是第一个；二、天宝十二载，郭子仪任天德军使。剧中将两事处理为同时发生。

[2]谒选：等候任用。

[3]杞天：意谓自己并非杞人忧天，无所作为。

[4]堂间处燕：喻不知所处的危险。

[5]屋上瞻乌：喻为国家的前途担忧。

[6]不提防柙虎樊熊，任纵横社鼠城狐：柙虎、樊熊，喻安禄山有野心，虽然一时驯服，有机会就要作乱；社鼠、城狐，喻倚势横行的奸臣，指杨国忠等。

[7]几回家听鸡鸣，起身独夜舞：闻鸡起舞，用东晋祖逖的故事，表示自己有救国的大志。

[8]乘除：消长、成败、兴衰。

[9]闹昏昏似醉汉难扶，哪里有独醒行吟楚大夫：醉汉，指认识不清时局的人；楚大夫，指屈原，只有他独醒行吟，知道国家的危机，这是郭子仪自喻。

[10]钓鱼人：吕尚，西周开国功臣；射虎人，李广，西汉名将；屠狗人，樊哙，汉初功臣。他们都是古代有作为的人物，郭子仪引为"同心伴侣"。

[11]也有吃寡酒的，吃案酒的：吃寡酒，光喝酒不买菜；案酒，下酒的小菜。

[12]青帘：酒旗。

[13]燕市酒人：指战国时的侠士荆轲。

[14]闲陶令：悠闲自在的陶渊明（曾任彭泽令）。

[15]莽灌夫：灌夫是西汉人，性刚直，曾在酒后骂丞相田蚡，因而被害。

[16]高阳酒徒：本指郦食其，刘邦的谋士，这里也是郭子仪自指。

[17]我问你咱："咱"和下文"我一面告诉你波"的"波"，都是语气
助词，相当于"啊"或"吧"。

[18]四家府门相连：据史载，除了杨国忠、三国夫人外，其实还有贵妃
的宗兄杨铦、杨锜共六家。

[19]地位：地步。

[20]怪私家恁僭窃：私家，指臣子；僭窃，滥冒名位，作非分的享受。

[21]折腰：卑躬屈节，奉迎权势。

[22]市附：赶集。

[23]舆情：公众意见。

[24]幺篇：北曲中指和前面一个乐调曲牌相同。

[25]端详：端相，细看。少祯符，不吉利。

[26]李遐周：相传是唐玄宗时的术士、预言家。

[27]多则是就里难言藏谶语：多半是（多则是）不好说出底细（就
里），只好把它们藏在谶语里面。

[28]猜诗谜杜家何处：懂得这几句诗意思的人在哪儿呢？

[29]早难道：难道。早，用来加强语气。

[30]头踏：古代官员出行时排在前面的仪仗队。

[31]杂种：安禄山的父亲是胡人，母亲是突厥人。

[32]气夯（háng）胸脯：气胀满了胸脯。

[33]迕（wǔ）：不顺遂，不满意。

[34]趷踏：即疙瘩，形容眉头紧皱。

[35]赤紧似尺水中展鬣鳞，枳棘中拂毛羽：赤紧似，正如；鱼游浅水、
鸟入荆棘丛，用来比喻自己处境之难。鬣，鱼头部附近的鳍。

[36]妖氛孽蛊：指安禄山。孽蛊（gǔ），祸害。

[37]肩担日月：担当国家大事。

[38]要津：政府中的重要职位。

[39]卑散：卑官散职，不重要的低级闲散官员。

第三本

# 第一出 闻 乐

【南吕 引子】【步蟾宫】（老旦扮嫦娥，引仙女上）清光独把良宵占，经万古纤尘不染。散瑶空风露洒银蟾[1]，一派仙音微飐[2]。

"药捣长生离劫尘[3]，清妍面目本来真。云中细看天香落[4]，仍倚苍苍桂一轮[5]。"吾乃嫦娥是也，本属太阴之主，浪传后羿之妻[6]。七宝团圞，周三万六千年内[7]；一轮皎洁，满一千二百里中。玉兔、金蟾，产结长明至宝；白榆、丹桂，种成万古奇葩。向有《霓裳羽衣》仙乐一部[8]，久秘月宫，未传人世。今下界唐天子，知音好乐。他妃子杨玉环，前身原是蓬莱玉妃，曾经到此。不免召他梦魂，重听此曲。使其醒来记忆，谱入管弦。竟将天下仙音，留作人间佳话，却不是好！寒簧过来。（贴）有。（老旦）你可到唐宫之内，引杨玉环梦魂到此听曲。曲终之后，仍旧送回。（贴）领旨。（老旦）"好凭一枕游仙梦，暗授千秋法曲音[9]。"（引丑下）（贴）奉着娘娘之命，不免出了月宫，到唐宫中走一遭也。（行介）

【南吕 过曲】【梁州序犯】【本调】明河斜映[10]，繁星微闪，俯将尘世遥觑。只见空濛香雾，早离却玉府清严。一任佩摇风影，衣动霞光，小步红云垫。待将天上乐授宫襜[11]，密召芳魂入彩蟾[12]。来此已是唐宫之内。【贺新郎】你看鱼钥闭[13]，龙帷掩，那杨妃呵，似海棠睡足增娇艳。【本序尾】轻唤起，拥冰簟。

（唤介）杨娘娘起来。（旦扮梦中魂上）

【渔灯儿】恰才的追凉后雨困云淹，畅好是酣眠处粉腻黄黏[14]。（贴）娘娘有请。（旦）呀，深宫之内，檐下何人叫唤？悄没个宫娥报轻来画檐。（贴）娘娘快请。（旦作倦态欠身介）我娇怯怯朦胧身欠，慢腾腾待自起开帘。

（作出见贴介）呀，原来是一个宫人！（贴）

【前腔】俺不是隶长门帚奉曾嫌[15]，（旦）不是宫人，敢是别院的美人？（贴）俺不是列昭容御座曾瞻[16]。（旦）这等你是何人？（贴）儿家月中侍儿[17]，名唤寒簧，则俺的名在瑶宫月殿金[18]。（旦惊介）原来是月中仙子，何因到此？（贴）恰才奉姮娥口敕亲传点，请娘娘到桂宫中花下消炎[19]。

（旦）哦，有这等事！（贴）娘娘不必迟疑。儿家引导，就请同行。（引旦行介）（合）

【锦渔灯】指碧落足下云生冉冉[20]，步青霄听耳中风弄纤纤。乍凝眸星斗垂垂似可拈，早望见烂辉辉宫殿影在镜中潜[21]。

（旦）呀，时当仲夏，为何这般寒冷？（贴）此即太阴月府，人间所传广寒宫者是也。就请进去。（旦喜介）想我浊质凡姿，今夕得到月府，好侥幸也。（作进看介）

【锦上花】清游胜满意饮[22]。（想介）这些景物都似曾见过来！环玉砌，绕碧檐，依稀风景漫猜嫌[23]。那壁桂花开的恁早！（贴）此乃月中丹桂，四时常茂，花叶俱香。（旦看介）果然好花也。看不足喜更添[24]，金英缀翠叶兼[25]，氤氲芳气透衣缣[26]，人在桂阴潜。

（内作乐介）（旦）你看一群仙女，素衣红裳，从桂树下奏乐而来，好不美听。（贴）此乃《霓裳羽衣》之曲也。（杂扮仙女四人、六人或八人，白衣、红裙、锦云肩、璎珞、飘带[27]，各奏乐，唱，绕场行上介）（旦、贴旁立看介）（众）

**【锦中拍】** 携天乐花丛斗拈，拂霓裳露沾。迥隔断红尘荏苒，直写出瑶台清艳。纵吹弹舌尖玉纤韵添，惊不醒人间梦魇，停不驻天宫漏签[28]。一枕游仙曲终闻盐[29]，付知音重翻检。

（同下）（旦）妙哉此乐。清高宛转，感我心魂，真非人间所有也！

**【锦后拍】** 缥缈中簇仙姿宛曾觑。听彻清音意厌厌，数琳琅琬琰；数琳琅琬琰，一字字偷将凤鞋轻点，按宫商揎记指儿尖。晕羞脸，枉自许舞娇歌艳，比着这钧天雅奏多是欺[30]。

请问仙子，愿求月主一见。（贴）要见月主还早。天色渐明，请娘娘回宫去罢。

**【尾声】** 你攀蟾有路应相念，（旦）好记取新声无欠，（贴）只误了你把枕上君王半夜儿闪[31]。

（旦下）（贴）杨妃已回唐宫，我索向月主娘娘复旨则个。

碧瓦桐轩月殿开，曹　唐　　还将明月送君回。丁仙芝

钧天虽许人间听，李商隐　　却被人间更漏催。黄　滔

注释 ————————————————————————————————————

[1]银蟾：银色的月光。相传月宫里有蟾蜍，因此用蟾来指月亮。

[2]飐（zhǎn）：飐，微微摇动。

[3]药捣长生：相传月宫里有白兔捣制长生药。

[4]天香：指月宫里的桂花。

[5]一轮：这里谓月中桂树。

[6]浪传后羿之妻：传说嫦娥是后羿之妻，偷吃了西王母的仙药，飞奔到
　　月宫。浪传，不可信的传说。

[7]七宝团圞：指月宫；周三万六千年内，指月宫由来已久。

[8]《霓裳羽衣》：唐代著名舞曲。

[9]法曲：原是道观所奏的音乐，唐明皇加以改造。

[10]明河：银河。

[11]宫襜（chān）：宫帷，此指杨贵妃。

[12]彩蟾：月宫。

[13]鱼钥：锁。古代锁多作鱼形。

[14]畅好是：正是。粉腻黄黏，形容脸上的残妆。黄，花黄，贴在脸
　　上。

[15]俺不是隶长门帚奉曾嫌：我不是失宠的宫女。

[16]俺不是列昭容：我不在昭容之列。昭容，比贵妃地位略低的一种女
　　官。

[17]儿家：我，女性自称。

[18]金：金名，注籍。

[19]消炎：避暑。

[20]碧落：天空。

[21]早望见烂辉辉宫殿影在镜中潜：已经看见了月亮里面明亮光辉的宫
　　殿影子。镜，指月亮。

[22]忺（xiān）：满意。

[23]漫猜嫌：徒然地猜疑。

[24]看不足：看不厌，看不够。

[25]金英缀：金黄色的花朵开了。

[26]氤氲芳气透衣襟：按曲牌，此句应为九字。

[27]锦云肩、璎珞：云肩，古代妇女的一种披肩；璎珞，用珍珠、宝石
串起来的项圈。

[28]纵吹弹舌尖玉纤韵添，惊不醒人间梦魇，停不驻天宫漏签：纵然
仙女们舌尖吹，纤手（玉纤）弹，风韵很美；（但是）既不能把人
（贵妃）从迷梦中惊醒，也不能让时间停住。漏签，即漏箭，古代
的计时器漏刻用漏箭表示时间。这几句曲文，有劝贵妃不要贪恋富
贵，及早回到天上做神仙之意。

[29]曲终闻盐：盐即艳，曲引，本在一支曲子的开头。这里似指《霓裳
羽衣曲》结尾的"长引"。

[30]枉自许舞娇歌艳，比着这钧天雅奏多是歉：徒然地自以为歌舞娇
艳，与天乐（钧天雅奏）一比，就自愧不如了。

[31]闪：丢下。

# 第二出 制 谱

【仙吕 过曲】【醉罗歌】【醉扶归】（老旦上）西宫才奉传呼罢，安排水榭要清佳。慢卷晶帘散朝霞[1]，玉钩却映初阳挂。奴家永新是也。与念奴妹子同在西宫，承应贵妃杨娘娘。我娘娘再入宫闱，万岁爷更加恩幸。真乃"三千宠爱在一身，六宫粉黛无颜色"。今早娘娘分付，收拾荷亭，要制曲谱。念奴妹子在那里伏侍晓妆，奴家先到此间，不免将文房四宝[2]，摆设起来。【皂罗袍】你看笔床初拂，光分素札[3]；砚池新注，香浮墨华——绿阴深处多幽雅。【排歌尾】竹风引，荷露洒，对波纹帘影弄参差[4]。

呀，兰麝香飘，佩环风定，娘娘早则到也。（旦引贴上）

【正宫 引子】【新荷叶】幽梦清宵度月华，听《霓裳羽衣》歌罢。醒来音节记无差，拟翻新谱消长夏。

"斗画长眉翠淡浓，远山移入镜当中[5]。晓窗日射胭脂颊，一朵红酥旋欲融。"我杨玉环自从截发感君之后，荷宠弥深。只有梅妃《惊鸿》一舞，圣上时常夸奖。思欲另制一曲，掩出其上。正在推敲，昨夜忽然梦入月宫。见桂树之下，仙女数人，素衣红裳，奏乐甚美。醒来追忆，音节宛然。因此分付永新，收拾荷亭，只待细配宫商，谱成新曲。（老旦）启娘娘：纸、墨、笔、砚，已安排齐备了。（旦）你与念奴一同在此伺候。

（老旦、贴应，作打扇、添香介）（旦作制谱介）

【正宫 过曲】【刷子带芙蓉】【刷子序】荷气满窗纱，鸾笺慢伸犀管轻拿，待谱他月里清音，细吐我心上灵芽。这声调虽出月宫，其间转移过度[6]，细微曲折之处，须索自加细审。安插，一字字要调停如法，一段段须融和入化。这几声尚欠调匀，拍𠆤怎下[7]？（内作莺啼，旦执笔听介）呀，妙阿！（作改介）【玉芙蓉】听宫莺、数声恰好应红牙[8]。

（搁笔介）谱已制完，永新，是什么时候了？（老旦）晌午了。（旦）万岁爷可曾退朝？（老旦）尚未。（旦）永新，且随我更衣去来。念奴在此伺候，万岁爷到时，即忙通报。（贴）领旨。（旦）"好凭晚镜增蛾翠，漫试香纱换蝶衣。"（引老旦随下）（生行上）

【渔灯映芙蓉】【山渔灯】散千官，朝初罢。拟对玉人，长昼闲话。寡人方才回宫，听说妃子在荷亭上，因此一径前来。依流水待觅胡麻[9]，把银塘路踏。（作到介）（贴见介）呀，万岁爷到了。（生）念奴，你娘娘在何处闲欢耍，怎堆香几有笔砚交加？（贴）娘娘在此制谱，方才更衣去了。（生）妃子，妃子！美人韵事，被你都占尽也。但不知制甚曲谱，待寡人看来。（作坐翻看介）消详从头觑咱。妙哉，只这锦字荧荧银钩小，更度羽换宫没半米差[10]。好奇怪，这谱连寡人也不知道。细按音节，不是人间所有，似从天下，果曲高和寡。妃子，不要说你娉婷绝世，只这一点灵心，有谁及得你来？【玉芙蓉】恁聪明，也堪压倒上阳花[11]。

【普天赏芙蓉】【普天乐】（旦换妆，引老旦上）换轻妆，多幽雅，试生绡添潇洒。（见生介）臣妾见驾。（生扶介）妃子坐了。（坐介）（生）妃子，看你晚妆新试，妩媚益增。似迎风袅袅杨枝，宛凌波濯濯莲花。芳兰一朵斜把云鬟压，越显得庞儿风流煞。（旦）陛下今日退朝，因何恁晚？（生）只为灵武太守员缺，地方紧要，与廷臣议了半日，难得其人。朕特擢郭子仪，补授此缺[12]，因此退朝迟了。（旦）妾候陛下不至，独坐荷亭，爱风来一弄明纱[13]，闲学谱新声奏雅。【玉芙蓉】怕输他舞《惊鸿》，曲终满座有光华。

（生）寡人适见此谱，真乃千古奇音，《惊鸿》何足道也！（旦）妾凭臆见，草草创成。其中错误，还望陛下更定[14]。（生）再同妃子，细细点勘一番。（老旦、贴暗下）（生、旦并坐翻谱介）

**【朱奴折芙蓉】**【朱奴儿】倚长袖香肩并亚[15]，翻新谱玉纤同把。（生）妃子，似你绝调佳人世真寡，要觅破绽并无毫发。再问妃子，此谱何名？（旦）妾于昨夜梦入月宫，见一群仙女奏乐，尽着霓裳羽衣。意欲取此四字，以名此曲。（生）好个"霓裳羽衣"！非虚假，果合伴天香桂花[16]。【玉芙蓉】（作看旦介）觑仙姿，想前身原是月中娃。

此谱即当宣付梨园，但恐俗手伶工，未谙其妙。朕欲令永新、念奴，先抄图谱，妃子亲自指授。然后传与李龟年等，教习梨园子弟，却不是好。（旦）领旨。（生携旦起介）天已薄暮，进宫去来。

**【尾声】**晚风吹，新月挂，（旦）正一缕凉生凤榻。（生）妃子，你看这池上鸳鸯，早双眠并蒂花。

| | | |
|---|---|---|
| （生） | 芙蓉不及美人妆， | 王昌龄 |
| （旦） | 杨柳风多水殿凉。 | 刘长卿 |
| （老旦） | 花下偶然歌一曲， | 曹　唐 |
| （合） | 传呼法部按《霓裳》。 | 王　建 |

## 注 释

[1]慢卷：即漫卷。

[2]文房四宝：纸、墨、笔、砚。

[3]素札：白纸。

[4]参差：这里为协韵，差读作chà。

[5]远山：画眉的一种式样，看起来好像淡淡的一弯远山。

[6]过度：音调转移。

[7]拍尒（qí）怎下：节拍差了，怎样安排呢？唱曲不合拍节，叫尒拍。

[8]红牙：拍板。

[9]依流水待觅胡麻：传说刘晨、阮肇到天台山采药，见水上流来胡麻饭，因此遇见仙女。

[10]更度羽换宫没半米差：作曲没半点儿差错。

[11]恁聪明，也堪压倒上阳花：且不说美貌，单凭这样聪明，也足以胜过后宫别的美女了。上阳，宫殿名。

[12]朕特擢郭子仪，补授此缺：据史载，郭子仪做灵武郡太守在安禄山叛乱爆发之后。

[13]一弄：一派。

[14]更定：改定。

[15]香肩并亚：挨着肩膀。亚，压。

[16]果合伴天香桂花：这样的曲子，果然只有天上月宫才配拥有。

# 第三出 权 讧[1]

【双调 引子】【秋蕊香】（副净引祗从上）狼子野心难料，看跋扈渐肆咆哮，挟势辜恩更堪恼，索假忠言入告[2]。

下官杨国忠。外凭右相之尊，内恃贵妃之宠。满朝文武，谁不趋承！独有安禄山这厮，外面假作痴愚，肚里暗藏狡诈。不知圣上因甚爱他，加封王爵！他竟忘了下官救命之恩，每每遇事欺凌，出言挺撞。好生可恨！前日曾奏圣上，说他狼子野心，面有反相，恐防日后酿祸，怎奈未见听从。今日进朝，须索相机再奏，必要黜退了他，方快吾意。来此已是朝门，左右回避。（从下）（内喝道介）（副净）呀，那边呵殿之声[3]，且看是谁？（净引祗从上）

【玉井莲后】宠固君心，暗中包藏计狡。

左右回避。（从下）（净见副净介）请了。（副净笑介）哦，原来是安禄山！（净）老杨，你叫我怎么？（副净）这是九重禁地，你怎敢在此大声呵殿？（净作势介）老杨，你看我："脱下御衣亲赐着，进来龙马每教骑。常承密旨趋朝数，独奏边机出殿迟。"我做郡王的，便呵殿这么一声，也不妨。比似你右相还早哩[4]！（副净冷笑介）好，好个"不妨"！安禄山，我且问你，这般大模大样是几时起的？（净）下官从来如此。（副净）安禄山，你也还该自去想一想！（净）想什么？（副净）你只想当日来见我的时节，可是这个模样

243

么？（净）彼一时，此一时，说他怎的。（副净）唉，
安禄山，

【仙吕入双调 过曲】【风入松】你本是刀头活鬼罪难逃，
那时节长跪阶前哀告。我封章入奏机关巧，才把你身躯全保。
（净）赦罪复官，出自圣恩。与你何涉？（副净）好，倒说得干
净！只太把良心昧了。恩和义付与水萍飘。

（净）唉，杨国忠，你可晓得，

【前腔】世间荣落偶相遭？休夸着势压群僚。你道我失机之
罪，可也记得南诏的事么[5]？胡卢提掩败将功冒[6]，怪浮云蔽遮
天表[7]。（副净）圣明在上，谁敢蒙蔽？这不是谤君么！（净）
还说不蒙蔽，你卖爵鬻官多少？贪财货竭脂膏。（副净）住了，
你道卖官鬻爵，只问你的富贵，是那里来的？（冷笑介）（净）
也非止这一桩。若论你、恃戚里，施奸狡，误国罪，有千条。
（副净）休得把、诬蔑语，凭虚造。（扯净介）我与你、同去面
当朝！

（净）谁怕你来，同去，同去！（作同扭进朝俯伏介）
（副净）臣杨国忠谨奏：

【前腔】（本调）禄山异志腹藏刀[8]，外作痴愚容貌，奸同石
勒倚东门啸[9]。他不拜储君公然桀傲[10]，这无礼难容圣朝。望吾
皇立赐罢斥，除凶恶早绝祸根苗。

（净伏介）臣安禄山谨奏：

【前腔】念微臣谬荷主恩高，遂使嫌生权要[11]，愚蒙触忤知
难保[12]。（泣介）陛下呵，怕孤立终落他圈套。微臣呵，寸心
赤只有吾皇鉴昭。容出镇犬马效微劳。（内）圣旨道来：杨国
忠、安禄山互相讦奏，将相不和，难以同朝共理。特命安禄
山为范阳节度使[13]，剋期赴镇。谢恩。（净、副净）万岁！

（起介）（净向副净拱手介）老丞相，下官今日去了，你再休怪我大模大样。朝门内，一任你、张牙爪，我去开幕府[14]，自逍遥。（副净冷笑介）（净欲下，复转向副净介）还有一句话儿，今日下官出镇，想也仗、回天力、相提调。（举手介）请了，我且将冷眼，看伊曹。

（下）（副净看净下介）呀，有这等事！

**【前腔】**（本调）一腔块垒怎生消[15]，我待把他威风抹倒，谁知反分节钺添荣耀[16]。这话靶教人嘲笑[17]。咳，但愿禄山此去，做出事来[18]，方信我忠言最早！圣上，圣上，到此际可也悔今朝[19]！

> 去邪当断勿狐疑，　周　昙　祸稔萧墙竟不知[20]。储嗣宗
>
> 壮气未平空咄咄，　徐　铉　甘言狡计奈娇痴！　郑　嵎

注　释

[1]本出所涉史实：天宝九载，安禄山封王，"是时，杨国忠为御史中丞，方承恩用事。禄山登降殿阶，国忠常扶掖之。"（《资治通鉴》卷二一六）这时候安禄山的权势本来比杨国忠大，两人之间还谈不上什么利害冲突。他们有时还联手对付共同的政敌李林甫。从开元二十二年到天宝十一载，李林甫一直担任宰相。杨国忠接替李林甫执政以后，他和安禄山才成为势均力敌的对手。一个是朝中的执政者，一个是当时最大的军事集团的首领，彼此都想削弱对方，以加重自己的权势。杨国忠几次告发安禄山有反心，皇帝也几次派中使去察看动静，但是安禄山对付得很好，博得玄宗更大的信任。另一方面，由于杨国忠的阻挠，安禄山也始终没有实现做宰相的野心，杨国忠在朝中得以大权独揽。

[2]索假忠言入告：杨国忠对安禄山不满，装作对皇帝尽忠，告发安禄山有反心。

[3]呵殿：前呼后拥，喝道而来。呵，从人在前面喝道；殿，殿后，从人在后面拥卫。

[4]"我做郡王的"四句：我受封为王，喝道一下，没有关系；至于你做右相的，要在宫殿里喝道，自然还谈不上。

[5]南诏的事："四月……剑南节度使鲜于仲通讨南诏（哀牢彝民族，在现在云南省西部），大败于泸南……士卒死者六万人，仲通仅以身免。杨国忠掩其败状，仍叙其功。"（《资治通鉴》卷二一六）同年冬季，杨国忠指使鲜于仲通，奏请遥领剑南节度使。

[6]胡卢提：糊里糊涂。

[7]怪浮云蔽遮天表：喻杨国忠蒙蔽玄宗的耳目。

[8]异志：有造反之心。

[9]奸同石勒倚东门啸：石勒"年十四，随邑人行贩洛阳，倚啸上东门。王衍见而异之，顾谓左右曰：'向者胡雏，吾观其声视有奇志，恐将为天下之患。'"（《晋书》卷一0四）石勒后自立为后赵国皇帝，他是羯人，所以用来比喻安禄山。

[10]他不拜储君：储君，太子。"（唐玄宗）又尝命见太子，禄山不拜。左右趋之拜，禄山拱立曰：'臣胡人，不习朝仪，不知太子者何官？'上曰：'此储君也。朕千秋万岁后，代朕君汝者也。'禄山曰：'臣愚，曏者唯知有陛下一人，不知乃更有储君。'不得已，然后拜。"（《资治通鉴》卷二一五）

[11]权要：指杨国忠。

[12]愚蒙：指自己。

[13]特命安禄山为范阳节度使：安禄山早在天宝三载就被任为范阳节度使、河北采访使兼平卢节度使，这时杨玉环还没有册为贵妃，杨国忠还没有登上政治舞台。

[14]开幕府：即开府，建立府署，独当一面。这里指担任节度使。

[15]块垒：郁积在心头的牢骚、不平。

[16]节钺：符节与斧钺，授给大将，以示其威权。

[17]话靶：即话把，话柄。

[18]做出事来：指造反。

[19]此际：那时。

[20]祸稔萧墙：内部祸患累积。稔，积久而成；萧墙，这里指宫廷内部的祸患。

# 第四出 偷 曲[1]

**【仙吕 过曲】【八声甘州】**（老旦、贴携谱上）（老旦）霓裳谱定，（贴合）向绮窗深处秘本翻誊。香喉玉口，亲将绝调教成。（老旦）奴家永新，（贴）奴家念奴。（老旦）自从娘娘制就《霓裳》新谱，我二人亲蒙教授。今驾幸华清宫，即日要奏此曲。命我二人，在朝元阁上，传谱与李龟年，连夜教演梨园子弟。（贴）散序俱已传习[2]，今日该传拍序了[3]。（老旦）你看月明如水，正好演奏。我和你携了曲谱，先到阁中便了。（行介）（合）凉蟾正当高阁升，帘卷薰风映水晶[4]。高清，恰称广寒宫仙乐声声。（下）

**【道宫 近词】【鱼儿赚】**（末苍髯，扮李龟年上）乐部旧闻名，班首新推独老成。早暮趋承，上直更番入内廷[5]。自家李龟年是也，向作伶官，蒙万岁爷点为梨园班首。今有贵妃娘娘《霓裳》新曲，奉旨令永新、念奴传谱出来，在朝元阁上教演，立等供奉。只得连夜趱习，不免唤齐众兄弟每同去。兄弟每那里？（副净扮马仙期上）仙期方响鬼神惊[6]，（外扮雷海青上）铁拨争推雷海青[7]。（净白须扮贺怀智上）贺老琵琶擅场屋[8]，（丑扮黄幡绰上）黄家幡绰板尤精[9]。（同见末介）李师父拜揖。（末）请了。列位呵，君王命，《霓裳》催演不教停。那永新、念奴呵，两娉婷，把红牙小谱携端正，早向朝元待月明。（众）如此，我每就去便了。（末）请同行。（同行介）趁迟迟宫漏夜凉生，把新腔敲订，新腔敲订。（同下）

【仙吕 过曲】【解三醒犯】（小生巾服扮李謩上[10]）【解
三醒】逞风魔少年逸兴，借曲中妙理陶情。传闻今夜蓬莱境，翻
妙谱奏新声。小生李謩是也，本贯江南，遨游京国。自小谙通音
律，久以铁笛擅名。近闻宫中新制一曲，名曰《霓裳羽衣》。乐
工李龟年等，每夜在朝元阁中演习。小生慕此新声，无从得其秘
谱。打听的那阁子，恰好临着宫墙，声闻于外。不免袖了铁笛，
来到骊山，趁此月明如昼，窃听一回。一路行来，果然好景致
也。（行介）林收暮霭天气清，山入寒空月彩横。真佳景，【八
声甘州】宛身从画里游行。

　（场上设红帷作墙，墙内搭一阁介）（小生）说话之间，
　　早来到宫墙下了。

【道宫调 近词】【应时明近】只见五云中，宫阙影，窈窕
玲珑映月明。光辉看不定，光辉看不定。想潜通御气，处处仙
楼，阑干畔有玉人闲凭。

　闻那朝元阁，在禁苑西首，我且绕着红墙，迤逦行去。
　（行介）

【前腔】花阴下，御路平，紧傍红墙款款行。（望介）只这垂
杨影里，一座高楼露出墙头，想就是了。凝眸重细省，凝眸重细
省，只见画帘缥缈，文窗掩映。（指介）兀的不是上有红灯[11]！

　（老旦、贴在墙内上阁介）（末众在内云）今日该演拍
　　序，大家先将散序，从头演习一番。（小生）你看上面
　　灯光隐隐，似有人声，一定是这里了。我且潜听一回。
　（作潜立听介）

【双赤子】悄悄冥冥[12]，墙阴窃听。（内作乐介）（小生作
袖出笛介）不免取出笛来，倚声和之[13]。就将音节，细细记明便
了。听到月高初更后，果然弦索齐鸣。恰喜禁垣夜深人静，玎璁

齐应[14]。这数声恍然心领，那数声恍然心领。

> （内细十番[15]，小生吹笛和介）（乐止，老旦、贴在内阁
> 上唱后曲，小生吹笛合介）（老旦、贴）

【画眉儿】骊珠散迸[16]，入拍初惊。云翻袂影，飘然回雪舞风
轻。飘然回雪舞风轻，约略烟蛾态不胜[17]。（小生接唱）这数声
恍然心领，那数声恍然心领。

> （内细十番如前，老旦、贴内唱，小生笛合介）（老旦、
> 贴）

【前腔】珠辉翠映，凤翥鸾停。玉山蓬顶，上元挥袂引双成。
上元挥袂引双成，萼绿回肩招许琼。（小生接唱）这数声恍然心
领，那数声恍然心领。

> （内又如前十番，老旦、贴内唱，小生笛合介）（老旦、
> 贴）

【前腔】音繁调骋，丝竹纵横。翔云忽定，慢收舞袖弄轻盈。
慢收舞袖弄轻盈，飞上瑶天歌一声。（小生接唱）这数声恍然心
领，那数声恍然心领。

> （内又十番一通，老旦、贴暗下）（小生）妙哉曲也。真
> 个如敲秋竹，似戛春冰[18]，分明一派仙音，信非人世所
> 有。被我都从笛中偷得，好侥幸也！

【鹅鸭满渡船】霓裳天上声，墙外行人听。音节明，宫商
正，风内高低应。偷从笛里写出无余剩。呀，阁上寂然无声，想
是不奏了。人散曲终红楼静，半墙残月摇花影。

> 你看河斜月落，斗转参横[19]，不免回去罢。（袖笛转行
> 介）

【尾声】却回身，寻归径。只听得玉河流水韵幽清，犹似《霓
裳》袅袅声。

倚天楼殿月分明，杜　牧　　歌转高云夜更清。赵　嘏
偷得新翻数般曲，元　稹　　酒楼吹笛有新声。张　祜

## 注 释

[1]本出李暮傍宫墙偷谱法曲事，本《全唐诗》元稹《连昌宫词》注。

[2]散序：《霓裳羽衣》舞的序曲。

[3]拍序：《霓裳羽衣》舞的一个组成部分。

[4]薰风：南风，和风。

[5]上直更番：上直，值班；更番，轮流。

[6]方响：古代打击乐器，主要由十六块铁片组成。

[7]铁拨：雷海青弹一种特制的琵琶，以铁拨代替指甲。

[8]擅场屋：压倒全场。场屋，奏乐的地方。

[9]板：拍板。

[10]李暮（mó）：唐代著名笛师。

[11]兀的：那边，含有表示惊异的语气。

[12]悄悄冥冥：暗地里。

[13]倚声和之：照听到的乐调吹奏。

[14]玎瑽：乐器声。

[15]细十番：即十番鼓，由笛、管、箫、弦、提琴、云锣、汤锣、木鱼、檀板、大鼓等十种乐器组成，可奏多种乐曲。

[16]骊珠散进：形容入拍以后的《霓裳羽衣》曲的音乐。骊珠，传说骊龙（黑色的龙）颔下有宝珠，叫骊珠。

[17]约略烟蛾：画成淡淡的黑色的眉毛。

[18]戛（jiá）：敲。

[19]斗转参横：形容夜深。斗，北斗星；参，参宿。

# 第五出 进 果

【过曲】【柳穿鱼】（末扮使臣持竿挑荔枝蓝，作鞭马急上）一身万里跨征鞍，为进离支受艰难[1]。上命遣差不由己，算来名利怎如闲！巴得个、到长安，只图贵妃看一看。

> 自家西州道使臣，为因贵妃杨娘娘。爱吃鲜荔枝，奉敕涪州[2]，年年进贡。天气又热，路途又远，只得不惮辛勤，飞马前去。（作鞭马重唱"巴得个"三句跑下）

【撼动山】（副净扮使臣持荔枝篮，鞭马急上）海南荔子味尤甘，杨娘娘偏喜唻。采时连叶包，缄封贮小竹篮。献来晓夜不停骖，一路里怕耽，望一站也么奔一站[3]！

> 自家海南道使臣。只为杨娘娘爱吃鲜荔枝，俺海南所产，胜似涪州，因此敕与涪州并进。但是俺海南的路儿更远，这荔枝过了七日，香味便减，只得飞驰赶去。

> （鞭马重唱"一路里"二句跑下）

【十棒鼓】（外扮老田夫上）田家耕种多辛苦，愁旱又愁雨。一年靠这几茎苗，收来半要偿官赋，可怜能得几粒到肚！每日盼成熟，求天拜神助。

> 老汉是金城县东乡一个庄家。一家八口，单靠着这几亩薄田过活。早间听说进鲜荔枝的使臣，一路上捎着径道行走，不知踏坏了人家多少禾苗！因此，老汉特到田中看守。（望介）那边两个算命的来了。（小生扮算命瞎子手持竹板，净扮女瞎子弹弦子，同行上）

【**蛾郎儿**】住褒城，走咸京，细看流年与五星[4]。生和死，断分明，一张铁口尽闻名[5]。瞎先生，真灵圣，叫一声，赛神仙，来算命。

（净）老的，我走了几程，今日脚疼，委实走不动。不是算命，倒在这里挣命了。（小生）妈妈，那边有人说话，待我问他。（叫介）借问前面客官，这里是什么地方了？（外）这是金城东乡，与渭城西乡交界。（小生斜揖介）多谢客官指引。（内铃响，外望介）呀，一队骑马的来了。（叫介）马上长官，往大路上走，不要踏了田苗！（小生一面对净语介）妈妈，且喜到京不远，我每叫向前去，雇个毛驴子与你骑。（重唱"瞎先生"三句走介）（末鞭马重唱前"巴得个"三句急上，冲倒小生、净下）（副净鞭马重唱前"一路里"二句急上，踏死小生下）（外跌脚向鬼门哭介[6]）天啊，你看一片田禾，都被那厮踏烂，眼见的没用了。休说一家性命难存，现今官粮紧急，将何办纳！好苦也！（净一面作爬介）哎呀，踏坏人了，老的啊，你在那里？（作摸着小生介）呀，这是老的。怎么不做声，敢是踏昏了？（又摸介）哎呀，头上湿渌渌的。（又摸闻手介）不好了，踏出脑浆来了！（哭叫介）我那天呵，地方救命[7]。（外转身作看介）原来一个算命先生，踏死在此。（净起斜福介[8]）只求地方，叫那跑马的人来偿命。（外）哎，那跑马的呵，乃是进贡鲜荔枝与杨娘娘的。一路上来，不知踏坏了多少人，不敢要他偿命。何况你这一个瞎子！（净）如此怎了！（哭介）我那老的呵，我原算你的命，是要倒路死的。只这个尸首，如今怎么断送！

（外）也罢，你那里去叫地方，就是老汉同你抬去埋了罢。（净）如此多谢，我就跟着你做一家儿[9]，可不是好！（同抬小生）（哭，诨下[10]）（丑扮驿卒上）

【小引】驿官逃，驿官逃，马死单单剩马膫[11]。驿子有一人，钱粮没半分。拚受打和骂，将身去招架，将身去招架！

自家渭城驿中，一个驿子便是。只为杨娘娘爱吃鲜荔枝，六月初一是娘娘的生日，涪州、海南两处进贡使臣，俱要赶到。路由本驿经过，怎奈驿中钱粮没有分文，瘦马刚存一匹。本官怕打，不知逃往那里去了，区区就便权知此驿。只是使臣到来，如何应付？且自由他！（末飞马上）

【急急令】黄尘影内日衔山，赶赶赶，近长安。（下马介）驿子，快换马来。（丑接马，末放果篮，整衣介）（副净飞马上）一身汗雨四肢瘫，趱趱趱，换行鞍。

（下马介）驿子，快换马来。（丑接马，副净放果篮，与末见介）请了，长官也是进荔枝的？（末）正是。（副净）驿子，下程酒饭在那里？（丑）不曾备得。（末）也罢，我每不吃饭了，快带马来。（丑）两位爷在上，本驿只剩有一匹马，但凭那一位爷骑去就是。（副净）唗，偌大一个渭城驿，怎么只有一匹马！快唤你那狗官来，问他驿马那里去了？（丑）若说起驿马，连年都被进荔枝的爷每骑死了。驿官没法，如今走了。（副净）既是驿官走了，只问你要。（丑指介）这棚内不是一匹马么？（末）驿子，我先到，且与我先骑了去。（副净）我海南的来路更远，还让我先骑。（末作向内介）

【惩麻郎】我只先换马，不和你斗口。（副净扯介）休恃强，惹着我动手。（末取荔枝在手介）你敢把**我**这荔枝乱丢！（副净取荔枝向末介）你敢把**我**这竹笼碎扭！（丑劝介）请罢休，免气吼，不如把这匹瘦马同骑一路走！（副净放荔枝打丑介）唗，胡说！

**【前腔】**我只打你、这泼腌臜死囚[12]！（末放荔枝打丑介）我也打你这放刁顽贼头！（副净）克官马嘴儿太油。（末）误上用胆儿似斗[13]。（同打介）（合）鞭乱抽，拳痛殴，打得你难捱那马自有！

**【前腔】**（丑叩头介）向地上连连叩头，望台下轻轻放手[14]。（末、副净）若要饶你，快换马来。（丑）马一匹驿中现有。（末、副净）再要一匹。（丑）第二匹实难补凑。（末、副净）没有只是打！（丑）且慢纽[15]，请听剖，我只得脱下衣裳与你权当酒！

（脱衣介）（末）谁要你这衣裳！（副净作看衣、披在身上介）也罢，赶路要紧。我原骑了那马，前站换去。（取果上马，重唱前"一路里"二句跑下）（末）快换马来我骑。（丑）马在此。（末取果上马，重唱前"巴得个"三句跑下）（丑吊场）咳，杨娘娘，杨娘娘，只为这几个荔枝呵！

铁关金锁彻明开，　　崔　液
黄纸初飞敕字回[16]。元　稹
驿骑鞭声砉流电[17]，李　郢
无人知是荔枝来。　杜　牧

## 注 释

[1]离支：即荔枝。

[2]涪（fú）州：今四川涪陵。

[3]也么：有声无义的语气助词。

[4]流年与五星："流年"、"五星"都是古代星相学术语。流年，一年
　　所行的运；五星，金、木、水、火、土，星相家根据一个人出生时
　　所值的星位，来推算他的禄命。

[5]铁口：自夸算命很准。

[6]鬼门：即古门，舞台上演员的出入口。

[7]地方：地保。

[8]福：即万福，妇女向人敛衽致敬。

[9]做一家儿：做夫妻。

[10]诨：打诨，调笑。

[11]马膫（diǎo）：马屌，牡马的生殖器。

[12]泼腌臜（ā zā）：肮脏。

[13]上：皇上。

[14]台下：对官长的尊称。意思近于"阁下"。

[15]纽：即扭，扭打。

[16]黄纸：唐代用黄麻纸写的皇帝敕令。

[17]砉（huā）：形容动作迅疾。

# 第六出 舞 盘

【仙吕 引子】【奉时春】（生引二内侍、丑随上）山静风微昼漏长，映殿角火云千丈。紫气东来[1]，瑶池西望，翩翩青鸟庭前降[2]。

朕同妃子避暑骊山。今当六月朔日，乃是妃子诞辰。特设宴在长生殿中，与他称庆，并奏《霓裳》新曲。高力士，传旨后宫，宣娘娘上殿。（丑）领旨。（向内传介）（内应"领旨"介）（旦盛妆，引老旦、贴上）

【唐多令】日影耀椒房，花枝弄绮窗，门悬小帨赭罗黄[3]。绣得文鸳成一对，高傍着五云翔。

（见介）臣妾杨氏见驾。愿陛下万岁，万万岁！（生）也妃子同之。（旦坐介）（生）紫云深处婺光明[4]，（旦）带露灵桃倚日荣。（老旦、贴）岁岁花前人不老，（丑合）长生殿里庆长生。（生）今日妃子初度[5]，寡人特设长生之宴，同为竟日之欢。（旦）薄命生辰，荷蒙天宠。愿为陛下进千秋万岁之觞。（丑）酒到。（旦拜，献生酒，生答赐，旦跪饮，叩头呼"万岁"，坐介）（生）

【高平 过曲】【八仙会蓬海】【八声甘州】风薰日朗，看一叶阶蓂摇动炎光[6]。华筵初启，南山遥映霞觞。【玩仙灯】（合）果合欢桃生千岁，花并蒂莲开十丈[7]。【月上海棠】宜欢赏，恰好殿号长生，境齐蓬阆。

（小生扮内监，捧表上）"手捧金花红榜子，齐来宝殿祝千秋。"（见介）启万岁爷、娘娘，国舅杨丞相，同韩、虢、秦三国夫人，献上寿礼贺笺，在外朝贺。（丑取笺送生看介）（生）生受他每。丞相免行礼，回朝办事。三国夫人，候朕同娘娘回宫筵宴。（小生）领旨。（下）（净扮内监捧荔枝、黄袱盖上）"正逢瑶圃十秋宴[8]，进到炎州十八娘[9]。"（见介）启万岁爷，涪州、海南贡进鲜荔枝在此。（生）取上来。（丑接荔枝去袱，送上介）（生）妃子，朕因你爱食此果，特敕地方飞驰进贡。今日寿宴初开，佳果适至，当为妃子再进一觞。（旦）万岁！（生）宫娥每，进酒。（老、贴进酒介）（旦）

**【杯底庆长生】【倾杯序】【换头】**盈筐，佳果香，幸黄封[10]，远敕来川广。爱他浓染红绡，薄裹晶丸[11]，入手清芬，沁齿甘凉。**【长生导引】（合）**便火枣交梨应让[12]，只合来万岁台前，千秋筵上，伴瑶池阿母进琼浆[13]。

高力士，传旨李龟年，押梨园子弟上殿承应。（丑）领旨。（向内传介）（末引外、净、副净、丑各锦衣、花帽，应"领旨"上）"红牙待拍筝排柱[14]，催着红罗上舞筵，换戴柘枝新帽子[15]，随班行到御阶前。"（见介）乐工李龟年，押领梨园子弟，叩见万岁爷、娘娘。（生）李龟年，《霓裳》散序昨已奏过，《羽衣》第二叠可曾演熟[16]？（末）演熟了。（生）用心去奏。（末）领旨。（起介）（暗下）（旦）妾启陛下，此曲散序六奏，止有歇拍而无流拍[17]。中序六奏，有流拍而无促拍，其时未有舞态[18]。

**【八仙会蓬海】【换头】**只是悠扬，声情俊爽。要停住彩云飞绕虹梁[19]。至羽衣三叠，名曰饰奏[20]。一声一字，都将舞态含藏。其间有慢声，有缠声，有衮声[21]，应清圆骊珠一串；有入破，有摊破，有出破<sup>[22]</sup>，合袅娜虺魁千状<sup>[23]</sup>；还有花犯，有道和，有傍拍，有间拍，有催拍，有偷拍<sup>[24]</sup>，多音响，皆与慢舞相生，缓歌交畅。

（生）妃子所言，曲尽歌舞之蕴。（旦）妾制有翠盘一面，请试舞其中，以博天颜一笑。（生）妃子妙舞，寡人从未得见。永新、念奴，可同郑观音、谢阿蛮伏侍娘娘，上翠盘来者。（老、贴）领旨。（旦起福介）告退更衣。"整顿衣裳重结束<sup>[25]</sup>，一身飞上翠盘中。"（引老、贴下）（生）高力士，传旨李龟年，领梨园子弟按谱奏乐。朕亲以羯鼓节之<sup>[26]</sup>。（丑）领旨。（向内传介）（生起更衣，末、众在场内作乐介）（场上设翠盘，旦花冠、白绣袍、璎珞、锦云肩、翠袖、大红舞裙，老、贴同净、副净扮郑观音、谢阿蛮，各舞衣、白袍，执五彩霓旌、孔雀云扇，密遮旦簇上翠盘介）（乐止，旌扇徐开，旦立盘中舞，老、贴、净、副唱，丑跪捧鼓，生上坐击鼓，众在场内打细十番合介）

**【羽衣第二叠】【画眉序】**罗绮合花光，一朵红云自空漾<sup>[27]</sup>。**【皂罗袍】**看霓旌四绕，乱落天香。**【醉太平】**安详，徐开扇影露明妆。**【白练序】**浑一似天仙，月中飞降。（合）轻扬，彩袖张，向翡翠盘中显伎长。**【应时明近】**飘然来又往，宛迎风菡萏，**【双赤子】**翩翩叶上。举袂向空如欲去，乍回身侧度无方。（急舞介）**【画眉儿】**盘旋跌宕，花枝招飐柳枝扬，凤影高骞鸾影翔<sup>[28]</sup>。**【拗芝麻】**体态娇难状，天风吹起众乐缤纷响。**【小桃红】**冰弦玉柱声嘹亮，鸾笙象管音飘荡，**【花药栏】**恰合着羯鼓低昂。按新腔，度新腔，**【怕春归】**褪金裙齐作留仙想<sup>[29]</sup>。（生住鼓，丑携去介）**【古轮台】**舞住敛霞裳，（朝上拜介）重低颡,山呼万岁拜君王[30]。

　　（老、贴、净、副扶旦下盘介）（净、副暗下）（生起,
　　前携旦介）妙哉,舞也!逸态横生,浓姿百出。宛若翩
　　风回雪,恍如飞燕游龙,真独擅千秋矣。宫娥们,看酒
　　来,待朕与妃子把杯。（老、贴奉酒,生擎杯介）

【千秋舞霓裳】【千秋岁】把金觞,含笑微微向,请一点点
檀口轻尝。（付旦介）休得留残,休得留残,酬谢你舞怯腰肢劳
攘[31]。（旦接杯谢介）万岁!【舞霓裳】亲颁玉酝恩波广,惟惭
庸劣怎承当!（生看旦介）俺仔细看他模样,只这持杯处,有万
种风流殢人肠。

　　（生）朕有鸳鸯万金锦十匹,丽水紫磨金步摇一事[32],
　　聊作缠头[33]。（出香囊介）还有自佩瑞龙脑八宝锦香囊
　　一枚,解来助卿舞佩。（旦接香囊谢介）万岁。（生携
　　旦行介）

【尾声】（生）霓裳妙舞千秋赏,合助千秋祝未央[34]。（旦）
徼幸杀亲沐君恩透体香。

　　（生）长生秘殿倚青苍,　吴融
　　（旦）玉醴还分献寿觞。　张说
　　（生）饮罢更怜双袖舞,　韩翃
　　（旦）满身新带五云香。　曹唐

## 注释

[1]紫气东来：相传函谷关吏尹喜看见有紫气从东方过来，知道要有
　　"真人"出现，果然遇到了欲出关的老子。

[2]瑶池西望，翩翩青鸟庭前降：传说西王母住在瑶池。她来看汉武帝
　　时，先有青鸟飞来报信。

[3]帨（shuì）：佩巾。

[4]紫云深处婺光明：喻贵妃在宫廷里得宠，并含有祝贺之意。婺光，女
　　宿（一个星座）的亮光。

[5]初度：生日。

[6]夐：莫莫，生在阶前。

[7]果合欢桃生千岁，花并蒂莲开十丈：两个果结在一起，即一个果实有
　　两个果仁，叫合欢果，这里指桃子；两朵花开在一个蒂上，叫并蒂
　　花，这里指莲花。

[8]正逢瑶圃千秋宴：瑶圃，传说是仙人住的地方，这里指宫殿；千秋
　　宴，指贵妃的寿筵。

[9]炎州十八娘：炎州，南方；十八娘，著名荔枝品种。

[10]黄封：这里指黄袱包裹。

[11]浓染红绡，薄裹晶丸：红绡，指荔枝的果皮；晶丸，指鲜荔枝的白
　　色果肉。

[12]火枣、交梨：道教所说的仙果。

[13]瑶池阿母：西王母，借喻贵妃。

[14]筝排柱：筝，乐器，有十三根弦线固定在小柱上。排柱，演奏前调
　　弦的动作。

[15]柘（zhé）枝：柘枝的色素所染成的黄颜色，是乐人帽子的颜色。

[16]叠：即遍，也即下文所说"六奏"的奏。

[17]歇拍：歇拍及下文提到的流拍、促拍都是用来表明节拍速度的古代
　　音乐术语。

[18]其时未有舞态：《霓裳羽衣》中序已有舞态，剧中这个说法不知何
据。

[19]飞绕虹梁：形容乐声悠扬，余音绕梁。

[20]饰奏：据现存文献，《霓裳羽衣》第三大段不叫"饰奏"。

[21][22][24]慢声、缠声、衮声、入破、摊破、出破，花犯、道和、傍
拍、间拍、催拍、偷拍等都是古代音乐术语。

[23]氍毹：地毯。全句形容地毯上演员的舞态。

[25]结束：穿戴起来。

[26]羯鼓：羯鼓，一种乐器，从羯族传来。据载唐明皇长于演奏此乐
器。

[27]一朵红云自空漾：指贵妃。以下两曲都用来描写她的舞态。

[28]高骞（qiān）：高飞。骞，飞举。

[29]齐作留仙想：据说有赵飞燕有一次舞蹈时，几乎乘风飞去，汉成帝
叫左右拖住她的裙子。这条裙子被称为留仙裙。

[30]山呼：高呼万岁，祝颂皇帝。据说汉武帝登嵩山，臣下听见空中有
呼"万岁"的声音三次。

[31]劳攘：辛苦。

[32]一事：一件。丽水紫磨金，最好的金子。丽水，即金沙江。

[33]缠头：赏给歌伎的财物。

[34]未央：没有完，这里是祝福长寿之意。

第四本

# 第一出 合 围

（外、末、副净、小生扮四番将上）（外）三尺镔刀耀雪光，（末）腰间明月角弓张。（副净）葡萄酒醉胭脂血，（小生）貂帽花添锦绣装。（外）俺范阳镇东路将官何千年是也[1]。（末）俺范阳镇西路将官崔乾祐是也。（副净）俺范阳镇南路将官高秀岩是也。（小生）俺范阳镇北路将官史思明是也。（各弯腰见科）请了，昨奉王爷将令，传集我等，只得齐至帐前伺候。道犹未了，王爷升帐也。（内鼓吹、掌号科）（净戎装引番姬、番卒上）

**【越调】【紫花拨四】**统貔貅雄镇边关。双眸觑破番和汉，掌儿中握定江山，先把这四周围爪牙迭办[2]。

我安禄山夙怀大志，久蓄异谋。只因一向在朝[3]，受封东平王爵，宠幸无双，富贵已极，咱的心愿倒也罢了。叵耐杨国忠那厮[4]，与咱不合，出镇范阳。且喜跳出樊笼，正好暗图大事。俺家所辖，原有三十二路将官，番汉并用，性情各别，难以任为腹心。因此奏请一概俱用番将[5]。如今大小将领，皆咱部落。（笑科）任意所为，都无所顾忌了。昨日传集他每俱赴帐前，这嗏敢待齐也[6]。（众进见科）三十二路将官参见。（净）诸将少礼。（众）请问王爷，传集某等，不知有何钧令？（净）众将官，目今秋高马壮，正好演习武艺。特召你等，同往沙地，大合围场，较猎一番[7]。多少是好！
（众）谨遵将令。（净）就此跨马前去。（同众作上马
科）（净）

**【胡拨四犯】**紫缰轻挽，（合）双手把紫缰轻挽，骗上马[8]，
将盔缨低按。（行科）闪旗影云殷，没揣的动龙蛇[9]，一直的通霄
汉。按奇门布下了九连环[10]，觑定了**这小中原在眼，消不得俺众
路强蕃**。（众四面立，净指科）这一员身材慓悍，那一员结束牢
拴，这一员莽兀喇拳毛高鼻[11]，那一员恶支沙雕目胡颜[12]，这
一员会急进格邦的弓开月满，那一员会滴溜扑碌的锤落星寒，这
一员会咭吒克擦的枪风闪烁，那一员会悉力飒剌的剑雨澎滩，端
的是人如猛虎离山涧，显英雄天可汗[13]！（众行科）（合）振军
威，扑通通鼓鸣，惊魂破胆；排阵势，韵悠悠角声，人疾马闲。
抵多少雷轰电转，可正是海沸**也那河翻**。折末的铜作壁[14]，铁作
垒，有什么攻不破、攻不破也雄关！（净）这里地阔沙平，就
**此摆开围场，射猎一回者**。（净同番姬立高处，众排围射猎下）
（净）摆围场这间、这间，四下里来挤趱、挤趱。马蹄儿泼剌剌
旋风赳[15]，不住的把弓来紧弯，弦来急攀。一回呵滚沙场兔鹿儿
无头赶，都难动弹，就地里踠跧[16]。（众射鸟兽上）（净）把
鹰、犬放过去者。（众应，放鹰、犬科，跑下）（净）呀呀呀，
疾忙里一壁厢把**翅摩霄的玉爪腾空散[17]**，一壁厢把**足驾雾的金
獒逐路拦，雾时间兽积、兽积如山**。（众上献猎物科）禀王爷，
众将献杀[18]。（净）打的鸟兽，散给众军。就此高坡上，把人马
歇息片时。大家炙肉暖酒，番姬每歌的歌，舞的舞，洒落一回
者[19]。（众）得令。（同席地坐，番姬送净酒，众作拔刀割肉，
提背壶斟酒，大饮啖科）（番姬弹琵琶、浑不是[20]，众打太平鼓
板[21]）（合）斟起这酪浆儿，满满的浮金盏，满满的浮金盏。更
**把那连毛带血肉生餐，笑拥着番姬双颊丹，把琵琶忒楞楞弹也么**

弹，唱新声《菩萨蛮》[22]。（净起科）吃了一会，酒醉肉饱。天色已晚，诸将各回汛地[23]。须要整顿兵器，练习军马，听候将令便了。（众应科）得令。（作同上马吹海螺，侧帽、摆手绕场疾行科）听罢了令，疾翻身跃登锦鞍，侧着帽、摆手轻偎[24]。各自里回还，镇守定疆藩。摆搦些旗竿，装折着轮辘[25]，听候传番，施逞凶顽。天降摧残，地起波澜。把渔阳凝盼[26]，一飞羽箭，争赴兵坛，专等你个抱赤心的将军、将军来调拣。

（众下）（净）你看诸路番将，一个个人强马壮，眼见得俺的羽翼已成。（笑科）唐天子，唐天子，你怎当得也！

【煞尾】没照会，先去了那掣肘汉家官[27]；有机谋，暗添上这助臂番儿汉。等不的宴华清《霓裳》法曲终，早看俺闹鼓鼙渔阳骁将反。

六州番落从戎鞍[28]，　薛　逢　　战马闲嘶汉地宽。刘禹锡
倏忽抟风生羽翼，　　骆宾王　　山川龙战血漫漫。胡　曾

注 释 ——————————————————————

[1]何千年：与下文的崔乾祐、高秀岩都是安禄山部下的将官。东、西、南、北路用来概括安禄山的所有部将，并非真正官衔。史思明，突厥人，和安禄山是同乡，原来同是张守珪的部下。天宝十载，他已经做到平卢兵马使，次年兼北平太守，充卢龙军使，地位比何千年等人高。至德二载，安庆绪杀死父亲安禄山而自立。乾元二年，史思明又杀安庆绪而自立。《长生殿》剧情在安禄山被刺之后，不再写安庆绪、史思明、史朝义等人的继续叛乱。

[2]先把这四周围爪牙迭办：爪牙，指何千年等人；迭办，准备好，布置好。

[3]只因一向在朝：安禄山是节度使，一向在范阳。"只因一向在朝"，是《长生殿》对这个人物际遇的处理。

[4]叵（pǒ）耐：无奈，可恨。

[5]一概俱用番将：《资治通鉴》卷二一七天宝十四载条："二月，辛亥，安禄山使副将何千年入奏，请以蕃将三十二人代汉将。上命立进画（立刻送皇帝签字批准）。给告身（委任状）。"

[6]这嗒：这时，这会儿。

[7]较猎：角猎，比赛猎杀野兽。

[8]骗上马：疾跳上马。

[9]没揣的劲龙蛇：没揣的，无端，有"忽然"之意。龙蛇，指旗上的图案；下接"一直的通霄汉"，龙蛇又是安禄山野心的象征。

[10]按奇门布下了九连环：奇门，即奇门遁甲，古代一种神秘的术数。九连环，即九宫连环八卦阵。

[11]莽兀喇拳毛：兀喇，用来加强语气，无意义。拳毛，鬈发。

[12]恶支沙雕目胡颜：恶支沙，凶狠的；支沙，也用来加强语气，无意义。雕，猛禽。胡颜，胡人的脸相。

[13]显英雄天可汗：这里安禄山以天可汗自居。天可汗，唐代时外族尊称中国皇帝为天可汗。

[14]折末的：不管。

[15]趈（shàn）：跳跃。

[16]踠跧（wán quán）：屈伏。

[17]玉爪：指猎鹰。下文金獒（áo）指猎犬。

[18]献杀：献猎获物。

[19]洒落：不拘束。

[20]浑不是：乐器名，一作吴拨四。

[21]太平鼓板：可能是太平宴时奏的乐曲，因主要乐器鼓板而得名。

[22]《菩萨蛮》：唐代教坊曲调。

[23]汛地：军队驻防的地方。

[24]轻儇（xuān）：轻快。

[25]輴（fān）：车旁障泥板。

[26]把渔阳凝盼：静待安禄山的命令。渔阳即范阳，指范阳节度使安禄山。

[27]没照会，先去了那掣肘汉家官：没有了汉人官员的牵制，朝廷上就不知道己方的动静了。照会，对勘，有知道之意。

[28]六州番落：六州的番人部落。六州，伊州（今新疆维吾尔自治区哈密境）、梁州（凉州，今甘肃武威）、甘州（今甘肃张掖）、石州（今山西离石）、胡渭州、氐州（都在甘肃境内）；这里泛指安禄山所统辖的各部落。

# 第二出 夜 怨

【正宫 引子】【破齐阵】【破阵子头】（旦上）宠极难拚轻舍，欢浓分外生怜[1]。【齐天乐】比目游双，鸳鸯眠并，未许恩移情变。【破阵子尾】只恐行云随风引，争奈闲花竞日妍[2]，终朝心暗牵。

（清平乐）"卷帘不语，谁识愁千缕。生怕韶光无定主，暗里乱催春去。 心中刚自疑猜，那堪踪迹全乖。凤辇却归何处？凄凉日暮空阶。"奴家杨玉环，久邀圣眷，爱结君心。叵耐梅精江采苹，意不相下[3]。恰好触忤圣上，将他迁置楼东。但恐采苹巧计回天，皇上旧情未断，因此常自堤防。唉，江采苹，江采苹，非是我容你不得，只怕我容了你，你就容不得我也！今早圣上出朝，日色已暮，不见回宫，连着永新、念奴打听去了。此时情绪，好难消遣也！

【仙吕入双调】【风云会四朝元】【四朝元头】烧残香串，深宫欲暮天。把文窗频启，翠箔高卷，眼儿几望穿。但常时此际，但常时此际，【会河阳】定早驾到西宫，执手齐肩。【四朝元】花映房栊，春生颜面，【驻云飞】百种耽欢恋。嗏，今夕问何缘，【一江风】芳草黄昏，不见承回辇？（内作鹦哥叫"圣驾来也"介）（旦作惊看介）呀，圣上来了！（作看介）呸，原来是鹦哥弄巧言，把愁人故相骗。【四朝元尾】只落得徘徊伫立，思思想想画栏凭遍。

（老旦上）"闻道君王前殿宿，内家各自撤红灯[4]。"

（见介）启娘娘：万岁爷已宿在翠华西阁了。（旦呆介）有这等事！（泣介）

【前腔】君情何浅，不知人望悬！正晚妆慵卸，暗烛羞剪，待君来同笑言。向琼筵启处，向琼筵启处，醉月觞飞，梦雨床连。共命无分，同心不舛，怎蓦把人疏远！（老旦）万岁爷今夜偶不进宫，料非有意疏远，娘娘请勿伤怀！（旦）嗏，若不是情迁，便宿离宫，阿监何妨遣。我想圣上呵，从来未独眠，鸳衾厌孤展，怎得今宵枕畔，清清冷冷竟无人荐[5]！

（贴上）"雪隐鹭鸶飞始见，柳藏鹦鹉语方知。"（见介）娘娘，奴婢打听翠阁的事来了。（旦）怎么说？

（贴）娘娘听启，奴婢方才呵，【月临江】"悄向翠华西阁，守将时近黄昏[6]，忽闻密旨遣黄门[7]。"（旦）遣他何处去呢？（贴）"飞鞭乘戏马，灭烛召红裙。"（旦急问介）召那一个？（贴）"贬置楼东怨女，梅亭旧日妃嫔。"（旦惊介）呀，这是梅精了。他来也不曾？（贴）"须臾簇拥那佳人，暗中归翠阁。"（老旦问介）此话果真否？（贴）"消息探来真。"（旦）唉，天那，原来果是梅精复邀宠幸了。（做不语闷坐、掩泪介）（老旦、贴）娘娘请免愁烦。（旦）

【前腔】闻言惊颤，伤心痛怎言。（泪介）把从前密意，旧日恩眷，都付与泪花儿弹向天。记欢情始定，记欢情始定，愿似钗股成双，盒扇团圆。不道君心，霎时更变。总是奴当谴。嗏，也索把罪名宣。怎教冻蕊寒葩，暗识东风面[8]。可知道身虽在这边，心终系别院。一味虚情假意，瞒瞒昧昧只欺奴善。

（贴）娘娘还不知道，奴婢听得小黄门说，昨日万岁爷

在华萼楼上，私封珍珠一斛去赐他，他不肯受。回献一
诗，有"长门自是无梳洗，何必珍珠慰寂寥"之句，所
以致有今夜的事。（旦）哦，原来如此，我那里知道！

**【前腔】**他向楼东写怨，把珍珠暗里传。直恁的两情难割，不
由我寸心如剪。也非咱心太褊，只笑君王见错；笑君王见错，把
一个罪废残妆，认是金屋婵娟。可知我守拙鸾凰，斗不上争春莺
燕！（老旦）万岁爷既不忘情于他，娘娘何不迎合上意，力劝召
回。万岁爷必然欢喜，料他也不敢忘恩。（旦）唉，此语休提。
他自会把红丝缠[9]。嗏，何必我重牵。只怕没头兴的媒人[10]，反
惹他憎贱。你二人随我到翠阁去来。（贴）娘娘去怎的？（旦）
我到那里，看他如何逞媚妍，如何卖机变，**取次把君情鼓动**[11]，
颠颠倒倒暗中迷恋。

  （贴）奴婢想今夜翠阁之事，原怕娘娘知道。此时夜将
  三鼓，万岁爷必已安寝。娘娘猝然走去，恐有未便。
  不如且请安眠，到明日再作理会。（旦作不语，掩泪叹
  介）唉，罢罢，只今夜教我如何得睡也！

**【尾声】**他欢娱只怕催银箭[12]，我这里寂寥深院，只索背着灯
儿和衣将空被卷。

  紫禁迢迢宫漏鸣， 戴叔伦  碧天如水夜云生。 温庭筠
  泪痕不与君恩断， 刘 皂  斜倚薰笼坐到明[13]。白居易

## 注释

[1]分外：格外，特别。

[2]争奈：怎奈。

[3]意不相下：争持不下，不肯退让。

[4]闻道君王前殿宿，内家各自撤红灯：内家，指后、妃、宫嫔等，她们在自己门口点起红灯，准备接待皇帝。皇帝到某一个妃嫔那儿去了，其他人就把红灯收起来。

[5]荐：荐枕席，同寝。

[6]守将：等到。

[7]黄门：太监。

[8]怎教冻蕊寒葩，暗识东风面：冻蕊寒葩，即梅花，指梅妃；冻、寒，含有贬损她的意思。东风，喻唐明皇。

[9]红丝：喻爱情、姻缘。

[10]没头兴：即没兴头，倒运。

[11]取次：随便，轻易。

[12]催银箭：时间很快过去。银箭，银制的漏箭。

[13]薰笼：用来薰衣的炉子，外罩竹笼或铁笼。

## 第三出　絮　阁

（丑上）"自闭昭阳春复秋，罗衣湿尽泪还流。一种蛾眉明月夜[1]，南宫歌舞北宫愁。"咱家高力士，向年奉使闽粤，选得江妃进御，万岁爷十分宠幸。为他性爱梅花，赐号梅妃，宫中都称为梅娘娘。自从杨娘娘入侍之后，宠爱日夺，万岁爷竟将他迁置上阳宫东楼。昨夜忽然托疾，宿于翠华西阁，遣小黄门密召到来。戒饬宫人，不得传与杨娘娘知道。命咱在阁前看守，不许闲人擅进。此时天色黎明，恐要送梅娘娘回去，只索在此伺候咱。（虚下）（旦行上）

【北黄钟】【醉花阴】一夜无眠乱愁搅，未拔白潜踪来到[2]。往常见红日影弄花梢，软咍咍春睡难消，犹自压绣衾倒[3]。今日呵，可甚的凤枕急忙抛，单则是那筹儿撇不掉[4]。

（丑一面暗上望科）呀，远远来的，正是杨娘娘，莫非走漏了消息么？现今梅娘娘还在阁里，如何是好？（旦到科）（丑忙见科）奴婢高力士，叩见娘娘。（旦）万岁爷在那里？（丑）在阁中。（旦）还有何人在内？（丑）没有。（旦冷笑科）你开了阁门，待我进去看者。（丑慌科）娘娘且请暂坐。（旦坐科）（丑）奴婢启上娘娘，万岁爷昨日呵，

南【画眉序】只为政勤劳，偶尔违和厌烦扰。（旦）既是圣体违和，怎生在此驻宿？（丑）爱清幽西阁，暂息昏朝。（旦）在里面做什么？（丑）偃龙床静养神疲。（旦）你在此何事？

（丑）守玉户不容人到。（旦怒科）高力士，你待不容我进去么？（丑慌叩头科）娘娘息怒，只因亲奉君王命，量奴婢敢行违拗！

**北【喜迁莺】**（旦怒科）哌，休得把虚脾来掉[5]，嘴喳喳弄鬼妆幺。（丑）奴婢怎敢？（旦）焦也波焦，急的咱满心越恼。我晓得你今日呵，别有个人儿挂眼稍，倚着他宠势高，明欺我失恩人时衰运倒。（起科）也罢，我只得自把门敲。

　　（丑）娘娘请坐，待奴婢叫开门来。（做高叫科）杨娘娘来了，开了阁门者。（旦坐科）（生披衣引内侍上，听科）

**南【画眉序】**何事语声高，蓦忽将人梦惊觉。（丑又叫科）杨娘娘在此，快些开门。（内侍）启万岁爷，杨娘娘到了。（生作呆科）呀，这春光漏泄怎地开交？（内侍）这门还是开也不开？（生）慢着。（背科）且教梅妃在夹幕中，暂躲片时罢。（急下）（内侍笑科）哎，万岁爷，万岁爷，笑黄金屋怎样藏娇，怕葡萄架霎时推倒[6]。（生上作伏桌科）内侍，我着床傍枕伴推睡，你索把兽环开了[7]。

　　（内侍）领旨。（作开门科）（旦直入，见生科）妾闻陛下圣体违和，特来问安。（生）寡人偶然不快，未及进宫。何劳妃子清晨到此。（旦）陛下致疾之由，妾倒猜着几分了。（生笑科）妃子猜着何事来？（旦）

**北【出队子】**多则是相思萦绕，为着个意中人把心病挑。

（生笑科）寡人除了妃子，还有甚意中人？（旦）妾想陛下向来钟爱，无过梅精。何不宣召他来，以慰圣情牵挂。（生惊科）呀，此女久置楼东，岂有复召之理！（旦）只怕悄东君偷泄小梅梢，单只待望着梅来把渴消。（生）寡人那有此意。（旦）既不沙[8]，怎得那一斛珍珠去慰寂寥！

（生）妃子休得多心。寡人昨夜呵，

南【滴溜子】偶只为微疴，暂思静悄。恁兰心蕙性，慢多度料，把人无端冥落。（作欠伸科）我神虚懒应酬，相逢话言少。请暂返香车，图个睡饱。

  （旦作看科）呀，这御榻底下，不是一双凤舄么？（生急起，作欲掩科）在那里？（怀中掉出翠钿科）（旦拾看科）呀，又是一朵翠钿！此皆妇人之物，陛下既然独寝，怎得有此？（生作羞科）好奇怪！这是那里来的？连寡人也不解。（旦）陛下怎么不解？（丑作急态，一面背对内侍低科）呀，不好了，见了这翠钿、凤舄，杨娘娘必不干休。你每快送梅娘娘，悄从阁后破壁而出，回到楼东去罢。（内侍）晓得。（从生背后虚下）（旦）

北【刮地风】子这御榻森严宫禁遥[9]，早难道有神女飞度中宵。则问这两般信物何人掉？（作将舄、钿掷地，丑暗拾科）（旦）昨夜谁陪陛下寝来？可怎生般凤友鸾交，到日三竿犹不临朝？外人不知呵，都只说殢君王是我这庸姿劣貌。那知道恋欢娱别有个雨窟云巢！请陛下早出视朝，妾在此候驾回宫者。（生）寡人今日有疾，不能视朝。（旦）虽则是蝶梦余，鸾浪中，春情颠倒，困迷离精神难打熬，怎负他凤墀前鹄立群僚！

  （旦作向前背立科）（丑悄上与生耳语科）梅娘娘已去了，万岁爷请出朝罢。（生点头科）妃子劝寡人视朝，只索勉强出去。高力士，你在此送娘娘回宫者。（丑）领旨。（向内科）摆驾。（内应科）（生）"风流惹下风流苦，不是风流总不知。"（下）（旦坐科）高力士，你瞒着我做得好事！只问你这翠钿、凤舄，是那一个的？（丑）

南【滴滴金】告娘娘省可闲烦恼[10]。奴婢看万岁爷与娘娘呵，百纵千随真是少。今日这翠钿、凤舄，莫说是梅亭旧日恩情好，就是六宫中新窈窕，娘娘呵，也只合佯装不晓，直恁破工夫多计较！不是奴婢擅敢多口，如今满朝臣宰，谁没有个大妻小妾，何况九重，容不得这宵！

北【四门子】（旦）呀，这非是衾裯不许他人抱，道的咱量似斗筲[11]！只怪他明来夜去装圈套，故将人瞒的牢。（丑）万岁爷瞒着娘娘，也不过怕娘娘着恼，非有他意。（旦）把似怕我焦，则休将彼邀。却怎的劣云头只思别岫飘[12]。将他假做抛[13]，暗又招，转关儿心肠难料。

  （作掩泪坐科）（老旦上）清早起来，不见了娘娘，一定在这翠阁中，不免进去咱。（作进见旦科）呀，娘娘呵，

南【鲍老催】为何泪抛，无言独坐神暗消？（问丑科）高公公，是谁触着他情性娇？（丑低科）不要说起。（作暗出钿、舄与老旦看科）只为见了这两件东西，故此发恼。（老旦笑，低问科）如今那人呢？（丑）早已去了。（老旦）万岁爷呢？（丑）出去御朝了。永新姐，你来得甚好，可劝娘娘回宫去罢。（老旦）晓得了。（回向旦科）娘娘，你慢将眉黛蹙，啼痕渗，芳心恼。晨餐未进过清早，怎自将千金玉体轻伤了？请回宫去寻欢笑。

  （内）驾到。（旦起立科）（生上）"媚处娇何限，情深妒亦真。且将个中意，慰取眼前人。"寡人图得半夜欢娱，反受十分烦恼。欲待呵叱他一番，又恐他反道我偏爱梅妃，只索忍耐些罢。高力士，杨娘娘在那里？

  （丑）还在阁中。（老旦、丑暗下）（生作见旦，旦背立不语掩泣科）（生）呀，妃子，为何掩面不语？（旦不

应科，生笑科）妃子休要烦恼，朕和你到华萼楼上看花
去。（旦）

北【水仙子】问、问、问、问华萼娇，怕、怕、怕、怕不似楼
东花更好。有、有、有、有梅枝儿曾占先春，又、又、又、又何
用绿杨牵绕。（生）寡人一点真心，难道妃子还不晓得！（旦）
请、请、请、请真心向故交，免、免、免、免人怨为妾情薄。
（跪科）妾有下情，望陛下俯听。（生扶科）妃子有话，可起来
说。（旦泣科）妾自知无状，谬窃宠恩。若不早自引退，诚恐
谣诼日加，祸生不测，有累君德鲜终[14]，益增罪戾。今幸天眷犹
存，望赐斥放。陛下善视他人，勿以妾为念也。（泣拜科）拜、
拜、拜、拜辞了往日君恩天样高。（出钗、盒科）这钗、盒是陛
下定情时所赐，今日将来交还陛下。把、把、把、把深情密意从
头缴。（生）这是怎么说？（旦）省、省、省、省可自承旧赐福
难消。

（旦悲咽，生扶起科）妃子何出此言，朕和你两人呵，

南【双声子】情双好，情双好，纵百岁犹嫌少。怎说到，怎说
到，平白地分开了。总朕错，总朕错，请莫恼，请莫恼。（笑觑
旦科）见了你这颦眉泪眼，越样生娇。

妃子可将钗、盒依旧收好。既是不耐看花，朕和你到西
宫闲话去。（旦）陛下诚不弃妾，妾复何言。（袖钗、
盒，福生科）

北【尾煞】领取钗盒再收好，度芙蓉帐暖今宵，重把那定情时
心事表。

（生携旦并下）（丑复上）万岁爷同娘娘进宫去了。咱
如今且把这翠钿、凤舄，送还梅娘娘去。
柳色参差映翠楼，司马札　君王玉辇正淹留。钱　起

岂知妃后多娇妒，段成式　　恼乱东风卒未休。罗　隐

**注 释**

[1]一种：同样是。

[2]拔白：天色发白，天亮。

[3]倒：卧。

[4]那筹儿：那一件事。

[5]虚脾来掉：献假殷勤。

[6]葡萄架霎时推倒：倒了葡萄架，元代以来的曲文中用来指争风吃醋。

[7]兽环：门上的装饰，指代宫门。

[8]既不沙：不然，否则。

[9]子：只，不过。

[10]省可：免得，不要。

[11]斗筲（shāo）：斗、筲，两种不大的容器，形容气量小。

[12]却怎的劣云头，只思别岫飘：劣云头，喻唐明皇；别岫，指梅妃。

[13]他：指梅妃。

[14]鲜终：即鲜克有终，语出《诗经·大雅·荡》："靡不有初，鲜克有终。"鲜，少。意思是凡事都有个开头，但很少能到终了。这里指有始无终。

# 第四出 侦 报

（外引末扮中军，四杂执刀棍上）"出守岩疆典巨城，风闻边事实堪惊。不知忧国心多少，白发新添四五茎。"下官郭子仪，叨蒙圣恩，擢拜灵武太守。前在长安，见安禄山面有反相，知其包藏祸心。不想圣上命彼出镇范阳，分明纵虎归山。却又许易番将，一发添其牙爪。卜官自天德军升任以来，日夜担忧。此间灵武，乃是股肱重地，防守宜严。已遣精细哨卒，前往范阳采听去了。且待他来，便知分晓。

【双调】【夜行船】（小生扮探子，执小红旗上）两脚似星驰和电捷，把边情打听些些。急离燕山，早来灵武。（作进见外，一足跪叩科）向黄堂爆雷般唱一声高喏[1]。

（外）探子，你回来了么？（小生）我"肩挑令字小旗红，昼夜奔驰疾似风。探得边关多少事，从头来报主人公。"（外）分付掩门。（众掩门科，下）（外）探子，你探的安禄山军情怎地，兵势如何？近前来，细细说与我听者。（小生）爷爷听启，小哨一到了范阳镇上呵，

【乔木鱼】见枪刀似雪，密匝匝铁骑连营列。端的是号令如山把神鬼慑。那知有朝中天子尊，单逞他将军令阃外阵嗻[2]。

（外）那禄山在边关，近日作何勾当？（小生）

【庆宣和】他自请那番将更来把那汉将撤，四下里牙爪排设。每日价跃马弯弓斗驰猎，把兵威耀也耀也！

（外）还有什么举动波？（小生）

【落梅花】他贼行藏真难料[3]，歹心肠忒肆邪。诱诸番密相勾结，更私招四方亡命者，巢窟内尽藏凶孽。

（外惊科）呀，有这等事！难道朝廷之上，竟无人奏告么？（小生）闻得一月前，京中有人告称禄山反状，万岁爷暗遣中使，去到范阳，瞰其动静[4]。那禄山见了中使呵，

【风入松】十分的小心礼貌假妆呆，尽金钱遍布盖奸邪。把一个中官哄骗的满心悦，来回奏把逆迹全遮。因此万岁爷愈信不疑，反把告叛的人，送到禄山军前治罪。一任他横行傲桀，有谁人敢再弄唇舌！

（外叹介）如此怎生是了也！（小生）前日杨丞相又上一本，说禄山叛迹昭然，请皇上亟加诛戮。那禄山见了此本呵，

【拨不断】也不免脚儿跌，口儿嗟，意儿中忐忑心儿里怯。不想圣旨倒说禄山诚实，丞相不必生疑。他一闻此信，便就呵呵大笑，骂这谗臣奈我耶，咬牙根誓将君侧权奸灭，怒轰轰急待把此仇来雪。

（外）呀，他要诛君侧之奸，非反而何？且住，杨相这本怎么不见邸抄[5]？（小生）此是密本，原不发抄。只因杨丞相要激禄山速反[6]，特着塘报抄送去的[7]。（外怒科）唉，外有逆藩，内有奸相，好教人发指也！（小生）小哨还打听的禄山近有献马一事，更利害哩！

【离亭宴带歇拍煞】他本待逞豺狼魆地里思抄窃[8]。巧借着献骅骝乘势去行强劫。（外）怎么献马？可明白说来者。（小生）他遣何千年赍表，奏称献马三千匹，每马一匹，有甲士

二人，又有二人御马，一人刍牧，共三五一万五千人，护送入京。一路里兵强马劣，闹汹汹怎提防！乱纷纷难镇压，急攘攘谁拦截。生兵入帝畿，野马临城阙，怕不把长安来闹者。（外惊科）唉，罢了，此计若行，西京危矣[9]。（小生）这本方才进去，尚未取旨[10]。只是禄山呵，他明把至尊欺，狡将奸计使，险备机关设。马蹄儿纵不行，狼性子终难帖。逗的鼙鼓向渔阳动也[11]，爷爷呵，莫待传白羽始安排[12]。小哨呵，准备闪红旗再报捷。

（外）知道了。赏你一坛酒，一腔羊，五十两花银，免一月打差。去罢。（小生叩头科）谢爷。（外）叫左右，开门。（众应上，作开门科）（小生下）（外）中军官。（末应介）（外）传令众军士，明日教场操演，准备酒席犒赏。（末）领钧旨。（先下）

（外）数骑渔阳探使回，　杜　牧
　　　威雄八阵役风雷。刘禹锡
　　　胸中别有安边计，曹　唐
　　　军令分明数举杯。杜　甫

## 注 释

[1]黄堂：太守。

[2]将军令阃（kǔn）外咔嗻（chē zhè）：阃，郭门门槛。都城之外都是将军所管，用来形容其威权之大。咔嗻，厉害，了不起。

[3]行藏：动静，行为。

[4]万岁爷暗遣中使，去到范阳，瞰其动静：天宝十四载二月，宰相韦见素、杨国忠奏告安禄山有反叛的阴谋。唐玄宗派中使辅璆琳以赐安禄山柑子为名，前去察看动静。璆琳受贿赂，竭力为安禄辩解，玄宗遂对安禄山更加信任不疑。

[5]邸抄：邸，唐代藩镇在京师的留守处。邸中抄诏、令、奏章等文件传送给藩镇，这种抄件叫邸抄或邸报。

[6]杨丞相要激禄山速反：《资治通鉴》天宝十四载十月条："杨国忠与禄山不相悦，屡言禄山且反，上不听。国忠数以事激之，欲其速反，以取信于上。"

[7]塘报：驿报。塘，古代官设的通信站。

[8]魆地里思抄窃：企图暗中偷袭。魆地里，暗地里。抄窃，绕道袭击。

[9]西京：唐以洛阳为东都，京师长安也称西京。

[10]这本方才进去，尚未取旨：《资治通鉴》天宝十四载七月条："禄山表献马三千匹，每匹执控夫二人，遣蕃将二十二人部送。河南尹达奚珣疑有变，奏请谕禄山，以进车马宜俟至冬，官自给夫，无烦本军。于是上稍悟，始有疑禄山之意。"

[11]逗的：到，等到。

[12]白羽：羽檄，古代征调军队的文书。

# 第五出 窥 浴

【仙吕入双调】【字字双】（丑扮宫女上）自小生来貌天然，花面；宫娥队里我为先，扫殿。忽逢小监在阶前，胡缠；伸手摸他裤儿边，不见。

> "我做宫娥第一，标致无人能及。腮边花粉糊涂，嘴上胭脂狼藉。秋波俏似铜铃，弓眉弯得笔直。春纤十个擂槌，玉体浑身糙漆。柳腰松段十围，莲瓣滩船半只。杨娘娘爱我伶俐，选做《霓裳》部色。只因喉咙太响，歌时嘴边起个霹雳。身子又太狼伉[1]，舞去冲翻了御筵桌席。皇帝见了发恼，打落子弟名籍[2]。登时发到骊山，派到温泉殿中承值。昨日銮舆临幸，同杨娘娘在华清驻跸。传旨要来共浴汤池[3]，只索打扫铺陈收拾。"道犹未了，那边一个宫人来也。

【雁儿舞】（副净扮宫女上）担阁青春[4]，后宫怨女，漫趺脚捶胸，有谁知苦。拚着一世没有丈夫，做一只孤飞雁儿舞。

（见介）（丑）姐姐，你说什么"雁儿"舞！如今万岁爷，有了杨娘娘的《霓裳》舞，连梅娘娘的《惊鸿》舞，也都不爱了。（副净）便是。我原是梅娘娘的宫人。只为我娘娘，自翠阁中忍气回来，一病而亡，如今将我拨到这里。（丑）原来如此，杨娘娘十分妒忌，我每再休想有承幸之日。（副净）罢了。（丑）万岁爷将次到来[5]，我和你且到外厢伺候去。（虚下）（末、小

283

生扮内侍，引生、旦、老旦、贴随行上）

**【羽调 近词】【四季花】**别殿景幽奇：看雕梁畔，珠帘外，雨卷云飞。逶迤，朱阑几曲环画溪，修廊数层接翠微。绕红墙，通玉扉。（末、小生）启万岁爷，到温泉殿了。（生）内侍回避。（末、小生应下）（生）妃子，你看清渠屈注，洄澜皱漪，香泉柔滑宜素肌。朕同妃子试浴去来。（老、贴与生、旦脱去大衣介）（生）妃子，只见你款解云衣[6]，早现出珠辉玉丽，不由我对你爱你，扶你觑你怜你！

（生携旦同下）（老旦）念奴姐，你看万岁爷与娘娘恁般恩爱，真令人羡杀也。（贴）便是。（老旦）

**【凤钗花络索】【金凤钗】**花朝拥，月夜偎，尝尽温柔滋味。**【胜如花】**（贴合）镇相连似影追形，分不开如刀划水。**【醉扶归】**千般捆纵百般随[7]，两人合一副肠和胃。**【梧叶儿】**密意口难提，写不迭鸳鸯帐[8]，绸缪无尽期。（老旦）姐姐，我与你伏侍娘娘多年，虽睹娇容，未窥玉体。今日试从绮疏隙处，偷觑一觑何如？（贴）恰好，（同作向内窥介）**【水红花】**（合）悄偷窥，亭亭玉体，宛似浮波菡萏，含露弄娇辉。**【浣溪纱】**轻盈臂腕消香腻，绰约腰身漾碧漪。**【望吾乡】**（老旦）明霞骨，沁雪肌。**【大胜乐】**（贴）一痕酥透双蓓蕾，（老旦）半点春藏小麝脐。**【傍妆台】**（贴）爱杀红巾韈，私处露微微。永新姐，你看万岁爷呵，**【解三酲】**凝睛睇，**【八声甘州】**恁孜孜含笑浑似呆痴。**【一封书】**（合）休说俺偷眼宫娥魂欲化，则他个见惯的君王也不自持。**【皂罗袍】**（老旦）恨不把春泉翻竭，（贴）恨不把玉山洗颒[9]，（老旦）不住的香肩呜喝[10]，（贴）不住的纤腰抱围，**【黄莺儿】**（老旦）俺娘娘无言匿笑含情对。（贴）意怡怡，**【月儿高】**灵液春风，澹荡恍如醉。**【排歌】**（老旦）波光暖，日影晖，一双龙戏出平池。**【桂枝香】**（合）

险把个襄王渴倒阳台下，恰便似神女携将暮雨归[11]。

> （丑、副净暗上笑介）两位姐姐，看得高兴啊，也等我
> 每看看。（老旦、贴）姐姐，我每伺候娘娘洗浴，有甚
> 高兴。（丑、副净笑介）只怕不是伺候娘娘，还在那里
> 偷看万岁爷哩。（老旦、贴）啐，休得胡说，万岁爷同
> 娘娘出来也。（丑、副净暗下）（生同旦上）

【二犯掉角儿】【掉角儿】出温泉新凉透体，睹玉容愈增光
丽。最堪怜残妆乱头，翠痕干晚云生腻[12]。（老旦、贴与生、旦
穿衣介）（旦作娇软态，老旦、贴扶介）（生）妃子，看你似柳
含风，花怯露。软难支，娇无力，俏人扶起。（二内侍引杂推小
车上）请万岁爷、娘娘上如意小车，回华清宫去。（生）将车儿
后面随着。（二内侍）领旨。（生携旦行介）妃子，【排歌】朕
和你肩相并，手共携，不须花底小车催，【东瓯令】趁扑面好风
归。

【尾声】（合）意中人，人中意。则那些无情花鸟也情痴，
一般的解结双头学并栖。

> （生）花气浑如百和香，杜　甫
> （旦）避风新出浴盆汤。王　建
> （生）侍儿扶起娇无力，白居易
> （旦）笑倚东窗白玉床。李　白

## 注 释

[1]狼伉：粗大，笨拙。

[2]子弟：这里指教坊子弟。

[3]汤池：指骊山温泉。

[4]担阁：即耽搁，耽误。

[5]将次：快要。

[6]款：慢慢地。

[7]捆纵：迁就、放任之意。

[8]写不迭：形容不尽。

[9]玉山洗颏：形容洗浴困倦。

[10]呜嗻（zuō）：吻。

[11]险把个襄王渴倒阳台下，恰便似神女携将暮雨归：襄王，楚襄王。
    襄王和神女指恋爱中的男女，云雨、阳台指男女欢会。

[12]晚云：指头发。

# 第六出 密 誓

【越调 引子】【浪淘沙】（贴扮织女，引二仙女上）云护玉梭儿，巧织机丝。天宫原不着相思，报道今宵逢七夕，忽忆年时[1]。

> 【鹊桥仙】"纤云弄巧，飞星传信，银汉秋光暗度。金风玉露一相逢，便胜却人间无数。柔肠似水，佳期如梦，遥指鹊桥前路。两情若是久长时，又岂在朝朝暮暮[2]。"吾乃织女是也。蒙上帝玉敕，与牛郎结为天上夫妇。年年七夕，渡河相见。今乃下界天宝十载[3]，七月七夕。你看明河无浪，乌鹊将填，不免暂撤机丝，整妆而待。（内细乐扮乌鹊上，绕场飞介）（前场设一桥，乌鹊飞止桥两边介）（二仙女）鹊桥已驾，请娘娘渡河。（贴起行介）

【越调 过曲】【山桃红】【下山虎头】俺这里乍抛锦字，暂驾香辎[4]。（合）趁碧落无云滓，新凉暮飔，（作上桥介）踹上这桥影参差，俯映着河光净沚。【小桃红】更喜杀新月纤，华露滋，低绕着乌鹊双飞翅也，【下山虎尾】陡觉的银汉秋生别样姿。（做过桥介）（二仙女）启娘娘，已渡过河来了。（贴）星河之下，隐隐望见香烟一簇，摇扬腾空，却是何处？（仙女）是唐天子的贵妃杨玉环，在宫中乞巧哩。（贴）生受他一片诚心[5]，不免同了牛郎，到彼一看。（合）天上留佳会，年年在斯，却笑他人世情缘顷刻时。（齐下）

【商调 过曲】【二郎神】（二内侍挑灯，引生上）秋光静，碧沉沉轻烟送暝。雨过梧桐微做冷，银河宛转，纤云点缀双星。（内作笑声，生听介）顺着风儿还细听，欢笑隔花阴树影。内侍，是那里这般笑语？（内侍问介）万岁爷问，那里这般笑语？（内）是杨娘娘到长生殿去乞巧哩。（内侍回介[6]）杨娘娘到长生殿去乞巧，故此笑语。（生）内侍每不要传报，待朕悄悄前去。撤红灯，待悄向龙墀觑个分明。（虚下）

【前腔】（换头）（旦引老旦、贴同二宫女各捧香盒、纨扇、瓶花、化生金盆上[7]）宫庭，金炉篆霭，烛光掩映。米大蜘蛛厮抱定[8]，金盘种豆[9]，花枝招飐银瓶[10]。（老旦、贴）已到长生殿中，巧筵齐备，请娘娘拈香。（作将瓶花、化生盆设桌上，老旦捧香盒，旦拈香介）妾身杨玉环，虔爇心香，拜告双星，伏祈鉴祐。愿钗盒情缘长久订，（拜介）莫使做秋风扇冷。（生潜上窥介）觑娉婷，只见他拜倒在瑶阶暗祝声声。

（老旦、贴作见生介）呀，万岁爷到了。（旦急转，拜生介）（生扶起介）妃子在此，作何勾当？（旦）今乃七夕之期，陈设瓜果，特向天孙乞巧。（生笑介）妃子巧夺天工，何须更乞。（旦）惶愧。（生、旦各坐介）

（老旦、贴同二宫女暗下）（生）妃子，朕想牵牛、织女隔断银河，一年才会得一度，这相思真非容易也。

【集贤宾】秋空夜永碧汉清，甫灵驾逢迎[11]，奈天赐佳期刚半顷，耳边厢容易鸡鸣。云寒露冷，又趱上经年孤另[12]。（旦）陛下言及双星别恨，使妾凄然。只可惜人间不知天上的事。如打听，决为了相思成病。

（做泪介）（生）呀，妃子为何掉下泪来？（旦）妾想牛郎织女，虽则一年一见，却是地久天长。只恐陛下与妾的恩情，不能够似他长远。（生）妃子说那里话！

【黄莺儿】仙偶纵长生，论尘缘也不恁争[13]。百年好占风流胜，逢时对景，增欢助情，怪伊底事反悲哽？（移坐近旦低介）问双星，朝朝暮暮，争似我和卿！

  （旦）臣妾受恩深重，今夜有句话儿……（住介）

  （生）妃子有话，但说不妨。（旦对生呜咽介）妾蒙陛下宠眷，六宫无比。只怕日久恩疏，不免白头之叹[14]！

【莺簇一金罗】【黄莺儿】提起便心疼，念寒微侍掖庭，更衣傍辇多荣幸。【簇御林】瞬息间，怕花老春无剩，【一封书】宠难凭。（牵生衣泣介）论恩情，【金凤钗】若得一个久长时死也应，若得一个到头时死也暝。【皂罗袍】抵多少平阳歌舞，恩移爱更[15]；长门孤寂，魂销泪零：断肠枉泣红颜命！

  （生举袖与旦拭泪介）妃子，休要伤感。朕与你的恩情，岂是等闲可比。

【簇御林】休心虑，免泪零，怕移时，有变更。（执旦手介）做酥儿拌蜜胶粘定，总不离须臾顷。（合）话绵藤，花迷月暗，分不得影和形。

  （旦）既蒙陛下如此情浓，趁此双星之下，乞赐盟约，以坚终始。（生）朕和你焚香设誓去。（携旦行介）

【琥珀猫儿坠】（合）香肩斜靠，携手下阶行。一片明河当殿横，（旦）罗衣陡觉夜凉生。（生）惟应，和你悄语低言，海誓山盟。

  （生上香揖同旦福介）双星在上，我李隆基与杨玉环，（旦合）情重恩深，愿世世生生，共为夫妇，永不相离。有渝此盟[16]，双星鉴之。（生又揖介）在天愿为比翼鸟，（旦拜介）在地愿为连理枝。（合）天长地久有时尽，此誓绵绵无绝期。（旦拜谢生介）深感陛下情

重，今夕之盟，妾死生守之矣。（生携旦介）

【尾声】长生殿里盟私订。（旦）问今夜有谁折证[17]？（生指介）是这银汉桥边双双牛女星。（同下）

【越调 过曲】【山桃红】（小生扮牵牛，云巾、仙衣，同贴引仙女上）只见他誓盟密矢[18]，拜祷孜孜，两下情无二，口同一辞。（小生）天孙，你看唐天子与杨玉环，好不恩爱也！悄相偎倚着香肩，没些缝儿。我与你既缔天上良缘，当作情场管领[19]。况他又向我等设盟，须索与他保护。见了他恋比翼，慕并枝，愿生生世世情真至也，合令他长作人间风月司[20]。（贴）只是他两人劫难将至，免不得生离死别。若果后来不背今盟，决当为之绾合。（小生）天孙言之有理。你看夜色将阑，且回斗牛宫去。（携贴行介）（合）天上留佳会，年年在斯，却笑他人世情缘顷刻时！

何用人间岁月催，罗　邺　星桥横过鹊飞回。李商隐

莫言天上稀相见，李　郢　没得心情送巧来。罗　隐

注 释

[1]年时：从前。

[2]"纤云弄巧"以下：宋秦观《鹊桥仙》词，根据剧情需要有所改动。

[3]天宝十载：以史实论，这个时间是不对的。之前《合围》、《侦报》中所提到的事件，大都发生在天宝十四载，下一出《陷关》之事则发生在天宝十五载。

[4]香辀：香车。

[5]生受：原有为难的意思。这里"生受他"作"亏得他"解，含有赞许之意。

[6]回：回复。

[7]化生金盆：唐俗，七月七日，妇女以蜡做的婴儿放在水中，用以求子。

[8]米大蜘蛛厮抱定：七月七日，把蟢子（蜘蛛）捉在小盒子里，第二天早上看蛛网多少。多的，乞来的巧就多些，这叫乞巧。厮，相；抱定，捉住。

[9]金盘种豆：以绿豆、小豆、小麦浸在盆内，芽长三、四寸时，再用彩色丝线绕起来，叫"种生"。

[10]招飐：招展。

[11]甫：刚才。

[12]趱上：赶上。

[13]仙偶纵长生，论尘缘也不恁争：仙偶，指牛郎织女。尘缘，指明皇和贵妃的爱情。不恁争，差不了多少。

[14]白头之叹：相传汉代辞赋家司马相如想娶妾，妻子卓文君写了《白头吟》，感叹夫妻之情不能始终如一。

[15]抵多少平阳歌舞，恩移爱更：抵多少，胜过。汉武帝的皇后卫子夫，原是平阳公主的歌女，得武帝宠爱，封皇后。后色衰爱弛，失宠。

[16]渝：改变，违背。

[17]折证：作证。

[18]矢：发誓。

[19]情场管领：管领爱情的神。

[20]风月司：管理风月（恋爱）的人。

第五本

# 第一出 陷 关[1]

【越调 引子】【杏花天】（净领二番将，四军执旗上）狼贪虎视威风大，镇渔阳兵雄将多。待长驱直把殽函破[2]，奏凯日齐声唱歌。

咱家安禄山，自出镇以来，结连塞上诸蕃，招纳天下亡命，精兵百万[3]，大事可举。只因唐天子待我不薄，思量等他身后方才起兵。叵耐杨国忠那厮，屡次说我反形大著，请皇上急加诛戮。天子虽然不听，只是咱在边关，他在朝内，若不早图，终恐遭其暗算。因此假造敕书，说奉密旨，召俺领兵入朝诛戮国忠。乘机打破西京，夺取唐室江山，可不遂了我平生大愿！今乃黄道吉日，蕃将每，就此起兵前去[4]。（众）得令。（发号行介）（净）

【越调 过曲】【豹子令】只为奸臣酿大祸，（众）酿大祸，（净）致令边镇起干戈，（众）起干戈。（合）逢城攻打逢人剁，尸横遍野血流河，烧家劫舍抢娇娥。（喊杀下）

【水底鱼】（丑白须扮哥舒老将引二卒上[5]）年纪无多，刚刚八十过。渔阳兵至，认咱这老哥。自家老将哥舒翰是也，把守潼关。不料安禄山造反，杀奔前来，决意闭关死守。争奈监军内侍，立逼出战。势不由己，军士每，与我并力杀上前去。（卒）得令。（行介）（净领众杀上）（丑迎杀大战介）（净众擒丑绑介）（净）拿这老东西过来。我今饶你老命，快快献关降顺。

（丑）事已至此，只得投降。（众推丑下）（净）且喜潼关已得，势如破竹，大小三军，就此杀奔西京便了。（众应，呐喊行介）跃马挥戈，精兵百万多。靴尖略动，踏残山与河，踏残山与河。

　　平旦交锋晚未休，王　道　　动天金鼓逼神州。韩　偓

　　潼关一败番儿喜，司空图　　倒把金鞭上酒楼。薛　逢

注释 ————————————————————

[1]天宝十四载十一月，安禄山在范阳起兵，次年六月初八攻破潼关。

[2]殽函：即函谷关，在潼关东面。安禄山要攻占长安，函谷关是必经之地。

[3]精兵百万：安禄山起兵时有十五万军队，号称二十万。

[4]以上这一段自述，和正史的有关记载基本相符。

[5]哥舒老将：指哥舒翰，原任河西、陇右两镇节度使。

## 第二出 惊 变

（丑上）"玉楼天半起笙歌，风送宫嫔笑语和。月殿影开闻夜漏，水晶帘卷近秋河。"咱家高力士，奉万岁爷之命，着咱在御花园中安排小宴，要与贵妃娘娘同来游赏，只得在此伺候。（生、旦乘辇，老旦、贴随后，二内侍引，行上）

【北中吕】【粉蝶儿】天淡云闲，列长空数行新雁。御园中秋色斓斑：柳添黄，蘋减绿，红莲脱瓣。一抹雕阑，喷清香桂花初绽。

（到介）（丑）请万岁爷娘娘下辇。（生、旦下辇介）

（丑同内侍暗下）（生）妃子，朕与你散步一回者。

（旦）陛下请。（生携旦手介）（旦）

南【泣颜回】携手向花间，暂把幽怀同散。凉生亭下，风荷映水翩翻。爱桐阴静悄，碧沉沉并绕回廊看。恋香巢秋燕依人，睡银塘鸳鸯蘸眼[1]。

（生）高力士，将酒过来，朕与娘娘小饮数杯。（丑）宴已排在亭上，请万岁爷娘娘上宴。（旦作把盏，生止住介）妃子坐了。

北【石榴花】不劳你玉纤纤高捧礼仪烦，子待借小饮对眉山[2]。俺与你浅斟低唱互更番，三杯两盏，遣兴消闲。妃子，今日虽是小宴，倒也清雅。回避了御厨中，回避了御厨中烹龙炮凤堆盘案，咿咿哑哑乐声催趱。只几味脆生生，只几味脆生生蔬和果清肴馔，雅称你仙肌玉骨美人餐[3]。

妃子，朕与你清游小饮，那些梨园旧曲，都不耐烦听
他。记得那年在沉香亭上赏牡丹，召翰林李白草《清平
调》三章，令李龟年度成新谱，其词甚佳。不知妃子
还记得么？（旦）妾还记得。（生）妃子可为朕歌之，
朕当亲倚玉笛以和。（旦）领旨。（老旦进玉笛，生吹
介）（旦按板介）

**南【泣颜回】** 花繁，秾艳想容颜。云想衣裳光璨。新妆谁似，
可怜飞燕娇懒。名花国色，笑微微常得君王看。向春风解释春
愁，沉香亭同倚阑干。

　　（生）妙哉，李白锦心，妃子绣口，真双绝矣。宫娥，
　　取巨觞来，朕与妃子对饮。（老旦、贴送酒介）（生）

**北【斗鹌鹑】** 畅好是喜孜孜驻拍停歌，喜孜孜驻拍停歌，笑
吟吟传杯送盏。妃子干一杯，（作照干介）不须他絮烦烦射覆
藏钩[4]，闹纷纷弹丝弄板。（又作照杯介）妃子，再干一杯。
（旦）妾不能饮了。（生）宫娥每，跪劝。（老旦、贴）领旨。
（跪旦介）娘娘，请上这一杯。（旦勉饮介）（老旦、贴作连劝
介）（生）我这里无语持觞仔细看，早子见花一朵上腮间。（旦
作醉介）妾真醉矣。（生）一会价软咍咍柳軃花欹[5]，软咍咍柳
軃花欹，困腾腾莺娇燕懒。

　　妃子醉了，宫娥每，扶娘娘上辇进宫去者。（老旦、
　　贴）领旨。（作扶旦起介）（旦作醉态呼介）万岁！（老
　　旦、贴扶旦行）（旦作醉态介）

**南【扑灯蛾】** 态恹恹轻云软四肢，影濛濛空花乱双眼，娇怯怯
柳腰扶难起，困沉沉强抬娇腕，软设设金莲倒褪，乱松松香肩軃
云鬟，美甘甘思寻凤枕，步迟迟，倩宫娥搀入绣帏间。

　　（老旦、贴扶旦下）（丑同内侍暗上）（内击鼓介）（生
　　惊介）何处鼓声骤发？（副净急上）"渔阳鼙鼓动地

来，惊破霓裳羽衣曲。"（问丑介）万岁爷在那里？
（丑）在御花园内。（副净）军情紧急，不免径入。
（进见介）陛下，不好了。安禄山起兵造反，杀过潼
关，不日就到长安了。（生大惊介）守关将士何在？
（副净）哥舒翰兵败，已降贼了。（生）

北【上小楼】呀，你道失机的哥舒翰……称兵的安禄山，赤紧
的离了渔阳，陷了东京，破了潼关。唬得人胆战心摇，唬得人胆
战心摇，肠慌腹热，魂飞魄散，早惊破月明花粲。

卿有何策，可退贼兵？（副净）当日臣曾再三启奏，禄
山必反，陛下不听，今日果应臣言。事起仓卒，怎生
抵敌？不若权时幸蜀，以待天下勤王[6]。（生）依卿所
奏。快传旨，诸王百官，即时随驾幸蜀便了。（副净）
领旨。（急下）（生）高力士，快些整备军马。传旨令
右龙武将军陈元礼，统领羽林军士三千，扈驾前行[7]。
（丑）领旨。（下）（内侍）请万岁爷回宫。（生转行叹
介）唉，正尔欢娱，不想忽有此变，怎生是了也！

南【扑灯蛾】稳稳的宫庭宴安，扰扰的边廷造反。冬冬的鼙鼓
喧，腾腾的烽火飐。的溜扑碌臣民儿逃散，黑漫漫乾坤覆翻，硃
磕磕社稷摧残[8]，硃磕磕社稷摧残。当不得萧萧飒飒西风送晚，
黯黯的，一轮落日冷长安。

（向内问介）宫娥每，杨娘娘可曾安寝？（老旦、贴内
应介）已睡熟了。（生）不要惊他，且待明早五鼓同
行。（泣介）天那，寡人不幸，遭此播迁，累他玉貌花
容，驱驰道路。好不痛心也！

南【尾声】在深宫兀自娇慵惯，怎样支吾蜀道难！（哭介）我
那妃子啊，愁杀你玉软花柔要将途路趱。

宫殿参差落照间，　　卢　纶
渔阳烽火照函关。　　吴　融
遏云声绝悲风起[9]，　胡　曾
何处黄云是陇山[10]。武元衡

## 注 释

[1]蘸（zhàn）眼：耀眼，引人注目。

[2]子待借小饮对眉山：子待，只待、只要。眉山，眉毛，与前句"玉纤
纤高捧"，暗用"举案齐眉"的典故。

[3]雅：甚。

[4]射覆藏钩：射覆，类似猜（射）字谜的一种酒令；藏钩，猜东西藏在
谁那儿的一种游戏。

[5]一会价软咍咍柳軃花敧：一会价，一会儿。软咍（hāi）咍，软绵绵
的。軃（duǒ），垂下。柳、花和下句的莺、燕都用来比喻杨贵妃。

[6]勤王：起兵援救危难中的朝廷。

[7]扈驾：随驾。

[8]碜磕（cǎn kē）磕：悲惨、惨痛之意。或作碜可可。磕磕，无意义。
碜，惨的同音异写。

[9]遏（è）云：停住了行云。形容音乐的美妙。

[10]何处黄云是陇山：陇山在陕西、甘肃一带，由长安往成都，经陇山
东麓而南行。

# 第三出 埋 玉

**【南吕 过曲】【金钱花】**（末扮陈元礼引军士上）拥旄仗钺前驱[1]，前驱；羽林拥卫銮舆，銮舆。匆匆避贼就征途。人跋涉，路崎岖。知何日，到成都。

> 下官右龙武将军陈元礼是也。因禄山造反，破了潼关。圣上避兵幸蜀，命俺统领禁军扈驾。行了一程，早到马嵬驿了。（内鼓噪介）（末）众军为何呐喊？（内）禄山造反，圣驾播迁，都是杨国忠弄权，激成变乱。若不斩此贼臣，我等死不扈驾。（末）众军不必鼓噪，暂且安营。待我奏过圣上，自有定夺[2]。（内应介）（末引军重唱"人跋涉"四句下）（生同旦骑马，引老旦、贴、丑行上）

**【中吕 过曲】【粉孩儿】**匆匆的弃宫闱珠泪洒，叹清清冷冷半张銮驾，望成都直在天一涯。渐行来渐远京华[3]，五六搭剩水残山，两三间空舍崩瓦。

> （丑）来此已是马嵬驿了，请万岁爷暂住銮驾。（生、旦下马，作进坐介）（生）寡人不道，误宠逆臣，致此播迁，悔之无及。妃子，只是累你劳顿，如之奈何！
> （旦）臣妾自应随驾，焉敢辞劳。只愿早早破贼，大驾还都便好。（内又喊介）杨国忠专权误国，今又交通吐蕃，我等誓不与此贼俱生。要杀杨国忠的，快随我等前去。（杂扮四军提刀赶副净上，绕场奔介）（军作杀副净，呐喊下）（生惊介）高力士，外面为何喧嚷？快宣

陈元礼进来。（丑）领旨。（宣介）（末上见介）臣陈
元礼见驾。（生）众军为何呐喊？（末）臣启陛下：杨
国忠专权召乱，又与吐蕃私通。激怒六军，竟将国忠杀
死了。（生作惊介）呀，有这等事。（旦作背掩泪介）
（生沉吟介）这也罢了，传旨起驾。（末出传旨介）圣
旨道来，赦汝等擅杀之罪。作速起行。（内又喊介）国
忠虽诛，贵妃尚在。不杀贵妃，誓不扈驾。（末见生
介）众军道，国忠虽诛，贵妃尚在，不肯起行。望陛下
割恩正法。（生作大惊介）哎呀，这话如何说起！（旦
慌牵生衣介）（生）将军，

【红芍药】国忠纵有罪当加，现如今已被劫杀。妃子在深宫自
随驾，有何干六军疑讶。（末）圣谕极明，只是军心已变，如
之奈何！（生）卿家，作速晓谕他，怎狂言没些高下。（内又喊
介）（末）陛下呵，听军中怎地喧哗，教微臣怎生弹压！

　　（旦哭介）陛下啊，

【耍孩儿】事出非常堪惊诧。已痛兄遭戮，奈臣妾又受波查[4]。
是前生，事已定薄命应折罚。望吾皇急切抛奴罢，只一句伤心
话……

　　（生）妃子且自消停。（内又喊介）不杀贵妃，死不扈
驾。（末）臣启陛下：贵妃虽则无罪，国忠实其亲兄，
今在陛下左右，军心不安。若军心安，则陛下安矣。愿
乞三思。（生沉吟介）

【会河阳】无语沉吟，意如乱麻。（旦牵生衣哭介）痛生生
怎地舍官家[5]！（合）可怜，一对鸳鸯，风吹浪打，直恁的遭强
霸！（内又喊介）（旦哭介）众军，逼得我心惊唬，（生作呆
想，忽抱旦哭介）贵妃，好教我难禁架[6]！

（众军呐喊上，绕场、围驿下）（丑）万岁爷，外厢军士已把驿亭围了。若再迟延，恐有他变，怎么处？（生）陈元礼，你快去安抚三军，朕自有道理！（末）领旨。

（下）（生、旦抱哭介）（旦）

**【缕缕金】**魂飞颤，泪交加。（生）堂堂天子贵，不及莫愁家[7]。（合哭介）难道把恩和义，霎时抛下！（旦跪介）臣妾受皇上深恩，杀身难报。今事势危急，望赐自尽，以定军心。陛下得安稳至蜀，妾虽死犹生也。算将来无计解军哗，残生愿甘罢，残生愿甘罢！

（哭倒生怀介）（生）妃子说那里话！你若捐生，朕虽有九重之尊，四海之富，要他则甚！宁可国破家亡，决不肯抛舍你也！

**【摊破地锦花】**任谳哗，我一谜妆聋哑，总是朕差。现放着一朵娇花，怎忍见风雨摧残，断送天涯。若是再禁加[8]，拼代你陨黄沙。

（旦）陛下虽则恩深，但事已至此，无路求生。若再留恋，倘玉石俱焚，益增妾罪。望陛下舍妾之身，以保宗社[9]。（丑作掩泪，跪介）娘娘既慷慨捐生，望万岁爷以社稷为重，勉强割恩罢。（内又喊介）（生顿足哭介）罢罢，妃子既执意如此，朕也做不得主了。高力士，只得但、但凭娘娘罢！（作哽咽、掩面哭下）（旦朝上拜介）万岁！（作哭倒介）（丑向内介）众军听着，万岁爷已有旨，赐杨娘娘自尽了。（众内呼介）万岁，万岁，万万岁！（丑扶旦起介）娘娘，请到后边去。

（扶旦行介）（旦哭介）

**【哭相思】**百年离别在须臾，一代红颜为君尽！

（转作到介）（丑）这里有座佛堂在此。（旦作进介）且住，待我礼拜佛爷。（拜介）佛爷，佛爷！念杨玉环啊，

【越恁好】罪孽深重，罪孽深重，望我佛度脱咱。（丑拜介）愿娘娘好处生天。（旦起哭介）（丑跪哭介）娘娘，有甚话儿，分付奴婢几句。（旦）高力士，圣上春秋已高，我死之后，只有你是旧人，能体圣意，须索小心奉侍。再为我转奏圣上，今后休要念我了。（丑哭应介）奴婢晓得。（旦）高力士，我还有一言。（作除钗、出盒介）这金钗一对，钿盒一枚，是圣上定情所赐。你可将来与我殉葬[10]，万万不可遗忘。（丑接钗盒介）奴婢晓得。（旦哭介）断肠痛杀，说不尽恨如麻。（末领军拥上）杨妃既奉旨赐死，何得停留，稽迟圣驾。（军呐喊介）（丑向前拦介）众军士不得近前，杨娘娘即刻归天了。（旦）唉，陈元礼，陈元礼，你兵威不向逆寇加，逼奴自杀。（军又喊介）（丑）不好了，军士每拥进来了。（旦看介）唉，罢、罢，这一株梨树，是我杨玉环结果之处了。（作腰间解出白练，拜介）臣妾杨玉环，叩谢圣恩。从今再不得相见了。（丑泣介）（旦作哭缢介）我那圣上啊，我一命儿便死在黄泉下，一灵儿只傍着黄旗下[11]。

（做缢死下）（末）杨妃已死，众军速退。（众应同下）

（丑哭介）我那娘娘啊！（下）（生上）"六军不发无奈何，宛转蛾眉马前死。"（丑持白练上，见生介）启万岁爷，杨娘娘归天了。（生作呆不应介）（丑又启介）杨娘娘归天了。自缢的白练在此。（生看大哭介）哎哟，妃子，妃子，兀的不痛杀寡人也[12]！（倒介）（丑扶介）（生哭介）

【红绣鞋】当年貌比桃花，桃花，（丑）今朝命绝梨花，梨

花。（出钗盒介）这金钗、钿盒，是娘娘分付殉葬的。（生看钗盒哭介）这钗和盒，是祸根芽。长生殿，恁欢洽；马嵬驿，恁收煞！

  （丑）仓卒之间，怎生整备棺椁？（生）也罢，权将锦褥包裹。须要埋好记明，以待日后改葬。这钗盒就系娘娘衣上罢。（丑）领旨。（下）（生哭介）

【尾声】温香艳玉须臾化，今世今生怎见他！（末上跪介）请陛下起驾。（生顿足恨介）咳，我便不去西川也值甚么！（内呐喊、掌号，众军上）

【仙吕入双调 过曲】【朝元令】（丑暗上，引生上马行介）（合）长空雾黏，旌旆寒风刮。长征路淹[13]，队仗黄尘染。谁料君臣，共尝危险。恨贼寇横兴逆焰，烽火相兼，何时得豺虎歼。遥望蜀山尖，回将凤阙瞻[14]，浮云数点，咫尺把长安遮掩，长安遮掩。

  翠华西拂蜀云飞[15]， 章 褐

  天地尘昏九鼎危[16]。 吴 融

  蝉鬓不随銮驾去[17]， 高 骈

  空惊鸳鸯忽相随。 钱 起

---

注释

[1]拥旄（máo）仗钺（yuè）：旄，旄节，毛编成竹节的样子；钺，大斧。两者都是古代帝王、元帅、将军所有，象征权威。

[2]定夺：决定。

[3]京华：京都。

[4]波查：波折。

[5] 官家：皇帝。

[6] 难禁架：难受，难以对付。

[7] 堂堂天子贵，不及莫愁家：爱上皇帝，不及古乐府中所描写的莫愁女那样爱上一个普通人，相爱到老。

[8] 若是再禁加：如果军队再闹下去。

[9] 宗社：宗庙、社稷，即国家。

[10] 将来：拿来。

[11] 黄旗下：指天子的行踪。

[12] 兀的不：表示惊叹的语气，犹如岂不、怎么不。兀的，本身没有意义。

[13] 淹：迟留，在路上走得缓慢。

[14] 回将凤阙瞻：回头看宫殿。

[15] 翠华：装饰着翠鸟羽毛的旗子，是天子所用。

[16] 九鼎：相传夏禹铸九鼎，成为历代传国之宝。这里代指国家。

[17] 蝉鬓：古代妇女鬓发的一种式样，梳得像蝉翼一样薄。这里指杨贵妃。

# THEORY ON LITERARY TRANSLATION OF THE CHINESE SCHOOL

The theory on literary translation of the Chinese school owes its origin to traditional Chinese culture, including the Confucian and the Taoist school of thought respectively represented by *Thus Spoke the Master* and *Laws Divine and Human*.

It is said in the first chapter of *Laws Divine and Human* that truth can be known, but it may not be the truth you know, and that things may be named, but names are not the things. When applied to literary translation, this may mean that the theory on literary translation can be known, but it may not the unproven theory on the one hand, nor the scientific theory on the other, for neither literary translation nor its theory is science. As the names are not equal to the things, the translation cannot be equal to the original. As there is more difference than equivalence between the Chinese and the English language, the principle of equivalence can not be applied to the translation between them as between two occidental languages.

It is said in the last chapter of *Laws Divine and Human* that truthful words may not be beautiful and beautiful words may not be truthful. That is to say, there is contradiction between truth and beauty or between equivalence and excellence. A translation where equivalents are used may be called a faithful or truthful translation. When no equivalent can be found between two languages, the translator should make use of the best expressions or excellent expressions of the target language. That may be called theory of excellence.

In *Thus Spoke the Master*, Confucius said, "At seventy, I can do what I will without going beyond what is right." Professor Zhu Guangqian said that this has shown the mature state of an artist. I think it may also show the mature state of a literary translator. The literal translator has used the equivalents without going beyond the original in sound; the liberal translator has described the image without going beyond the original in sense; the literary translator has described the scene without going beyond reality. Not to go beyond the original is to be truthful or faithful, and the translator has reached the ordinary level of translation. To do what one will without going beyond the original is not only to be faithful but also to make his translation beautiful, in that case the translator has attained a higher level. To excel the original without going beyond the reality it describes is to attain the highest level.

What is literary translation? It is an art of solving the contradiction between faithfulness (or truth) and beauty. How to solve it? There are three methods, namely, equalization, generalization and particularization. When there is little or no contradition between truth and beauty, equalization or equivalents may be used. When there is contradction between them, generalization may be used to make the meaning clear, and particularization to make a deeper impression.

Confucius said in *Thus Spoke the Master* that it would be good to be understandable, better to be enjoyable and best to be delectable or delightful. When applied to literary translation, this principle means that an understandable translation is good, an enjoyable one is better and a delightful one is best. The ontology or theory of contradition between truth and beauty, the methodology or theory of equalization, generalization and particularization, and the teleology or theory of the understandable, the enjoyable and the delectable, all owe their origin to the Confucian and Taoist schools of thoughts.

But Confucius said less about what delight is and more about how to be delightful. In the beginning of *Thus Spoke the Master* he said it is delightful to acquire knowledge and put it into practice; In Chapter Six he told us how Yan Hui could find delight in reading though living in a humble lane with only a handful of rice to eat and a gourdful of water to drink; In Chapter Eleven, Zeng Xi told us his delight in an spring excursion. From these examples we can see Confucius' theory on delight or teleology, and his theory on practice or methodology. His theory is not scientific but artistic. Since literary translation is an art but not a branch of science, his theory can not only be applied to the practice but also to the theory of literary translation. As his theory has stood the test of time, it is as durable as scientific theories. A theorist on science who studies truth and the truthful should not go beyond what is truthful. A theorist on art or an artist who studies beauty and the beautiful may go beyond what is truthful and faithful.

The contradiction between truth and beauty in Chinese theory on literary translation has developed into a contradiction between equivalence and excellence. As Keats said, "Beauty is truth, truth beauty," we may even say beauty is a virtue, a kind of excellence. When we cannot find the equivalent, we may resort to generalization or particularization.

In short, literary translation is an art to create the beautiful.

长生殿

This is the epistemology of the Chinese school. The contradition between truth and beauty or between equivalence and excellence is its ontology; the theory on equalization, generalization and particularization is its triple methodology; and the theory of the understandable, the enjoyable and the delectable or delightful is its triple teleology.

Xu Yuanchong
Oct. 2011

# 代后记：中国学派的文学翻译理论

中国学派的文学翻译理论源自中国的传统文化，主要包括儒家思想和道家思想，儒家思想的代表著作是《论语》，道家思想的代表著作是《老子道德经》。

《老子道德经》第一章开始就说："道可道，非常道；名可名，非常名。"联系到翻译理论上来，就是说：翻译理论是可以知道的，是可以说得出来的，但不是只说得出来而经不起实践检验的空头理论，这就是中国学派翻译理论中的实践论。其次，文学翻译理论不能算科学理论（自然科学），与其说是社会科学理论，不如说是人文学科或艺术理论，这就是文学翻译的艺术论，也可以说是相对论。后六个字"名可名，非常名"应用到文学翻译理论上来，可以有两层意思：第一层是原文的文字是描写现实的，但并不等于现实，文字和现实之间还有距离，还有矛盾；第二层意思是译文和原文之间也有距离，也有矛盾，译文和原文所描写的现实之间，自然还有距离，还有矛盾。译文应该发挥译语优势，运用最好的译语表达方式，来和原文展开竞赛，使译文和现实的距离或矛盾小于原文和现实之间的矛盾，那就是超越原文了。这就是文学翻译理论中的优势论或优化论，超越论或竞赛论。文学翻译理论应该解决的不只是译文和原文在文字方面的矛盾，还要解决译文和原文所反映的现实之间的矛盾，这是文学翻译的本体论。

一般翻译只要解决"真"或"信"或"似"的问题，文学翻译却要解决"真"或"信"和"美"之间的矛盾。原文反映的现实不只是言内之意，还有言外之意。中国的文学语言往往有言外之意，甚至还有言外之情。文学翻译理论也要解决译文和原文的言外之意、言外之情的矛盾。

《论语》说："知之者不如好之者，好之者不如乐之者。"知之，好之，乐之，这"三之论"是对艺术论的进一步说明。艺术论第一条原则要求译文忠实于原文所反映的现实，求的是真，可以使人知之；第二条原则要求用"三化"法来优化译文，求的是美，可以使人好之；第三条原则要求用"三美"来优化译文，尤其是译诗词，求的是意美、音美和形美，可以使人乐之。如果"不逾矩"的等化译文能使人知之（理解），那就达到了文学翻译的低标准，如从心所欲而不逾矩的浅化或深化的译文既能使人知之，又能使人好之（喜欢），那就达到了中标准；如果从心所欲的译文不但能使人知之，好之，还能使人乐之（愉快），那才达到了文学翻译的高标准。这也是中国译者对世界译论作出的贡献。

翻译艺术的规律是从心所欲而不逾矩。"矩"就是规矩，规律。但艺术规律却可以依人的主观意志而转移，是因为得到承认才算正确的。所以贝多芬说：为了更美，没有什么清规戒律不可打破。他所说的戒律不是科学规律，而是艺术规律。不能用科学规律来评论文学翻译。

孔子不大谈"什么是"（What?）而多谈"怎么做"（How?）。这是中国传统的方法论，比西方流传更久，影响更广，作用更大，并且经过了两三千年实践的考验。《论语》第一章中说："学而时习之，不亦说（悦，乐）乎！""学"是取得知识，"习"是实践。孔子只说学习实践可以得到乐趣，却不说什么是"乐"。这就是孔子的方法论，是中国文学翻译理论的依据。

总而言之，中国学派的文学翻译理论是研究老子提出的"信"（似）"美"（优）矛盾的艺术（本体论），但"信"不限原文，还指原文所反映的现实，这是认识论，"信"由严复提出的"信达雅"发展到鲁迅提出"信顺"的直译，再发展到陈源的"三似"（形似，意似，神似），直到傅雷的"重神似不重形似"，这已经接近"美"了。"美"发展到鲁迅的"三美"（意美，音美，形美），再发展到林语堂提出的"忠实，通顺，美"，转化为朱生豪"传达原作意趣"的意译，直到茅盾提出的"美的享受"。孔子提出的"从心所欲"发展到郭沫若提出的创译论（好的翻译等于创作），以及钱钟书说的译文可以胜过原作的"化境"说，再发展到优化论，超越论，"三化"（等化，浅化，深化）方法论。孔子提出的"不逾矩"和老子说的"信言不美，美言不信"有同有异。老子"信美"并重，孔子"从心所欲"重于"不逾矩"，发展为朱光潜的"艺术论"，包括郭沫若说的"在信达之外，愈雅愈好。所谓'雅'不是高深或讲修饰，而是文学价值或艺术价值比较高。"直到茅盾说的："必须把文学翻译工作提高到艺术创造的水平。"孔子的"乐之"发展为胡适之的"愉快"说（翻译要使读者读得愉快），再发展到"三之"（知之，好之，乐之）目的论。这就是中国学派的文学翻译理论发展为"美化之艺术"（"三美"，"三化"，"三之"的艺术）的概况。

许渊冲

2011年10月

**图书在版编目（CIP）数据**

长生殿: 汉英对照 / 许渊冲译. —2版. —北京: 五洲传播出版社, 2018.8
（许译中国经典诗文集）
ISBN 978-7-5085-4029-0

Ⅰ.①长… Ⅱ.①许… Ⅲ.①汉语－英语－对照读物
②传奇剧（戏曲）－剧本－中国－清代 Ⅳ.①H319.4：I

中国版本图书馆CIP数据核字（2011）第199469号


# 长生殿

译　　者：许渊冲　许　明
策划编辑：荆孝敏　郑　磊
责任编辑：王　峰
中文编辑：常　征
英文编辑：马培武　程　阳
装帧设计：北京正视文化艺术有限责任公司
出版发行：五洲传播出版社
地　　址：北京市海淀区北三环中路31号生产力大楼B座6层
邮　　编：100088
电　　话：010-82005927，010-82007837
网　　址：http://www.cicc.org.cn http://www.thatsbooks.com
印　　刷：中煤（北京）印务有限公司
版　　次：2012年1月第1版　2019年1月第2版第1次印刷
开　　本：140mm×210mm　1/32
印　　张：10.25
字　　数：260千字
书　　号：ISBN 978-7-5085-4029-0
定　　价：89.00元